GW00384680

Critical Enquiries

Critical Enquiries

Essays on Literature

W.W. ROBSON

THE ATHLONE PRESS
LONDON

First published 1993 by
THE ATHLONE PRESS LTD
1 Park Drive, London NW11 7SG

© W.W. Robson 1993

British Library Cataloguing in Publication Data
*A catalogue record for this book is available
from the British Library*

ISBN 0 485 11441 0

Typeset by
Bibloset

Printed and bound in Great Britain by the
University Press, Cambridge

Wallace Robson

20th June 1923 – 31st July 1993

Contents

Preface

The essays in this collection are not united by a single theme. They were written for a variety of purposes. Some were originally introductions to editions (such as those on *The Portrait of a Lady* and *The Golden Bowl*); some were written for particular occasions (the first essay, for example, on an episode in *Hamlet*, was my inaugural lecture at Edinburgh University); others commemorate anniversaries. I have assembled them all under the general heading *Critical Enquiries* as this seemed an appropriate title for a representative selection of my writings from the past twenty years.

There have been great changes in literary criticism since I gave my *Hamlet* lecture in 1972. The expression 'literary criticism' has itself come to seem rather dated. The language of published critical debate, at least in the universities, has been strongly influenced by 'theory'. This movement is surveyed by Terry Eagleton in his *Literary Theory: An Introduction* (1983), though he says more about the Continental than about the Anglo-American tradition. Since then theory has been much attacked: a recent hostile critique may be found in David Lehman's *Signs of the Times* (1992). But its predominance still seems to continue. Trevor Tolley, of Carleton University in Canada, opines that theory has helped to contribute to a schism between the writing of literature and the study of it – 'something that happily used not to exist in Great Britain', where we have had a long, distinguished and still not obsolete tradition of poet-critics. But the leading proponents of literary theory avoid expressing their views in the way I have expressed mine here. Many of them would disclaim the notion of 'views' altogether. They hold that analyses of texts and theories of criticism demand the use of quasi-scientific terminology which is (and should be) inaccessible to the non-specialist. This position is bolstered by a dislike of what are perceived as 'bourgeois' conceptions of literary argument, said to be carried on in an outmoded, complacent fashion.

I do not propose to account for the reasons for this hostility. That is not the scope or purpose of this book. While much lively debate can and does continue among literary journalists and other readers who like discussing their ideas about books, there is no doubt that the serious critical essay has changed beyond recognition during my lifetime. I began work as a university teacher at London and Oxford before criticism was regarded as the preserve of small professional groups. It was still viewed as a humane activity, welcome to lovers of literature everywhere. The literary critic aspired to be a humanist in the sense described by Gregory Vlastos in his *Socrates* (1991): 'a scholar . . . trying first to find the relevance of his individual work to our common humanity; secondly, to state his findings in common speech – not folksy talk, just the Queen's English, unassisted by a suitcaseful of technical glossaries'. And I continue to think that it is possible to alert readers to things of value in an author's work without recourse to arcane language or outlandish speculations. At any rate it is in that conviction that I have reprinted these essays.

I will now take the opportunity to mention a few theoretical controversies. The first of these appears at present not to have much life in it. Glancing at a famous pronouncement on Milton by F.R. Leavis, John Carey remarks that 'the dislodgment of "evaluation" has been effected with remarkably little fuss' (*Original Copy*, 1987). This statement seems open to the objection that readers of literature cannot but evaluate (unless their sole concern is with bibliography or scholarly hardware). And their evaluations may well be of interest to others. While accepting this, Carey comments: 'The real usefulness of value judgments can emerge only when we have acknowledged that they are subjective. Their usefulness lies not in anything they can tell us about the people making the judgments, including ourselves' (*ibid.*). I would only qualify this by suggesting that we should distinguish two senses of 'evaluation'. In one sense – that deprecated by Carey – it means the effort to give final, 'objective' answers to questions of good and bad, better and worse. I agree with him that this effort seems futile. It serves no useful purpose, except perhaps to relieve the reader's feelings. This is because there are no valid general descriptive criteria for excellence in literature or any other art. Indeed this may well be a defining characteristic of art (see Sir Peter Strawson, 'Aesthetic Appraisal', *The Oxford Review*, Michaelmas 1966). To suppose otherwise would be to commit both art and criticism to Byzantine immobility. On the other hand 'evaluation' may mean appraisal, an enquiry into the distinctive qualities of authors and their works. This sense seems to escape the objection levelled by Carey. And I think many people today take it for granted that it is not the purpose of criticism to impose standards or lay down principles, or to draw up laws and rules. As for 'ideological' (i.e. politically motivated) criticism, once officially enforced in the now defunct USSR, it is now so widely discredited, except in China, Cuba, and so on, that to attack it would be to flog a dead horse. But the impulse that prompted it is by no means dead; it can be relied on to appear in some other form. In the mean time the reading of René Wellek's majestic *History of Modern Criticism* may be confidently recommended to those who, whether *idéologues* or not, conceive the task of criticism too narrowly.

Another controversy, still continuing, appears at the moment to have reached a deadlock. I refer to the disagreement about literary meaning and the relevance (or possibility) of knowing an author's intentions. So far as I am aware this began, in English-speaking countries, with the celebrated essay by W.K. Wimsatt and M. Beardsley, 'The Intentional Fallacy' (reprinted in 1976 in 'On Literary Intention', edited by D.N. de Molina). Since then the argument has been reinforced in French thought of the 1970s – not always with proper clarity – by a refurbished psychoanalysis and by modern linguistics. And there has been a spectacular development of similar ideas in the USA. The work of the chief exponent of ultra-modern anti-intentionalism, the French thinker Jacques Derrida, a mixture of exegete, philosopher, and Jewish cabbalist, is still a subject of heated dispute. Estimates of the value and significance of deconstruction, the most influential critical movement of modern times, vary greatly. It has aroused fierce disagreement in Great Britain, as was shown by the opposition not long ago to the proposal to confer on Derrida an honorary degree at Cambridge University. Many doubts have been raised about his thought (some powerful criticisms of it may be found in John M. Ellis's book *Against Deconstruction* (Princeton, 1989)). Meanwhile we may ponder the hopefully eirenic words of one of his distinguished admirers, J. Hillis Miller, in *The Ethics of Reading* (New York, 1987):

Deconstruction is nothing more or less than good reading as such . . . attacks on it misread the plain sense of what Derrida or [Paul] de Man say about the relation of reader to text. Neither has ever asserted the freedom of the reader to make the text anything he or she wants it to mean. Each has in fact asserted the reverse.

But while welcoming the assurance that deconstructive criticism *has* a 'plain sense' (some baffled would-be readers might not agree) I fear that this is an *aporia* which is likely to go on for some time.

The controversy that stirs the most lively interest (not to say passion) at present, among writers and ordinary readers quite as much as among theorists, concerns the relation between criticism and biography. Here the half- (or quarter-) truth in Roland Barthes's 'death of the author' has to be recognized. Criticism cannot require biographical facts about writers, otherwise there would be no possibility of discussing many anonymous works (the *Odyssey*, the great folktales, the Gospels) or the work of authors such as Shakespeare, of whose lives little is known. And in cases where materials do exist for the biographical study of an author, they have been known to prove an especially seductive temptation to critical irrelevance, as in many discussions of Shelley's private conduct, or Dickens's double life, or, more recently, the personal qualities of the late Philip Larkin. We should not forget the sensible warning given many years ago by Sir Arthur Conan Doyle, irritated no doubt by the insistent identification of him with Sherlock Holmes, that 'the doll and its maker are not identical'. But it seems only good sense to judge that what an author has created will be better appreciated by those who have some insight into the mind of its creator. The anti-historical and anti-biographical tendency of modern academic criticism enforces a separation between an 'Eric Blair' and a 'George Orwell' which I find difficult to apply in practice. The doctrine of 'nothing outside the text', taken strictly, would lead to the absurd conclusion that in thinking about *Animal Farm* we should forget there was someone called Stalin, and that his existence greatly affected what Orwell was writing about and how Orwell wrote about it.

I will end with a few notes on the individual essays.

'Did the King See the Dumb-Show?' (1972) suggests that Shakespeare was experimenting with 'multiple perspective' in depicting the struggle between Hamlet and the King. (Later reflection has led me to suspect that I was guilty of 'thinking too precisely on the event'.)

The essay on *The Faerie Queene* (1982) offers a concise survey of Spenser interpretation down to 1982.

The essay on *Paradise Lost* (1982) attempts to perform the same service for Milton's poem.

The essay on Pope's 'Coronation Epistle' (1988) suggests a way in which, without resort to biographical information from outside, this poem can be shown to reveal different facets of the poet's feeling about the heroine.

'Johnson as a Poet' (1984) explores some neglected aspects of Johnson's verse. For instance, it may not be known that he wrote beautifully of music, of which (on his own private admission) he knew nothing.

The short discussion of 'Romantic Narrative Verse' (1984) makes some observations on the poetry of Scott and Byron.

'Tennyson and Victorian Balladry' (1992) is a plea for a revaluation (upwards) of the 'domestic' dimension (once very popular) of Tennyson's poetry.

The essay on *Nicholas Nickleby* (1975) is a discussion of 'reality' and 'unreality' in Dickens's novel. It was written before the Royal Shakespeare Company's successful dramatization (1980), which I would otherwise have referred to.

The essay on *The Mystery of Edwin Drood* (1983) proposes what I think is a new solution to the 'Datchery' problem. If this solution is accepted the hypothetical presence of the author here takes on a special sense.

The essay on *The Portrait of a Lady* (1983) deals with some problems in the plot of James's novel.

The essay on *The Golden Bowl* (1984) consists of an analysis of the great critical division over this puzzling work.

The essay on Kipling's *Jungle Books* (1992) discusses the element of allegory in them and tries to define the exact quality of their 'imperialism'.

The essay on E. Nesbit's *The Book of Dragons* (1989) shows how she mixes Fabian socialism with Kipling while remaining within the fairytale genre.

The essay on the Father Brown stories (1974) contains some suggestions about the Chestertonian philosophy of language implied in them.

The essay on Raymond Chandler's letters (1987) urges that whatever Chandler's status as a novelist he deserves high marks as a critical theorist (mainly, of course, of crime fiction). I argue that his thoughts have a more general bearing on the problem he informally discussed about description and evaluation in criticism, and the relationship between technical and moral judgments on literature.

The essay on the poetry of C.S. Lewis (1991) considers this question: if Lewis (as is often said) failed as a poet, can any lessons be learnt from this about his work in general?

W.W. Robson

Acknowledgements

The author gratefully acknowledges the editors and publishers of the books and journals in which these essays first appeared for their permission to reproduce the following:

'Did the King See the Dumb-Show?' *Cambridge Quarterly*, vol. VI (1972–5).

'Spenser and *The Faerie Queene*', *New Pelican Guide to English Literature*, vol. 2 (1982).

'*Paradise Lost*: Changing Interpretations and Controversy', *New Pelican Guide to English Literature*, vol. 3 (1982).

'Text and Context: Pope's "Coronation Epistle"' from *Alexander Pope: Essays for the Tercentenary*, ed. Colin Nicholson (1988).

'Johnson as a Poet' from *Samuel Johnson 1709–84*, ed. Kai Kin Yung (1984).

'Tennyson and Victorian Balladry' from *Tennyson: Seven Essays*, ed. P. Collins (1992).

'On *The Portrait of a Lady*', introduction to the Everyman edn (1983).

'On *The Golden Bowl*', introduction to the Everyman edn (1984).

'On *The Jungle Books*', prefaces in the World's Classics series (1992).

'E. Nesbit and *The Book of Dragons*' from *Children and their Books*, ed. G. Avery and J. Briggs (1989).

'Father Brown and Others' from *G.K. Chesterton: A Centenary Appraisal*, ed. John Sullivan (1974).

'"A Home for the Truth": Literary Criticism in the Letters of Raymond Chandler' from *Prose Studies*, vol. 10 (1987).

'The poetry of C.S. Lewis', *The Chesterton Review*, Aug–Nov 1991.

It is with sadness that the Publishers have to record the death of Wallace Robson, July 1993, during the production of this book.

Chapter 1
Did the King See the Dumb-Show?

Dover Wilson said that the interpretation of *Hamlet* was 'the supreme problem of English literature', and if anything the difficulties seem to have grown more radical in the years since *What Happens in Hamlet* appeared. To many of us the play is still the play described[1] by 'an Old Playgoer' in 1884. (The old playgoer was Matthew Arnold.)

> To the common public *Hamlet* is a famous piece by a famous poet, with crime, a ghost, battle, and carnage; and that is sufficient. To the youthful enthusiast *Hamlet* is a piece handling the mystery of the universe, and having throughout cadences, phrases, and words full of divinest Shakespearian magic; and that, too, is sufficient. To the pedant, finally, *Hamlet* is an occasion for airing his psychology; and what does pedant require more? But to the spectator who loves true and powerful drama, and can judge whether he gets it or not, *Hamlet* is a piece which opens, indeed, simply and admirably, and then: 'The rest is puzzle!'

It seems possible to distinguish the problem of *Hamlet* from those which commonly arise in the interpretation of old texts, and old plays in particular. We know less about Elizabethan theatrical conditions than we could wish; and we have little or no information about the nature of the Elizabethan audience's responses. Modern scholars' reconstructions must be largely guesswork. Then there is often uncertainty about the exact words Shakespeare wrote, and difficulty in interpreting the sense of what he wrote, in part because of general changes in the English language, and in part because of Shakespeare's very idiosyncratic way of using it. Moreover, *Hamlet* has more than its share of the usual Shakespearean difficulties – at any rate of those features which appear difficult when the plays are subjected to the kind of thoroughgoing analytic scrutiny which there is no reason to think the poet ever meant his work to undergo. Thus the play is silent on many matters which those who 'consider curiously' are curious about: for example, why Hamlet did not become King on his father's death; or whether the marriage of Gertrude and Claudius was regarded as incestuous by anyone besides Hamlet and the Ghost; or why Hamlet feigned madness; or – what for many people is still the problem of problems – whether Hamlet delayed his revenge because he was too weak, or because he was too wise, or for some other reason. Critics may try to fill in these gaps, but the fact is that the play simply does not tell us.

The distinctive problem of *Hamlet* is the problem of the action. 'We cannot too often remind ourselves,' says Waldock[2] that 'the difficulty, in ultimate terms, is to know what the play is really about.' 'This is what is so very strange,' he adds, 'that it should be difficult, or should have become difficult, to grasp the central drift of a play that has always been popular and successful.' Now, whatever the play is 'really about', it will not be disputed that the pivot of the action is the Play Scene. And the greatest puzzle of the Play Scene is the dumb-show. This famous Shakespearean difficulty was perhaps more discussed in the nineteenth century than it is today. It might seem dispiritingly similar to the problems considered by A.C. Bradley in the Notes to his *Shakespearean Tragedy* – problems which have not been so much *solved*, as *dropped*, by modern Shakespeareans. That consideration does not trouble me. But I do regret that the part of the text I shall discuss contains no poetry, only a stage-direction, and, in so far as it bears upon 'character', seems to bear upon the character of the King rather than that of Hamlet. I can only hope that it makes a small contribution to that fundamental reconsideration of *Hamlet* which I believe to be needed.

Let us transport ourselves into the theatre at *Hamlet* III. ii. 134 ff.

The trumpet sounds. Hautboys play. The Dumb Show enters.

Enter a *King* and a *Queen*, very lovingly; the Queen embracing him and he her. She kneels, and makes show of protestation unto him. He takes her up, and declines his head upon her neck. He lies him down upon a bank of flowers; she, seeing him asleep, leaves him. Anon comes in a *Fellow*, takes off his crown, kisses it, pours poison into the sleeper's ears, and leaves him. The *Queen* returns; finds the King dead, and makes passionate action. The *Poisoner*, with some two or three Mutes, comes in again, seeming to condole with her. The dead body is carried away. The Poisoner woos the Queen with gifts: she seems harsh awhile, but in the end accepts his love. (Exeunt.)

Dumb-shows were a popular feature of plays of the Elizabethan–Jacobean period, and scholars have endeavoured to trace their origin and to elucidate the purposes for which they were used. It has been suggested that their origin is to be found in the Morality plays; but the view of Cunliffe[3] has been more widely accepted. He thinks they descend from the *intermedii*, interludes of dance and song treating some allegorical or mythical theme, which occur between the acts of Italian dramas towards the close of the fifteenth century. The dumb-show in the earlier Elizabethan drama, as in *Gorboduc* or *The Spanish Tragedy*, is a fairly cryptic charade of allegorical figures, which throws out a veiled hint at what the play itself is to be about. Thus each act of *Gorboduc* was preceded by such a pantomime, and, in the printed version, these are described and explained.

Hereby was signified that a state knit in unity doth continue strong against all force, but being divided is easily destroyed; as befell upon Duke Gorboduc dividing his land to his two sons, which he before held in monarchy, and upon the dissension of the brethren to whom it was divided.

In *The Spanish Tragedy* also the dumb-show is a parade of allegorical figures, who might not even be fully recognizable to the end. But whereas in *Gorboduc* the explanation is not given, so that the audience have to interpret the dumb-show for themselves, in *The Spanish Tragedy* there is a presenter, Revenge, sitting (often asleep) beside the Ghost on the stage, who explains who the allegorical figures are and what they are doing, so that the Ghost can interpret the 'mystery' for himself. It is to be noted, however, that the audience might not be fully enlightened even after the presenter's speech, since they do not have the Ghost's private knowledge of what has happened before the play opens.

The older dumb-shows are thus dire foreshadowings of what is to come, sometimes hinting at it so obscurely and symbolically as to deserve Hamlet's contemptuous reference to them as 'inexplicable'. But in later Elizabethan drama the dumb-shows tend to have a different function. They no longer indicate what is to occur in the future, but look back to what has happened in the past, or is happening elsewhere in the present. (Famous examples are to be found in *The White Devil* and *The Changeling*.) These dumb-shows have become a more integral part of the play; they add to the 'business' which the Elizabethan dramatists loved, without the delay of dialogue; they find their place within the acts instead of between them.

Now it has long been recognized that the dumb-show in *Hamlet* is peculiar. B.R. Pearn[4] summarizing the results of his investigation of 57 plays of the period, which contain in all 120 dumb-shows, comes to the striking conclusion that 'the dumb-show in *Hamlet* is unique'. Its uniqueness lies in the fact that the show rehearses, without words, exactly the action which is immediately afterwards repeated in dialogue. It falls, therefore, within none of the categories among which other dumb-shows can be classified. It is true that the earliest examples of dumb-show also foreshadow the theme of the play. But this is invariably effected by means of symbolism; whereas in the dumb-show in *Hamlet* there is none. Pearn has found no other instance of a dumb-show which enacts in silence exactly the action which is afterwards repeated with vocal acting.

Finally it should be noted that the dumb-show in *Hamlet*, while differing from both the old and the new types of dumb-show in all the extant plays, combines features of each. For the *stage* audience it looks forward to the future – the action of the 'Murder of Gonzago' – as in the older dumb-shows, but without their cryptic symbolism. For the *actual* audience, the audience of *Hamlet* itself, it looks back at the past – the murder of King Hamlet – as in the newer kind.

So much for the peculiarities of this dumb-show. We now come to the problem. The usual and obvious interpretation of the action, in the central part of the play, is of course well known. King Claudius, who has disposed of his brother and predecessor by the very peculiar device of pouring poison into his ears, is witnessing the performance of a play which Hamlet jokingly calls 'The Mouse-trap' (III ii. 236), and which is 'to catch the conscience of the king' (II. ii. 601). This playlet reproduces in a remarkably complete manner the circumstances of his own crime. When the critical moment arrives and the King sees the intimate details of the murder displayed before the assembled Court, his nerve breaks and he leaves in confusion. It should be noted that his consternation appears to be due solely to the action of the play, since there is nothing particularly significant in the language used by the Poisoner.

But this interpretation seems to be contradicted by the presence of the dumb-show, which precedes the playlet and sets forth its whole action in detail. So far as the action is concerned – and on the usual assumption it is the action which alone is significant – the spoken play adds nothing whatsoever. Consequently, if this assumption is correct, either the King must have betrayed himself over the dumb-show, or there is no imaginable reason why he should betray himself at all.

Clearly there is something odd here. And the oddity is heightened by a strange remark of the King's. During the performance of the spoken play, and some time after he has (presumably) seen the dumb-show, which, as has been noted, presents the 'argument' of the Gonzago play, the King asks Hamlet whether Hamlet has 'heard' the argument and if there is no offence in it. This question seems unnaturally placed. If the King was now worried enough to put it to Hamlet, why was he apparently not worried at all when there was presented before him the whole story of what was to come? It is interesting to contrast this with the more natural placing of the question in *Der Bestrafte Brudermord*, a German play extant in a MS of 1710 which is obviously related in some way to Shakespeare's play. In the *Brudermord* the King asks his question where one would expect him to ask it, if he was going to ask it at all: *before* he has seen the dumb-show (the *Brudermord* gives no dialogue). The problem of the dumb-show in *Hamlet* therefore seems to me to turn on how we explain the King's question at III. ii. 231: 'Have you heard the argument? is there no offence in't?'

There seem to be two main ways in which this problem can be

dealt with. It can be *dissolved*, that is, prevented from arising. Or we can accept that it does arise, and attempt to solve it.

One way of dissolving the problem is to regard it as merely a textual muddle. A.A. Jack[5] suggests how it might have arisen. We are to suppose that Shakespeare was revising an old play, the outline of which may be preserved in the *Brudermord*. His raw material for the Play Scene might have been something like this (from the *Brudermord*).

> *King.*   Prince Hamlet, we understand that some actors have arrived who are to act a comedy for us this evening. Tell us, is that so?
>
> *Hamlet.*   Yes, my father, it is. They applied to me and I gave them permission. I hope your Majesty will also approve.
>
> *King.*   What kind of a plot is it? There is nothing, I suppose, offensive in it or rude?
>
> *Hamlet.*   It is a good plot. We who have good consciences are not touched by it.
>
> *Here enters the Play. The King with his consort. He wishes to lie down to sleep; the Queen begs him not to do so; he lies down, nevertheless; the Queen takes leave of him with a kiss, and exit. The King's brother comes with a phial and pours something into his ear, and exit.*
>
> *Hamlet.*   That is King Pyrrus (*sic*) who goes into the garden to sleep. The Queen begs him not to; however, he lies down. The poor little wife goes away; see, there comes the King's brother ['nephew' in Shakespeare] with the juice of Ebeno and pours it into his ear which, as soon as it mixes with the blood of man, destroys the body.
>
> *King* (alarmed). Torches, lanterns here! the play does not please us.

Here there is no problem about whether the King saw the dumb-show: the King saw nothing else. It seems a reasonable possibility, then, that the duplication in Shakespeare was unintentional. Shakespeare decided to replace the dumb-show in his original by a playlet with full dialogue, but omitted to delete the dumb-show from his revised draft.

But all this is pure speculation. We have only the most meagre information about what the old play of *Hamlet* contained, and certainly no evidence that it can be reconstructed from the *Brudermord*. (Attempts to support the *Brudermord* by adducing possible parallels from the 'bad' quarto of *Hamlet* are gravely weakened by the fact that the provenance of the 'bad' quarto itself is so dubious.) Secondly, the textual tradition is unassailable: the dumb-show is found in both the 'bad' and the 'good' quarto (Q2), as well as the folio. Finally, the spectators in *Hamlet* explicitly comment on the dumb-show (Ophelia seems puzzled by it) and so draw this feature of the proceedings to the audience's attention. It would appear, then, that we cannot excise the dumb-show.

The other way of eliminating the problem is to dismiss it as much ado about nothing. This is a way often taken, with similar Shakespearean difficulties, by those critics who insist that Shakespeare's plays are above all *poems*. Thus Dover Wilson is reproved by L.C. Knights because his interest is said to be in the 'events and the characters' rather than in the 'poetry'. And certainly if our interest in *Hamlet* is centred upon the general reflections on life in which the play abounds, and which are quoted wherever the English language is spoken, or upon its vivid details of language and imagery, we shall have no time for such inquiries. But it seems to me that our interest even in Shakespeare's poetry can only be diminished if we have no idea what kind of person is speaking, or in what dramatic situation. However, the advocates of the study of Shakespeare's plays as poems would presumably not go so far as to rule out such considerations as irrelevant. I imagine the line they might take, over the problem of the dumb-show, would be this. No doubt the *producer* has a problem here, in deciding what the King should do. Perhaps he was just not paying attention; or perhaps he was firmly controlling himself. It doesn't matter. The Play Scene is not an episode from real life, dramatically transcribed. The King does not betray himself at the point when, in real life, it would be natural for him to do so, but at the point when it suits Shakespeare's theatrical purposes. Shakespeare has good *dramatic* reasons for including both the dumb-show and the spoken playlet. He used the dumb-show to remind the audience of the Ghost's story, and to heighten the tension while we watch the spoken playlet. He added the spoken playlet to give the opportunity for Hamlet to make his barbed comments and mutter his cryptic jests. In short, the word *convention* is invoked; and for some readers, and perhaps some playgoers, that, nowadays, may be enough to settle the question.

Now I have no wish to deny that many Shakespearean difficulties may arise from our misunderstanding of the conventions Shakespeare uses. But I doubt whether this one can be removed so simply. If we have no interest in the plot of *Hamlet*, either because we think we know it already, or because we regard it as a mere peg on which to hang general reflections on life, vivid imagery, or 'character-acting' by the star performer, then the behaviour of the King during the Play Scene is of no interest. But if the elaborate preparation for the Play Scene has any point, then it seems clear that the King will be the central figure of the Play Scene; so that his reactions throughout are of the greatest interest. We are, of course, also interested in Hamlet during this scene, in Ophelia, in the Queen. But if the plot of *Hamlet* has any importance at all (and I suppose some critics would deny that it has) what happens to the King in the Play Scene must belong to the essence of the drama. We are to watch a psychological experiment to settle, in the only conceivable way open to Hamlet, one which was provided for him by the accident of the Players' arrival, the question which the consensus of Shakespearean scholarship increasingly instructs us to regard as very much an open question at least until III.ii: was the Ghost an honest Ghost? I cannot believe that anyone following the clear guidelines of the play could fail to comply with Hamlet's appeal to Horatio: 'Even with the very comment of thy soul/Observe my uncle.'

I now turn to attempted solutions of the problem. The first is simple. The King did not see the dumb-show. This was the suggestion of Halliwell-Phillips, and of Tieck in 1824:

> While waiting for the play to commence, the King is friendly towards Hamlet; he jests with the Queen or with other ladies and persons of the court; he is so absorbed in merry talk that he does not observe the dumb-show . . . Hamlet's repeated hints and the accents of Hamlet's voice at last arrest the King's notice.

Dover Wilson[6] developed this suggestion into a theory of great ingenuity. Some of his points seem very good. His explanation of why the dumb-show was included at all seems more convincing than the notion that it is a mere relic of the old play which Shakespeare left in without realizing the difficulty it would cause. The dumb-show indicates to the audience *how* the King is to be tested, so that the audience may watch for the moment of the King's self-betrayal. This is surely right. But Dover Wilson's theory goes beyond this, and for many readers becomes incredible. Shakespeare, he thinks, needed the dumb-show, but Hamlet did not. Hamlet's attack on the King was to occur in the play itself; the dumb-show was an unexpected addition by the players. His 'Marry, this is miching mallecho, it means mischief' (III. ii. 134) is angrily directed against them. When the Prologue appears Hamlet takes him for a 'presenter' (as in the *Spanish Tragedy*) and observes in agitation: 'The players cannot keep counsel; they'll tell all' (III. ii. 139). But they do keep counsel, and Hamlet shows his relief at the Prologue's innocuous 'posy'. He is relieved too because he now realizes that the dumb-show had not betrayed his intention; the King had not seen it, as is shown by his later question: 'Have you heard the argument? Is there no offence in't?' (III. ii. 231). Dover Wilson regards this question as unwittingly repeating Ophelia's word ('Belike this show imports the argument of the play'), which the King did not hear because it was spoken only to Hamlet. The audience is thereby made to realize that the King cannot have seen the dumb-show, which, as it knows, *is* the argument of the play.

Dover Wilson thinks that the King did not see the dumb-show not because, as older proponents of this view had held, he was talking to the Queen, but because he was talking to Polonius. We are to infer this from the remark of Polonius (III. ii. 109) 'Oho! do you mark that?' when Hamlet throws himself at Ophelia's feet, thereby strengthening Polonius's conviction that he is love-distraught. There has already been discussion between the King and Polonius about the cause of Hamlet's madness, and it is now resumed; the Queen is drawn into it, to hide her own embarrassment, by Hamlet's pointed remark: 'for look you how cheerfully my mother looks, and my father died within's two hours' (III. ii. 132).

Perhaps the scene may be played in this way. But the objections to Dover Wilson's theory seem insuperable. S.L. Bethell[7] observes

that Hamlet's remark about 'miching mallecho' is too much a part
of the 'antic' manner to be taken so seriously: its obvious meaning
is a dark reference to the play's function as 'Mouse-trap'. Again,
'The players cannot keep counsel' has its obvious meaning: the
players' job is to disclose things. If Shakespeare had meant the
dumb-show to be an untimely interpolation by the players he
would have made this unequivocally clear in the text. Similarly
with the behaviour of Claudius. The Elizabethan drama relies
fundamentally on words; any special 'business' is indicated in the
dialogue; it is not left to stage-directions or the discretion of the
actor. The fact that Claudius, becoming disturbed at the pointed
references to second marriages, asks Hamlet: 'Have you heard the
argument? Is there no offence in't?' seems to show that he is *not*
referring to the dumb-show; if he had missed it, he would surely
have said 'Have you *seen* the argument?' The only cogent argument
against the King's having seen the dumb-show is the negative one
from which the whole problem arose. He cannot have seen it,
because he shows no sign of having understood its significance.
As for the conversation which Dover Wilson thinks absorbed
the King at the critical moment, Bethell asks how on earth can
the actors indicate – without the use of dialogue, and while the
dumb-show is naturally focusing the main attention – that they
are discussing whether Hamlet's madness originated in frustrated
love, or in frustrated ambition? Not one word of this conversation
is recorded! In short, Dover Wilson has fallen into what Waldock
was to call 'the documentary fallacy': he is envisaging *Hamlet* not
as a play, but as a piece of history. (Granville-Barker[8] adds the
authority of a great producer to the dismissal of the idea that
Hamlet's plan was betrayed by the Players: 'such an irrelevancy . . .
springing from nowhere, leading nowhere, would be dramatically
meaningless.') There is thus no positive evidence that the King did
not see the dumb-show, and we are bound to assume that he did,
along with the rest of the Court. Yet, although it reproduced the
murder he had committed, he gave no sign of alarm, uttered no
revealing word. He sat tight, until the same action was repeated
with dialogue. Then he left the room, angered or alarmed, at the
point when the poisoning was again enacted. So we are back with
the difficulty.

Bethell has his own suggestion for getting round it. He accepts the view of Dover Wilson that Shakespeare needed the dumb-show to inform the (actual) audience. But he suggests that the dumb-show the actual audience sees, and the dumb-show the King sees, are, so to speak, not the same. This sounds like an extravagant subtlety of interpretation. But Bethell, in accordance with the general argument of his book, considers it, on the contrary, a 'popular' feature of Shakespeare's art, something that can be found in old Hollywood films and light entertainment at the present day. This feature he calls 'multi-consciousness'. Suppose a film is made about some amateurs putting on a play. What is actually shown as the play they are doing is in fact presented with the full resources of Hollywood. But the cinema audience is not for a moment deceived into supposing that the play the amateurs are 'really' putting on is like this. They know perfectly well what the real thing would be like. But they happily accept a convention which maintains the continuity of the story while providing them with superior entertainment. Assuming, then, that this untroubled 'multi-consciousness' was shared by an Elizabethan audience and a modern one, we can reconstruct the original performance thus. The audience sees the actual dumb-show, which informs them what Hamlet's trap is going to be. But they take it for granted that what the *King* is supposed to be seeing is the usual 'inexplicable' dumb-show, veiled and symbolic, which would not betray the trap prematurely.

The most usual solution of the problem,[9] however, comes closer to taking the text as it stands. This solution represents the Play Scene as a sustained ordeal for the King. On this view the playlet would be more aptly titled 'The Turn of the Screw'. The emphasis falls on the *gradual* realization by the King of what is going on. We must remember that the King has no reason for suspecting a Mouse-trap. For him the play was to be a Court device to divert Hamlet and lighten his melancholy. Nothing had yet happened to arouse his suspicion. Polonius had introduced the players to Hamlet and heard all their conversation except the hurried words between Hamlet and the First Player as he was leading them to their quarters (II. ii. 540). The play was one of those rapid decisions characteristic of Hamlet; the vital question whether the King will be present is asked casually (III. ii. 45). Hamlet's meeting with the Players immediately before the play was unknown to the King, who in any case, as we know, had other things on his mind. There was therefore no reason why the King, on seeing the dumb-show, should at once be certain that Hamlet knew his secret.

But what was Hamlet's attitude? Did he think the mere representation of the murder enough by itself to force the King to self-betrayal? Probably not. At any rate, he thought it necessary to insert a dozen lines of his own. Commentators are not agreed which these are; but it was this *speech*, whatever it was, not the representation of the King's *deed*, which he expected to make Claudius's guilt unkennel itself. Hamlet takes great pains to ensure that the acting is as realistic as possible. His directions to the Players, on this view, are part of the essential drama, and not, or not merely, an opportunity for Shakespeare to air his own ideas. The Players must hold up the mirror to nature as he himself later held a glass before his mother. Since Hamlet took such immense care over the preparation of the Mouse-trap, we should regard with distrust the suggestion that the dumb-show came as a surprise to him. The fact that the dumb-show is unique in anticipating the action of the play suggests that it had a special purpose. Hamlet knew the Gonzago play (II. ii. 54), and he used it to establish the King's guilt.

On this view, then, all the elaborate structure raised to explain away the King's silence during the dumb-show is unnecessary. It was a *speech* that Hamlet expected to give the final blow. When he first conceived the plan he may have jumped to the optimistic conclusion that the King would betray himself flagrantly. But such phrases as 'Even with the very comment of thy soul/Observe my uncle' suggest that he had come to realize that this was unlikely. Indeed, the King's self-betrayal may actually have been more flagrant than Hamlet had come to expect; this may be the explanation of his 'What, frighted with false fire?'

So the reconstruction of what happens is like this. There is nothing to arouse suspicion in the first scene of the playlet: it shows a queen vowing oaths of fidelity to her lord. It is Hamlet's comments ('If she should break it now!') which begin to give an ominous tinge to the play. After this scene Hamlet turns to the Queen with the question which gives the whole play an offensive meaning.

Hamlet.   Madam, how like you this play?
Queen.   The lady doth protest too much, methinks.
Hamlet.   O, but she'll keep her word.
King.   Have you heard the argument? Is there no offence in't?

The King's question reveals that his latent fear of Hamlet has been aroused by Hamlet's pointed remarks to the Queen. The playlet is now no mere diversion. But is it a weapon pointed at him by his nephew? His question gets down to fundamentals. Did Hamlet know beforehand about the embarrassing applicability of the Gonzago play? If so, it is Hamlet's plot, and the Players are his tools. The dumb-show now begins to appear in a more sinister light.

But what is the 'offence'? The King cannot be referring to the murder. How could he ask such a question about a crime known only to himself, without admitting his guilt? What the King wants to find out is whether Hamlet intended the first scene of the playlet to be an insult to his mother. Once the King suspects this, the play is changed for him, because he suspects that Hamlet had a hand in planning it. He continues probing: 'What do you call the play?' The answer 'The Mouse-trap' removes any doubt (III. ii. 236). From now on the King must endure the torment, during the rest of the Play Scene, not only of seeing again the representation of the parallel crime which he now knows to be modelled on his own, but the thrusts of Hamlet who 'tents him to the quick'. That he has seen the dumb-show is important, because he *now* can guess at Hamlet's intentions.

On this view, then, it is the '*talk* of the poisoning' that shatters the King. Previous discussions have turned on the supposition that there was one particular moment when the King discerned the trap, and that that moment was enough to overcome him. But Hamlet's attack is cumulative: 'poison in jest . . . your majesty and we that have free souls. . . . He poisons him i' the garden for his estate . . . *you shall see anon* . . .' The King cannot stand any more. He rises, and the turning-point of *Hamlet* has been reached: from now on the King knows that Hamlet is his deadly enemy.

This reconstruction seems the most attractive of those I have so far discussed. It has two great merits. The first is that it is much the most in keeping with the character of the self-controlled and resourceful King. He is capable, we know, of deep guilt and remorse, but he is not a jumpy, panic-stricken figure. What finally overcomes him is not the mere representation of his own crime, but the growing realization that Hamlet knew he had committed it. There was nothing in the dumb-show itself to bring this home to him; what brought it home to him was Hamlet's behaviour during the spoken playlet. The second advantage of the theory is that it views the Play Scene as an epitome of the whole action of *Hamlet*: the long, secret duel between Hamlet and the King. In the Play Scene Hamlet has won the first round.

Nevertheless, I find the theory hard to accept. With all its merits, it suffers from the same drawback as all those reconstructions that proceed by way of filling up gaps. And this drawback is that there is not one word in the text to indicate that the King realized Hamlet knew his secret. The opportunity for such a word is obviously the self-revealing soliloquy at III. iii. 46 ff. ('O, my offence is rank, it smells to heaven'). But there is nothing here, or later. Everything in the text is consistent with the view that the King's interpretation of the Play Scene was the same as the Court's: the Queen had been grossly insulted and, perhaps, the King's life threatened – if we are to assume that the King heard Hamlet's 'This is one Lucianus, nephew to the king' and that, as Babcock[10] suggests, 'nephew' is a Freudian slip.

And this brings me to the most striking feature of the dumb-show, as of the pre-story of *Hamlet* it re-enacts: the poisoning through the ears. This has always struck me as most peculiar. Perhaps it was in the old play, but the old play here as elsewhere is merely an *asylum ignorantiae*. The incident, it has been shown,[11] is based on something that really happened, an 'Italianate' crime; yet I have sometimes wondered how it is possible to poison someone with intact tympana in this way. Perhaps King Hamlet had damaged his tympana with all that banging of guns and sounding of trumpets which we know him to have been fond of? (I. iv. 12). But such speculations are frivolous. Medical considerations apart, the *aesthetic* aptness of the poisoning through the ears is plain. The horrible passage of the Ghost's speech which describes it is unforgettable. It is no wonder that psychoanalysts have been interested in the 'latent' significance of this method of murder.

(Ernest Jones's interpretation receives pre-Freudian support from a picture by Fuseli of the poisoning of King Hamlet, which is itself said to be based on a pederastic incident depicted on a Greek vase.) But for our present purpose the interest of the poisoning through the ears is its very great peculiarity: the *peculiarity* which puts it beyond reasonable doubt, for a spectator familiar with the event, that the dumb-show re-enacts the alleged method of murdering the late King.

If we lay stress, then, on this very spectacular and singular feature of the dumb-show, together with the complete silence of the King about Hamlet's knowledge of his secret, we shall want to give serious consideration to the last, and most sensational, solution I shall discuss that has been proposed for the problem. The King saw the dumb-show, but did not recognize the representation of his own crime. This solution is sensational because if it is correct the Ghost's story was untrue, at least in this particular, and the whole action of *Hamlet* must be seen differently.

In 1876 H. von Struve[12] put forward the theory that the Ghost of Hamlet's father was a hallucination. 'Hamlet's talk with his father is merely a soliloquy.' Struve supports his theory in a way characteristic of the documentary, Germanizing nineteenth century; he tries to reconstruct how Hamlet came to 'transform the figment of his fancy into the lively contours and plastic outline of reality', upon the 'trifling incitement from some superstitious soldiers'. 'Many an observation,' speculates Struve, 'made by chance and lost to memory, of his uncle's and his mother's conduct after his father's death; many a piece of gossip, which here and there reached his ears, and which by itself was insufficient to give his suspicions shape; many a significant shaking of the head by one or another of his father's faithful servants; many a fleeting observation which he had made unconsciously in connection with the numberless reports concerning the details of this mysterious event' – all these things, which the dramatist has admittedly neglected to record, 'suddenly took consistent shape in Hamlet's mind and stood out before his consciousness as an external image'.

This kind of analysis is not today in fashion with Shakespeareans, and I do not propose its revival. But I must say, at this point, that I do not like, either, the *a priori* dismissal, on pseudo-logical grounds, of the drawing of inferences about the past of Shakespearean characters. What *would* be logically absurd would be to take the characters for persons in real life whose history could be investigated in memoirs or other documentation going beyond the data provided by the play. But it seems to me quite wrong to lay it down as a critical doctrine that a play by Shakespeare can never be supposed to invite inferences about the characters' past. It may indeed be argued that in a particular case Shakespeare is not asking us to do this: but that is a separate argument, and must be judged on its own merits. By arguing that the Ghost scenes should be seen in this way Struve has not 'gone outside the play' or relegated himself automatically to the lunatic fringe.

The reason for not bothering with Struve's argument is not that it is 'documentary', but because it has no bearing on the essential play. For Struve accepts that the Ghost's story was true; his only innovation is to suggest an unusual interpretation of how Hamlet learned it. The argument of Greg[13] accepts Struve's suggestion, but develops it in a way which really does alter the essential drama. Greg lays great stress on the peculiarities of the Ghost scenes. He notes the element of rhetorical rant, of fustian, in the Ghost's speeches (a point made also by George Santayana). The Ghost leaves him sceptical and unconvinced. He finds it impossible to take the 'fellow in the cellarage' business seriously. He observes that none of the witnesses is really persuaded that the Ghost is genuine.

Greg seems to me particularly interesting when he examines the reactions of Hamlet to the Ghost. I have often wondered at the absence here of the normal reaction – if one can speak of normality in such a context – of a son who loved his father so greatly as Hamlet did. The beloved one has returned, in bodily form, but, as Struve says, there is no expression of love, no joy: 'he seeks from the Ghost nothing else but that it inform him *why* it appears, what it requires of him, what he must do to allay his tormenting disquiet.' (Of course that one should wonder at this at all is a tribute to Shakespeare for making the character of Hamlet so lifelike; no one would want to raise these questions about other Elizabethans' ghost scenes.) Greg sees Hamlet as suffering a mental shock when he sees the Ghost, but notes that he is at first cautious and critical. 'I'll *call* thee Hamlet,/King, father, royal Dane.' But, as so often happens, he is excited by his own ardour and eloquence. 'He waxes desperate with imagination.'

On the other hand, there are 'documentary' elements in Greg's account which leave me sceptical. He puts too much weight, in my view, on the great improbability of the Players' happening to have with them the text of a play which, by an astonishing coincidence, reproduces the exact circumstances of King Hamlet's murder. Such things are allowed to happen in fiction. And, as Dover Wilson soon pointed out, Greg's argument becomes very weak when he has to demolish the credibility of the witnesses in the first scene of the play (in which Hamlet does not appear at all). The 'superstitious soldiery' may be suspect, but we cannot ignore the central part played by Horatio in this scene, as the spokesman for the level-headed and intelligently agnostic. Greg's attempt to dispose of Horatio is the nadir of his essay. He points out that Horatio, on his own admission, had only seen the late King once, and that, as he is Hamlet's fellow-student at Wittenberg, he can have been at most a boy at the time of the Norwegian war. We are here in the world of *Baker Street Studies* rather than of serious scholarship.

Greg's argument has the advantage over all the others I have discussed in paying attention to the *poetic* quality of *Hamlet* (in this case, the writing in the Ghost scenes). But as it stands it is *prima facie* incredible. I have never met anyone who believed it, and I wonder if Greg himself did. Nevertheless, it does have the virtue of alerting us not to take the Ghost too much for granted. It is a great pity that the Ghost is so poorly treated in modern productions. 'As far as I can remember,' said the actor David William recently, 'the one thing which all the productions I have seen or played in lacked was a sense of the reality of the supernatural. I have never seen the ghost.' Moreover, it is quite common to find in modern productions that the Ghost's more horrifying and shocking language has been expunged. And in general the part is not played with due recognition of the fact that the Ghost is *sui generis*, as unique a creature of Shakespeare's imagination as Caliban or Ariel. Other ghosts in Shakespeare may with great plausibility be argued to be subjective visions; the ghosts of Kyd, Chapman and all the other Elizabethans are pantomime figures. The Ghost in *Hamlet*, whatever he is, animated corpse or invulnerable phantasm, 'spirit of health' or 'goblin damned', is, like other things in *Hamlet*, in a class by himself. But if the producers have done shabbily by the Ghost the scholars have not neglected him. Eleanor Prosser's *Hamlet and Revenge*[14] carries on further the attempt by Dover Wilson and others to elucidate him by reference to Elizabethan demonology. The general trouble with these historical inquiries, from the point of view of the plain reader, is that they are apt to result only in the laborious confirmation of what we had already assumed to be the case: that people in the past, like us, differed in opinion about matters on which no one can claim certain knowledge. Thus it seems likely that some Elizabethans were agnostic about the reality of ghosts; others were disbelievers; others believed that *some* reports of ghostly visitations were true; others, again, believed that queer beings did appear, but ascribed their origin to demonic powers. Is the situation very different today? But Eleanor Prosser's work does seem to take us a step forward from the position Dover Wilson established in *What Happens in Hamlet*. Where he had invited us to take the Ghost as an ambiguous figure, she provides substantial documentation for the view that Shakespeare's audience was overwhelmingly likely to have taken him for an evil spirit. Even Catholics were more likely to think him sent to entrap the soul. There are signs in the play that the Ghost is evil. It disappears (I. i. 49) when Horatio adjures it 'by heaven', and again when the cock crows (138). According to Horatio, it 'started like a guilty thing/Upon a fearful summons.' And on Miss Prosser's reading of the cellarage scene (I. v) it is manifestly behaving like a demon. But what proves its wickedness, for her, is that it tells Hamlet to avenge its murder. From the end of the first act, then, till the beginning of the fifth, Hamlet is to be seen as infected by the evil of the Ghost; most obviously in the scene (III. iii) when he spares the kneeling King, lest his soul should go to heaven, in a speech which Johnson thought 'too horrible to be read or uttered'.

To discuss this view would require a discussion of the whole play, and I can only register my opinion that it raises more questions than it solves. In particular, I find it difficult to agree with Miss Prosser in connecting the Ghost with the 'delay' motive. The most powerful expression of the 'delay' motive, which has stamped itself indelibly in the memory of all lovers of *Hamlet*, is the soliloquy in IV. iv. 33 ('How all occasions do inform against me'). But at this point the Ghost's part in the play is over; he has faded out as completely as Christopher Sly in *The Taming of the Shrew*. It is of course open to us to discard this speech, which is not in the folio, as belonging to a *Hamlet* different in conception. But I think there is a good case for preferring theories which attempt a coherent interpretation of the *Hamlet* of the second quarto, before we fall back on such expedients.

All that we can be certain of is that the Ghost, whatever else it may be, is a *portent*. A passage in I. i. 112 ff. shows that the spectacular phenomena which were said to have occurred before the murder of Caesar were in Shakespeare's mind when he wrote the first scene of *Hamlet*, and in the third act of *Julius Caesar* there is this dialogue:

> *Casca.* When these prodigies
> Do so conjointly meet, let not men say
> 'These are their reasons, they are natural';
> For, I believe, they are portentous things
> Unto the climate that they point upon.
> *Cicero.* Indeed, it is a strange-disposed time:
> But men may construe things after their fashion
> Clean from the purpose of the things themselves.

I believe we should see in the Ghost a 'portentous thing' which Hamlet 'construed after his fashion', and that if we do so we are following the play's repeated hints that what happens in *Hamlet* is the result of incompatible, yet complementary, ways of apprehending events.

It is in the spirit of this interpretation that I propose yet another solution for the problem of the dumb-show. I suggest that the evidence points strongly towards a *quiet* treatment of the Play Scene. There is no sign that the King was *publicly* exposed, and much to indicate that he was not. F.C. Kolbe's[15] objections to Irving's performance seem to me well grounded (they are also valid against Olivier's).

'All the stage Hamlets I have seen are unable to resist the chance of a great splash, and reveal the King's guilt to the public at large, thus ruining the whole logic of the play. I saw Henry Irving do it in his first great production of *Hamlet* at the Lyceum. The speech 'He poisons him i' the garden', instead of being quietly spoken to Ophelia by way of "chorus", was turned into a public accusation of murder. While uttering it, Hamlet crawled across the stage like a vengeful dragon stalking his prey. . . . 'He poisons him i' the garden for's estate (crawl). His name's Gonzago (wriggle); the story is extant, and writ in very choice Italian (crawl). You shall see anon (crescendo) how the murderer (threatening gesture) gets the love of Gonzago's wife (rush at the now vacated throne, collapse upon it with an unearthly cry, ah . . . grr . . . hoo!!).' This of course brings down the house. It also brings down the curtain in the middle of the scene, against all the laws of art. As a bit of histrionic energy, as a demonstration how far hysterical passion can go without becoming an absolute fit, as an appeal to the gallery, as a melodramatic thrill, it is superb. But it is not Shakespeare. And it is not human. And in order to gain this 'effect', two very important little speeches were either altogether left out or completely smothered. Ophelia says 'The King rises', showing that *she* sees no proofs of guilt; and the Queen says 'How fares my lord?' showing her own innocence of blood-guiltiness (which Hamlet has yet to probe) and also that the King's rising is merely taken as a passing indisposition. And all this marring of the play is by a man who in the same scene had admonished the players - 'for there be of them that will them-selves laugh, to set on some quantity of barren spectators to laugh too, though in the meantime some necessary question of the play be then to be considered; that's villainous.' Then he himself goes and does this. . . . And when we do go on with this scheme, we find an absolute contradiction of the Irving idea. Hamlet says anxiously to Horatio, 'Didst perceive?' In the Irving production (which in many other respects was the finest bit of stage-work I have ever seen) this is to me quite the funniest thing Hamlet says in the play. You fire off a pistol right under a man's nose, and then ask him, 'By the way, did you notice anything?"

That the duel between Hamlet and the King remains secret till the very end seems consistent with Hamlet's refusal throughout to play a *political* role (contrary to Soviet criticism, which insists on seeing him as the scourge and cleanser, with much blood, of a corrupt society). By the fifth act one almost feels the hidden struggle as a bond between them: 'I am constant to my purposes, they follow the king's pleasure. If his fitness speaks, mine is ready' (V. ii. 199.) This dialogue in II. ii. 246 ff. seems to me very significant.

Hamlet.   Denmark's a prison.
Rosencrantz.   Then is the world one.
Hamlet.   A goodly one, in which there are many confines, wards and dungeons; Denmark being one of the worst.
Rosencrantz.   We think not so, my lord.
Hamlet.   Why, then 'tis none to you; for there is nothing either good or bad, but thinking makes it so: to me it is a prison.

I am reminded of Wittgenstein's[16] saying: 'The world of the happy man is a different one from that of the unhappy man.' Need Hamlet's view of the Court be ours? The second act, for example, *can* be interpreted as a world of spying and corruption; but it can also be seen as a depiction of normal and sympathetic people genuinely concerned for Hamlet's welfare (including, at this point, the King).

The Play Scene may have resolved Hamlet's doubt, though his way of conveying this ('I'll take the ghost's word for a thousand pound') is curiously flippant. At any rate, it is clear that, as he saw it, the King *had* blenched, and he knew his course. But the Play Scene resolves Hamlet's doubt on this point without resolving the doubt of the thoughtful spectator. And here we come to a well-known difficulty in *Hamlet*: the Queen. The most peculiar aspect of the dumb-show, and of the dialogue that follows, is this. Neither suggests that the Queen was party to the murder or involved in adultery with the murderer. This shows a clear disparity with the account of the crime given by the Ghost (I. v. 42–57). What is happening here? Are we to think that she is guilty, but Hamlet is protecting her from exposure? Or is she innocent (in which case the Ghost's version of the crime is unreliable)?

This at least seems clear, where so much is enigmatic: Hamlet's mother, unlike the mother in *Coriolanus*, is not shown in a strong light. The strong light is on Hamlet himself, when in III. iv, in the most scathing language, he attempts to make Gertrude *feel* the truth about her relations with Claudius. But the interpretation of what has really happened *in the past* is left open. All that we can be *sure* of is, that in Hamlet's eyes, the Queen had gone from Hyperion to a satyr.

It has been seen as an essential characteristic of *Hamlet* – and a matter for adverse criticism – that the various points of view in the play are not subordinated to a single synoptic vision. But what if this was the dramatist's purpose? If so, perplexities about the conduct of the action may be as misguided as objections, by champions of academic perspective, to Cubism.

But now the inevitable question must be faced. Is it 'to consider too curiously, to consider so'? (V. i. 200). Is it not much more likely that what the audience saw was merely another Senecan revenge-melodrama, and that this is what Shakespeare meant to give them? Is it credible that he should have created a new dramatic technique to give expression, in terms of the theatre, to the thought that 'the world of the happy man is quite different from the world of the unhappy man'? Surely such speculations, while they may be appropriate to the drama of Ibsen or Pirandello, are out of place, because historically impossible, when brought to bear on the work of a popular Elizabethan dramatist. They belong among those numerous literary fantasias which *Hamlet* has inspired, not to responsible study of the plays.

In short, we have reached the impasse of Shakespearean criticism. 'With Shakespeare,' wrote Eliot,[17]

> we seem to be moving in an air of Cimmerian darkness. The conditions of his life, the conditions under which dramatic art was then possible, seem even more remote from us than those of Dante. . . . We dare not treat him as completely isolated from his contemporary dramatists, as we can largely isolate Dante. . . . The danger of studying him alone is the danger of working into the essence of Shakespeare what is just convention and the dodges of an overworked and underpaid writer; the danger of studying him together with his contemporaries is the danger of reducing a unique vision to a mode.

It seems to me that at the moment Shakespearean criticism has fallen apart. On the one hand there is a hard-headed historical school; on the other hand, theologians who treat the text as a source for what passes at the present day for religious wisdom. And at a time when, according to Marvin Mudrick, an American book club is offering *either* the works of Shakespeare *or* the Bible as the foundation for the subscriber's library, the latter school is likely to be in the ascendent. After reading what they write, with its academic *fumisterie* about symbols, image-clusters and so on, it is a positive relief to go back to the indignant iconoclasm of Tolstoy:[18]

> Shakespeare . . . destroys all that forms Hamlet's character in the legend. Throughout the whole tragedy Hamlet does not do what he might wish to do, but what is needed for the author's plans: now he is frightened by his father's ghost, now he begins to chaff it, calling it 'old mole'; now he loves Ophelia, now he teases her, and so on. There is no possibility of finding any explanation of Hamlet's actions and speeches. . . . In none of Shakespeare's figures is, I will not say his inability, but his complete indifference to giving his people characters, so strikingly noticeable as in the case of *Hamlet*.

At least Tolstoy realizes (whatever may be valid in the retorts to him by George Orwell or Wilson Knight) that he is dealing with a very *strange* phenomenon.

> However arbitrary the positions in which he puts his characters, however unnatural to them the language he makes them speak, however lacking in individuality they may be, the movement of feeling itself, its increase and change and the combination of many contrary feelings, are often expressed correctly and powerfully in some of Shakespeare's scenes.

It is a remarkable, if reluctant, tribute from the great realist; for the moment, if only for the moment, he joins hands with Samuel Johnson.

So everything turns on what sort of author we take Shakespeare to be. It seems to me not impossible to adopt, with regard to the mystery of *Hamlet*, something like the view which Philip Vellacott[19] takes of another problematic work, the *Oedipus Tyrannus*. Sophocles, he thinks, wrote the play in a form which would appear to most of his audience, and perhaps to most readers, to present the traditional story convincingly. But at the same time he wove into his fabric, from beginning to end, his consciousness of another, more sophisticated, view, containing all that the accepted view contained and something more. At any rate the publication of the second quarto of 1604, with its remarkable *length*, opens the possibility that Shakespeare wrote for readers as well as spectators. And no convincing explanation, based on the assumption that his handling of the Hamlet story was guided by pure expedience, has ever been found for the less 'natural' order of some of the incidents in Q2 as compared with that in the *Brudermord* and the first quarto.

And there is at least one hard fact which the most tough-minded historical critic has to accept. In the plays written probably after 1600 Shakespeare, whoever he was, established himself in the opinion of the world as one of the world's greatest writers – perhaps its greatest writer. If Shakespeare had not lived it may be that some other writer of his period, Marlowe possibly, might have been canonized instead; but the fact remains that he did live and has been judged to be of a different order from his fellow-dramatists. And *Hamlet* seems to have been the first of the plays in which the supreme Shakespeare appears.

I recently came across a passage in a book by John Berger[20] which struck me as oddly adaptable to *Hamlet*. Berger is writing of Picasso and the painting of his *Les Demoiselles d'Avignon* in 1907.

> The picture went through many stages and remains unfinished. Originally the composition included two men. One was a sailor, and the other entered the room carrying a skull. The room is in a brothel and the women are prostitutes. . . . The original presence of the man with a skull has prompted some critics to compare the subject with *The Temptations of St. Anthony*. It seems as likely to have been another private reference to Picasso's own recent fears about venereal disease. *In the final version of the picture the subject as such is hard to identify.* [Italics mine.] We see simply five naked women, painted more brutally than any woman had been painted since the eleventh or twelfth century, since that time when women were seen as a symbol of the flesh, of the physical purgatory in which man was condemned to suffer until he died.

Some of the great writers who have concerned themselves with

Hamlet have noticed the marked presence in it of disgust, of horror (Johnson, 'too horrible to be read or uttered', Eliot, 'inexpressibly horrible'). Yet critics also speak of a bursting of the dikes, the release of a flood of passionate poetry; as if the filter of human beings, through which Shakespeare's imaginative utterance had had to pass, had now almost given way, so that it pours out, inundating and fertilizing great tracts of country. And it seems to me that Eliot is right, in his much criticized essay, to find the emotional centre of the play in the effect of a mother's guilt upon her son.

> *Queen.* What have I done that thou dar'st wag thy tongue
> In noise so rude against me?

> *Hamlet.* Such an act
> That blurs the grace and blush of modesty,
> Calls virtue hypocrite, takes off the rose
> From the fair forehead of an innocent love,
> And sets a blister there; makes marriage-vows
> As false as dicers' oaths. O, such a deed
> As from the body of contraction plucks
> The very soul, and sweet religion makes
> A rhapsody of words: Heaven's face doth glow,
> And this solidity and compound mass
> With heated visage, as against the doom,
> Is thought-sick at the act.

> *Queen.* Ay me, what act,
> That roars so loud and thunders in the index?

> *Hamlet.* Look here upon this picture and on this,
> The counterfeit presentment of two brothers . . .

We are on the way to the Shakespeare of *Othello* and *King Lear*. And, however dubious we may be about speculations on the personal crisis underlying his tragic period, the astonishing development of his poetry and dramaturgy cannot be gainsaid. I return to the words of Berger.

> Blunted by the insolence of so much modern art, we probably tend to underestimate the brutality of the *Demoiselles d'Avignon*. All his friends who saw it in Picasso's studio (it was not exhibited publicly until 1937) were at first shocked by it. . . . It was a

raging, frontal attack, not against sexual 'immorality', but against life as Picasso found it – the waste, the disease, the ugliness and the ruthlessness of it. . . . It is in a direct line of descent from his previous paintings, only it is far more violent, and the violence has transformed the style.

Chapter 2
Spenser and The Faerie Queene

For many Elizabethan readers Edmund Spenser (?1552–99) was 'our principal poet', 'divine Master Spenser', 'the prince of poets in his time'. Since those days he has always been ranked with the great English poets, and so far as I know his place among them has never been formally challenged; there has been no 'dislodgment' of Spenser, no 'Spenser controversy'. Scholarly study of him has certainly been abundant, especially in the twentieth century. Yet it is difficult to feel that his work is really alive today. It seems to be unpopular with university students, and it is being gradually dropped from school syllabuses.

In part this decline of interest in Spenser may be connected with the growing neglect of English Renaissance literature as a whole, apart from the drama. The sixteenth-century part of Elizabeth I's reign – that is to say, most of it – is a blank period to more and more students. But there may be other reasons for it, more specifically related to Spenser's own peculiarities. His poems tend to be long, and his main work, The Faerie Queene, is enormously long. It is the longest good poem in English, longer than Jerusalem Delivered and Paradise Lost put together. Perhaps English-speaking readers do not really care for any long poem, however much they are told to admire it. Modern poets like Pound or Auden have tried to revive the long poem. But they are not essentially narrative poets. The modern reader tends to go to the novel for fictitious narrative, and for disquisition and sustained reflection he goes to the prose treatise or essay. From poetry we want something more tense and concentrated.

Less voluminous poets of that time may have a more direct appeal to us. Poems like 'The Lie' and 'The Passionate Man's Pilgrimage', once attributed to Spenser's friend and patron Sir Walter Ralegh, (?1552–1618) speak to us with greater immediacy.

In the best of the Tudor Court poetry we hear a familiar and forceful voice. In comparison, the impact of Spenser is vague and blurred. And the Tudor Court poets are in continuity with those better-known Stuart Court poets who inhabit a different mental world which, rightly or wrongly, has seemed to modern readers more like our own.

What troubles some readers is that 'Edmund Spenser' hardly exists for them as a human being. The modes and conventions he uses keep his own character and individuality at a distance. Whether in pastoral costume or not, he seems always to write in a sort of literary code, which is most difficult to penetrate. He is only an implied author, not a real historical person. With other writers – Milton, Kipling, D.H. Lawrence – we have the sense of a strong personality behind the work. We can feel this even in historically remote poets like Catullus, of whose life nothing is known. This personality may be liked or disliked, but it is always *there*, something to bump up against. With Spenser there is nothing.

It would seem that as a man Spenser made little or no impression on his contemporaries. To them he was 'the new poet', 'Immerito', 'Colin Clout', almost anonymous. Anecdotes about him are few and unrevealing. There are personal references in his work, but they are incidental, and mixed with fiction. We never learn the inner facts. The most important event in Spenser's public career was his appointment, through the patronage of the Earl of Leicester, Elizabeth's close friend and adviser, to a post in Ireland. But we do not learn from Spenser whether he saw this as a splendid opportunity or as exile. There is little sense of a changing individual in his work. His poems are difficult to date on internal grounds. The differences among them are differences of poetic kind and style, not of 'periods', phases of development.

But perhaps the heart of the Spenser problem is that modern readers, even those who still read poetry, simply find him tedious. He is certainly voluminous, and he might be more admired if he had written less. He is also temperamentally diffuse. He does not seem to have had the instinct for concentration which some other poets have had.

> I hate the heaven, because it doth withhold
> Me from my love, and eke my love fro me;

I hate the earth, because it is the mold
Of fleshy slime and fraile mortalitie;
I hate the fire, because to nought it flyes,
I hate the Ayre, because sighes of it be,
I hate the Sea, because it teares supplyes.

I hate the day, because it lendeth light
To see all things, and not my love to see;
I hate the darknesse and the drery night,
Because they breed sad balefulnesse in me;
I hate all times, because all times do flye
So fast away, and may not stayed be.
But as a speedie post that passeth by.

Daphnaida

And so Spenser goes on weaving his verbal patterns, day/night, man/woman, life/death, past/future, hate/love. His stanza forms may be simple, as here or in *Four Hymns*, or complicated, as in the *Epithalamion*, but they are never hurried, always graceful. Each stanza must be complete in itself: Spenser thinks in stanzas, not in single lines. It is significant that the word 'Spenserian' has passed into the language to describe the beautiful stanza he invented for *The Faerie Queene*. In lines like these (*F.Q.* II.xii.71) we see what English poetry gained from Spenser's love of pattern-making. As W.L. Renwick says in his book (1925), they represent a brilliant transference into words of the effects of polyphonic music: the entry of the different voices can be heard.

The joyous birdes shrouded in chearefull shade,
Their notes unto the voyce attempred sweet;
Th'Angelicall soft trembling voyces made
To th'instruments divine respondence meet:
The silver sounding instruments did meet
With the base murmur of the waters fall:
The waters fall with difference discreet,
Now soft, now loud, unto the wind did call:
The gentle warbling wind low answered to all.

Spenser's deliberateness, his refusal to crowd his thoughts, the slow and gradual development of his rhythms, can yield marvellous results in *The Faerie Queene*. But the question has to be raised whether much else of his is worth reading, except for historical reasons. The leading Spenserian of our time, C.S. Lewis, remarked that while Virgil would still be thought a great poet without the *Aeneid*, or Milton without *Paradise Lost*, or Goethe without *Faust*, Spenser without *The Faerie Queene* would probably have been forgotten. And in recent times Spenser scholarship and criticism have concentrated on it almost exclusively. In the Penguin English Poets series Spenser is represented only by *The Faerie Queene* (edited 1978 by Roche and O'Donnell). This isolation of Spenser's chief poem from all his others may be based on sound judgment but it does tend to make *The Faerie Queene* seem even more a bizarre curiosity than it is already. And while it may be admitted that much in the minor poems does not greatly appeal to us, there are elements in them that are more interesting and poetically alive than some things in *The Faerie Queene*. (Readers may be reminded of the similar situation in Pound criticism, with its overwhelming emphasis on the *Cantos*.) And even the reader who cares only about *The Faerie Queene* will find plenty of material in Spenser's other work to help him understand the author's characteristic thought and temper of mind.

The most famous of these other works is *The Shepherd's Calender* (1579), often compared with the *Lyrical Ballads* of Wordsworth and Coleridge as heralding a poetic revival. But it is likely to affect many readers as it affected the young Stephen Potter, coming to it with happy anticipation of pristine pleasure from 'the poet's poet'. His disappointment was complete.

> Instead of breath-taking images, there was smooth poetistical language. Instead of apprehensions of nature (making me see something as if for the first time) there was talk of *oaten stop*, and the shepherds' *fleecy care*. Instead of naivete and idealism, confident force (my conception, then, of what a young poet's.poetry was likely to possess) there was a careful imitation, use of classics chosen from models for which I still had a schoolboy antipathy.
>
> (*The Muse in Chains*, 1937)

Potter's reaction is understandable. He had not yet enough literary experience to realize that the 'poetic diction' he found so objectionable would not have had, for Spenser and his friends, the hackneyed, unfresh quality which it came to have in the eighteenth century; it had still something of the excitement of a new discovery. But though historical extenuations are possible, the *Calender* has been traditionally much overrated. The pastoral convention is dead for most of us, and it has been plausibly argued that Spenser's use of it is not happy: he gives us neither the sense of real country life, such as we find in the work of Homer or John Clare, nor a completely idyllic world, such as Michael Drayton portrays in his later poetry. The experiments in language and metre have some historical interest, but they represent on the whole a dead end for Spenser and for English poetry generally. The attempt to combine the neo-Chaucerian (evident in the rugged metre and archaic spelling) with the neo-classical produces an incongruous effect, and criticism of the 'old rustic' language goes back as far as Sidney's *Apology for Poetry*. But there are fine things in the *Calender*. The song on Elizabeth in 'April' shows Spenser as already a remarkable 'word-musician'; and these lines from 'December' have the freshness of real experience in them, for all the 'pastoral' costume:

> Whilome in youth, when flowrd my joy full spring,
> Like Swallow swift I wandred here and there:
> For heat of heedless lust* me so did sting,
> That I of doubted danger had no feare.
> I went the wastefull woodes and forest wyde
> Withouten dread of Wolves to bene espyed.
>
> I wont to raunge amydde the mazie thickette,
> And gather nuttes to make me Christmas game;
> And joyed ofte to chace the Trembling Pricket†,
> Or hunt the hartless‡ hare, till shee were tame.
> What wreaked I of wintry ages waste,
> Tho deemed I, my spring wold ever laste.
>
> How often have I scaled the craggie Oke,
> All to dislodge the Raven of her neste:
> How have I wearied with many a stroke
> The stately Walnut tree, the while the rest
> Under the tree fell all for nuts at strife:
> For ylike to me was libertee and lyfe.
>
> * pleasure   † young buck   ‡ timid

Much more immediate pleasure can be got from other poems of Spenser. There is strong plain writing in *Mother Hubberds Tale* (1591), a beast-fable in heroic couplets (it is in fact a group of stories). Here Spenser is the heir of the comic Chaucer, and his verse-manner looks forward to Dryden's satires. In *The Ruins of Time* there is some moving elegiac writing, as the poet commemorates the deaths of Sidney, Leicester and Walsingham. It is notable that the lines which seem to reveal the strongest feeling are not on Sidney, but on his uncle Leicester, to most of us a less attractive figure:

> He now is dead, and all with him is dead,
> Save what in heavens storehouse be uplaid:
> His hope is faild, and come to pass his dread,
> And evil men, now dead, his deeds upbraid:
> Spite bites the dead, that living never baid*.
> He now is gone, the whiles the Foxe is crept
> Into the hole, the which the Badger swept.
>
>   * barked

These bitter lines were to stick in the mind of Yeats (see 'The Municipal Gallery Revisited'). There is real observation behind them: the fox is a dirty feeder, the badger clean and neat. This earthy simplicity is characteristic of Spenser. Quite different is the sunny poem, the miniature epic *Muiopotmos; or the Fate of the Butterflie* – in its graceful charm suggesting a temporary release from puritan ethics and piety:

> What more felicitie can fall to creature
> Than to enjoy delight with liberty . . .

The full extent of Spenser's powers as a lyric poet is shown in a volume of 1595, containing the sonnet sequence *Amoretti*, together with *Epithalamion*. It seems clear that he meant this volume to be read as the poetic record of his courtship of and marriage to his second wife, Elizabeth Boyle. The sonnets themselves are too much in one key, and do not consistently rise above the level of average Elizabethan sonneteering. Spenser does not bring to this verse-form the force and originality of the English masters of the sonnet, Shakespeare, Milton, Wordsworth, Rossetti, Hopkins and Auden. It is the *Epithalamion* that is unique and unsurpassable, conveying something of the exultation to be felt in poems like Smart's *Song to David* or Hopkins's *The Wreck of the Deutschland*: the joy of a technical accomplishment which is at the same time an emotional satisfaction. The structure of this marriage ode is based on the progression of a summer day, from dawn to nightfall. Modern scholarship has discovered an elaborate astrological and numerological symbolism in the poem. But whether or not the secrets of Spenser's art can be discovered in this way, no lover of English poetry can miss the musical pattern of the stanzas and the interweaving of Christian and pagan motifs, the association of sensuousness and spirituality. In this exalting of marriage the 'Renaissance' and the 'puritan' elements of Spenser's temperament are at one.

> Now al is done; bring home the bride againe,
> Bring home the triumph of our victory,
> Bring home with you the glory of her gaine,
> With joyance bring her and with jollity.
> Never had man more joyfull day than this,
> Whom heaven would heape with blis.
> Make feast therefore now all this live long day,
> This day for ever to me holy is,
> Poure out the wine without restraint or stay,
> Poure not by cups, but by the belly full,
> Poure out to all that wull*,
> And sprinkle all the postes and walls with wine,
> That they may sweat, and drunken be withall.
> Crowne ye God Bacchus with a coronall,
> And Hymen also crowne with wreathes of vine,
> And let the Graces daunce unto the rest;
> For they can doe it beste:
> The whiles the maydens to their carroll sing,
> To which the woods shall answer and theyr eccho ring.
>   * will

Prothalamion (1596), written for the weddings of the two daughters of the Earl of Worcester, is on a smaller scale and does not have so much emotional unity. But its refrain ('Sweet

Themmes, runne softly till I end my song') is one of the few lines of Spenser that are well known, perhaps because of T.S. Eliot's use of it in *The Waste Land*.

To know the marriage odes is to know Spenser as a poet of celebration. In other poems he is the poet of complaint and elegy, of pastoral and satire. But it was to be in epic and romance – a peculiar mixture of them – that he was to achieve his most lasting fame, with *The Faerie Queene*. It is clear that this was his life work, and all his other poems were, in some sense, interruptions of it. But its status now appears ambiguous. One of the few things that can be said with confidence about *The Faerie Queene* is that it is enigmatic, problematic, protean.

To see *The Faerie Queene* as part of English poetic history is to realize what different things it has meant to different poets. It was extolled during Spenser's lifetime, though there are signs that his contemporaries really preferred *The Shepherd's Calender*, and for long Spenser was more esteemed as a pastoral than as an epic poet. And the seventeenth-century 'Spenserians' are not the liveliest poets of that time. Already in Cowley and Milton there are signs of the divided, divergent response to *The Faerie Queene* which is the central problem of Spenser criticism. Cowley as a boy was delighted by it, 'the stories of the Knights and Giants, and Monsters', and for many readers this level of response is the only true one. For Milton, on the other hand, the poet was 'our sage and serious Spenser', 'a better teacher than Scotus or Aquinas'. Spenser's first critic, Sir Kenelm Digby (1603–65), did something to bring these two aspects of *The Faerie Queene* together. But on the whole it was Spenser's fantasy, and his curious style, plain and forceful yet flavoured with archaism, that appealed to later poets. In the eighteenth century Spenser's poem contributed substantially to the romantic medievalism of the time. And its influence is plain in the work of the poets of the late eighteenth and early nineteenth century. Wordsworth admired Spenser as a teacher and moralist, and he felt the beauty of Spenser's poetry keenly. Keats and Shelley use the Spenserian stanza, and Keats especially was drawn to Spenser's erotic world, as we see in *The Eve of St Agnes*. Byron imitates Spenser's style in *Childe Harold's Pilgrimage*, and uses his stanza; but Byron's temperament was too unlike Spenser's for him to keep up the imitation for very long, and the slow-moving

Spenserian stanza was not so suited to him as the *ottava rima* he adopted in *Don Juan*. Tennyson in *The Lotos-Eaters* was better able to make a more positive use of Spenser, the Spenser of the Despair episode and the house of Morpheus. But after Tennyson and the Pre-Raphaelites the presence of Spenser, as part of the English poetic consciousness, seems less palpable. The last major modern poet to show much interest in him was Yeats (the others, if they were interested in sixteenth-century poetry at all, have preferred other poets, such as Skelton or Wyatt). And Yeats's essay makes it clear that he was bored and repelled by much in Spenser; his final verdict is not enthusiastic. Apart from isolated figures like C.M. Doughty there seems to be no twentieth-century poet for whom Spenser has counted for much.

The history of scholarly study and interpretation of *The Faerie Queene* is quite different. It began early in the eighteenth century with writers like Upton and Hughes, who are still well worth reading, though Upton was committed to the hopeless opinion that *The Faerie Queene* has a single 'story' (that of Prince Arthur), with beginning, middle and end. Eighteenth-century criticism was much concerned with questions about the form of Spenser's poem: what kind of poem is it? Many modern ideas, such as those expounded by Rosemond Tuve in *Allegorical Imagery* (1966) about its 'interlaced' narratives, are anticipated in commentators of that time who maintained that *The Faerie Queene* is to be understood (and enjoyed) as an example of 'Gothic', not 'classical', form. The romantic movement brought something of a reaction against Spenser commentators. Hazlitt advised readers not to bother with the allegory and moral significance but to enjoy *The Faerie Queene* as a glorious verbal symphony. What it was 'about' was not of any great consequence. The likeness to great Renaissance paintings which Spenser had never seen was expounded in extensive detail by Leigh Hunt, who called Spenser England's greatest painter. It was the colour work, not the themes, of this particular Old Master that interested Hunt. The 'escapist' view was carried further by James Russell Lowell, who found the didactic element in *The Faerie Queene* irrelevant or distasteful. But he was opposed firmly by the Irish critic Edward Dowden. And there were other critics who took Spenser's allegory seriously. Ruskin in *The Stones of Venice* supplied a point-by-point interpretation of Book I of *The Faerie*

Queene which anticipates much modern work of this kind. The topical, or historical, allegory has of course always been a matter for controversy. The great American scholar Greenlaw played it down, as did C.S. Lewis, the most influential of modern Spenserians; but it has been revived in recent times by Frank Kermode, with special emphasis on Books I and V.

The Variorum edition of 1949 can be seen as a landmark in traditional Spenser scholarship. Up till then the critics, though increasingly scholarly, had been within the 'genteel', men-of-letters tradition. After the Second World War there appeared the modern academic specialist and the new development of 'Renaissance studies'. Spenser was now to be 'read' as Panofsky or Edgar Wind taught us to 'read' Renaissance paintings. Iconography, rhetoric and other technical studies of language, astrology and numerology, and other recondite aspects of Renaissance thought, were brought to bear. The emblem-books, the shows and heraldry of the age were studied, as well as the inner politics and cultural life of the world Spenser knew. And the interconnections of symbolism, ambiguity and word-play within the poem were more and more studied; all this, it must be remembered, at a time when Freudian dream-interpretation and all its ramifications had spread into literary criticism, and the widely held view that speculation about a poet's intentions is irrelevant seemed to license the utmost extravagances of subjective interpretation. Today the reader in search of guidance to Spenser's work is caught between some experts using freedom of association ever more and more widely, and others demanding a heavier and heavier burden of esoteric knowledge.

All this is understandable. *The Faerie Queene* was said by the poet, in his prefatory letter to Ralegh, to contain an allegory, or 'dark conceit', and it has long been a rich mine for symbol-seekers, allusion-spotters, and source-hunters. As with Dante's *Divine Comedy*, the crossword-puzzle appeal is strong. But the question does arise: what is the purpose of all this activity? In an age which has produced *The Road to Xanadu* and *Finnegans Wake*, it may be that intellectual complications are enjoyed for their own sake. In the mean time, however, the question why Spenser matters, why his poem rather than, say, Phineas Fletcher's *The Purple Island* (1633), is the pretext for all this, goes unanswered. The Spenserian scholars do occasionally venture into evaluation. They admit faults, or judge one book of *The Faerie Queene* inferior to another. But the whole enterprise of *The Faerie Queene* goes unquestioned, as does its status relative to works which are admitted to be less problematically 'great'. How does it compare in value and significance with the plays of Shakespeare, or even with one of Shakespeare's major plays?

The stock answer to such evaluative questions has been that the poem must be understood before it can be judged. But the quest for a 'correct' understanding of *The Faerie Queene*, even with the full resources of modern scholarship, seems illusory. Studies multiply, often repetitive; one scholar may differ from another, but no interpretation gets eliminated; more and more are added. And as this is a world without a common reader, there is no commonsense check on these interpretations, no public opinion that need be attended to. It is not a healthy state of affairs for a supposedly 'classic' poet.

There has, however, been one hopeful development, as far as the general reader of poetry is concerned. Up to the 1940s Spenser scholars tended to be either indifferent to modern poetry and criticism, or actually hostile to it. Since then there have been good books by scholars like Nelson (1963), Alpers (1967) and Sale (1968), who are in sympathy with modern taste as well as aware of the many historical and exegetic problems which Spenser presents.

It should be clear, then, that in our time the status of *The Faerie Queene* is problematic, and an innocent, 'told to the children' account of it is not only insulting, but impossible. Until the old question 'What kind of poem is it?' is answered, we cannot read the poem; and the question is not easy to answer. Any assertions about the poem must therefore remain provisional and tentative.

But it might be asked why we should not simply go to the poet himself for an account of his intentions. There is the letter to Ralegh to be consulted. However, this document itself requires so much interpretation that it is no use simply passing it on to new readers as a helpful introduction to the poem. It is full of words and phrases that are themselves highly problematic and the interpretation of which is controversial.

And it describes only what may have been the poet's plan at the time of writing it: a twelve-book poem (with, perhaps, another twelve-book poem as its sequel) which we do not possess. What we have appears to be two fragments of that design, Books I, II and III, published together in 1590, and Books IV, V and VI, published together in 1596. (There is also the mysterious fragment known as the Mutability Cantos, published posthumously in 1609, which appears to be part of another Book, not extant.) The letter to Ralegh is prefixed to the first of these fragments. But it does not, on the face of it, fit even that part of the poem very well. The sketch of Book I is correct, but the sketch of Book II is not. Scholars have tried to reconcile the poem as we have it with the letter to Ralegh, but this is difficult to do. It would be wrong to say that the letter is not of great interest and historical value. But the problems of the poem as it actually exists, empirically, still remain.

What is reasonably uncontroversial is Spenser's choice of basic form for his narrative: the romance of knight-errantry. The Italian chivalrous epics of Boiardo and Ariosto are also based on this material, and Spenser's debt to the Italian poets is obvious. But he also draws directly on the traditions of this kind of romance as it came down to them. It has often been remarked that he creates a world of his own, Fairyland, even more remote from real history or geography than the world of the Italians. These are 'the brave days of old', exempt, as Coleridge said, from any particular space and time: an enchanted forest, a land of knights and fair ladies, castles and bowers and temples, vile witches, cunning enchantresses, sorcerers ('He to his studie goes'), demons and goddesses, ogres and monsters, nymphs and satyrs.

Why Spenser chose to write about knights and their adventures is not completely clear. Apart from references to his old-world romanticism and antiquarian, backward-looking disposition, the only explanation that used to be given was his ambition to emulate or to 'overgo' Ariosto, whose *Madness of Roland* (1532) had long delighted Renaissance readers and puzzled Renaissance critics. But it now seems reasonable to connect *The Faerie Queene* with the Elizabethan passion for tourneys in which nobles took part for royal entertainment, and the deliberate idealiza-

tion of life and times under an imaginary 'Arthurian' chivalry
which is mixed up with contemporary politics and ideology. In
Astraea (1975) Frances Yates has explored the 'imperial theme'
of the sixteenth century, with many of its ramifications extend-
ing into the world of Spenser's poems – another link with
Ariosto.

The *Madness of Roland*, of all famous poems, is the one most obviously like *The Faerie Queene*. And Spenser clearly knew Ariosto's
poem intimately, and adapts or imitates much of its contents. But
he is very different. It was for long a critical commonplace that the
English poet was grave, even humourless, that he took seriously
incidents and reflections which in the Italian poet were ironical.
It was regretted that the other great sixteenth-century Italian
poet, Tasso, came too late with his *Jerusalem Delivered* (1581,
1583) to influence Spenser greatly, though Spenser was able to
draw on him, with exquisite results, for the beautiful song in
the Bower of Bliss (II. xii. 75). Tasso was as devout and serious
a child of the Catholic Counter-reformation as Spenser was of
the Protestant Reformation, and no doubt they have much in
common. But why was Spenser attracted to Ariosto? Is it not
possible that he understood Ariosto perfectly well, but used him
for his own purposes and in his own way? The really great
difference between Spenser and Ariosto is that we very soon
come to know the implied author as we never know Spenser.
One of the charms of Ariosto's extravaganza is that we are
always aware of his presence beside us. Spenser is enigmatic: he
has reverted to the manner of the old, anonymous storytellers.
Even in the moralizing poems and explicit comments on the
action there is no 'Spenser voice'. Or rather, there are many
'Spenser voices'.

The next unchallengeable observation about *The Faerie Queene*
is that though the world of the poem is obviously an imaginary world, a dream-landscape, there is considerable realism of
presentation within its confines. Fairyland may contain angels,
goblins, giants, but it is full of observations of humanity and
nature, detailed and always visualized. This peculiar realism of
The Faerie Queene is perhaps the only respect in which it resembles a novel. Here is Britomart suspicious of her lover's good
faith:

One while she blam'd her selfe; another whyle
She him condemn'd, as trustlesse and untrew;
And then, her griefe with errour to beguile,
She fayn'd to count the time againe anew,
As if before she had not counted trew,
For houres but dayes; for weekes, that passed were,
She told but months, to make them seeme more few;
Yet when she reckned them, still drawing neare,
Each hour did seem a month, and every month a yeare.

                                              (V. vi. 5)

But if in some ways the characters of *The Faerie Queene* may
be said to inhabit an ordinary world, it is the ordinary world of
romance, in which strange adventures, misunderstandings, magic,
taboos respected and violated, are routine. In this respect it is very
unlike the 'classical-realist' novel. Metamorphosis, shape-shifting,
dream-like projections of states of mind and soul, which in the
realistic novel have an awkward status, flourish in *The Faerie
Queene*. At no point is the distinction between characters and
their 'inner world' a distinct one. It is a piquant irony that
Spenser, who has been relegated by some literary historians to
an antiquarian backwater even in his own time, should turn
out to have much in common with some ultra-modern writers
who have undermined the classic realism, the three-dimensional
'illusionism', of the traditional novel. But for the most part, and
for most people, English literature has remained a literature of
characters as the realistic novelist understands them; and this may
in part account for the uncertain position of Spenser's work.

Finally, there can be no doubt that *The Faerie Queene* is not
offered merely as a series of romantic tales. It has another dimension
of meaning for which the poet himself uses the word 'allegory'.
Innumerable books and articles have been written about this aspect
of the matter: what he, and Renaissance poets and critics and
readers generally, understood by allegory, the different types and
modes of it, different 'depths' at different places, the emblematic
details which are lost on the reader who merely reads the poem
as he finds it, without benefit of Natalis Comes or all the other
mythographers Spenser may or may not have drawn on. That much
in the poem points to other levels than the literal is obvious. It is full

of symbolic names, some transparent, like Sansloy and Sansfoy and Sansjoy, or Mammon, or Despair, some more opaque but none the less meaningful, like Archimago. The actual words of the poem, the odd spellings, constantly reflect Spenser's conviction that, at the linguistic level no less than the level of images, nothing is merely accidental or arbitrary. Contrary to the ideas of a modern thinker like Saussure, he sees nothing that is only contingent in the etymology and phonology of words as he understood them. Hence no paraphrase of an episode in *The Faerie Queene* can bring out its meaning, unless attention is paid to its puns and wordplay.

Nevertheless Hazlitt was not wholly wrong in advising us not to bother with the allegory: 'it will not bite us'. It must be understood that all interesting and significant works of art have more than one meaning, that they all contain elements which function in complex ways. The British film-maker Lindsay Anderson has said that no film-maker likes being asked what his work 'means'. What does *Gulliver's Travels* mean? What do *The Arabian Nights* mean? Is *Dick Whittington* 'real'? It may be guessed that Spenser, in his own way, wanted to fend off such questions. But the tone of Tudor high culture was ethical and didactic. We may think of the austere religious practices of even a worldly statesman like Lord Burghley, who seems to have been displeased by something non-moral, some element of eroticism he found in *The Faerie Queene*. Faced with 'mighty peers' and critics who demanded explicit ethical teaching from poetry, Spenser had no choice but to use the critical idiom of his day and talk about 'allegory', and Aristotle's twelve private moral virtues, and 'fashioning' a virtuous gentleman. Not that his avowed didactic aims should be dismissed as hypocritical, merely a sop to 'puritan' readers while the 'Renaissance' readers enjoyed his gallery of beautiful nudes, or goddesses in *déshabillé*. If Spenser aspired to emulate Ariosto, he also wanted to be an English Virgil. And Virgil, like all great poets, was credited with numerous allegorical meanings, moral and religious. He held up images of good to be cherished, of evil to be reprobated. Spenser does this in the temptation of Mammon (II. vii), one of the trials to which the hero of Book II, the representative of Temperance, is subjected. The incident echoes the descent of Aeneas, led by the Sibyl, to the world of shades (*Aeneid* VI). As they enter, they are surrounded by shadowy figures – Grief, Care, Disease, Old Age –

which we associate with the thought of death. Spenser makes the
scene a correlative for the evil of Money-lust.

> Before the dore sat selfe-consuming Care,
> Day and night keeping wary watch and ward,
> For feare lest Force or Fraud should unaware
> Breake in, and spoil the treasure there in gard;
> Ne would he suffer Sleepe once thither-ward
> Approch, albe his drowsy den were next;
> For next to Death is sleepe to be compared;
> Therefore his house is unto his annext;
> Here Sleep, there Richesse, and Hell-gate them both betwixt.

Besides the classical allusion, Spenser in this episode dwells on the
teaching of the Bible: 'How hardly shall they that have riches enter
into the kingdom of heaven!' And the triple temptation of Guyon,
which follows, alludes to Biblical temptations: Adam and Eve in
the Garden of Eden, Jesus in the wilderness. The ethical allegory
in such incidents has to be recognized, and taken seriously.

But it is important also to recognize that these classical, 'moral'
episodes, like the romantic tales, represent only what Spenser
started with. His poem is full of enigmas, and it seems clear that
there is an element in his work of the deliberately enigmatic.
At one time interest in this centred on the topical allegory, the
significances that may have been there for court readers, if not
for Spencer's printed-book public. All we can be certain of here
is what Spenser vouches for in the letter to Ralegh, that Gloriana
is Queen Elizabeth, who is also alluded to in 'Belphoebe'. It can
be regarded as reasonably certain that the episode of Timias and
Belphoebe refers to Ralegh's relations with the Queen. And
that Duessa refers, in Book V, to Mary Queen of Scots may
be taken as highly probable, since the identification was made
so early (King James VI protested, or affected to protest, at
the insult to his mother). But Duessa in Book I seems to
be the Church of Rome, rather than a particular individual.
And in general the historical allusions of the poem are fugitive.
The longest stretch of topical allegory is in the last five cantos
of Book V, almost a sustained commentary on foreign affairs
and events in Ireland. But that these allusions are so obvious
suggests that the search for other topical references is misguided.

To look for one main meaning in the poem is to fall into a sort of critical monism. Its character is to be protean. It is unlike all other famous Western poems in having no clear 'profile'. No brief account can suggest what it is about. In sources, allusions, mythology it is eclectic. Everything that goes through the Spenserian looking-glass is transformed, mutated. We can guess, however, that the main characters are human beings, not personified abstractions, or cardinal virtues. They encounter allegorical beings; they can even *become* them, as the jealous Malbecco 'becomes' Jealousy at the end of that blackly farcical story (III. ix. x). But the essential subject-matter is the inner life, the psychological landscapes, of men and women.

The presentation and tone vary in different Books. Books I and II have a similar pattern: the knight hero on his quest in company with a super-ego or conscience figure. The problems are perhaps too explicitly religious and ethical to be attractive to modern readers. Book I is the story of Redcrosse, a combination of the legend of St George with a sustained use of imagery drawn from the Book of Revelation. This is the book of Holiness, and the tone appropriately is one of high gravity, though the stories are of romantic enchantments: some of the deeper meanings in the Book depend upon both Redcrosse and Una mistaking an evil replica, the work of magic, for the beloved. Book II is more concerned with psychological than theological problems: the knight of Temperance is tempted by violence and lust. The lengthy and bloody fighting in this Book suggests that it is largely a study in the repressed sadism of the chilly hero. The things that 'happen' to him are the fantasies that are appropriate to such a personality. The great closing canto, culminating in the destruction of the bower of Acrasia, Spenser's version of Homer's Circe – the canto is an *Odyssey* in miniature – seems best read in such a way, rather than as an expression of Spenser's personal prurience. The violence with which Guyon destroys the Bower of Bliss seems to be a substitute for the climax of sexual enjoyment which is forbidden to him.

It is a pity that these Books are perhaps the best known. They contain some fine things, but they do not represent the whole of Spenser. Books III and IV have a less clear-cut quality. They are free from the anti-Catholic propaganda of Book I, the black-and-white moral tones of Book II. Here we are in

a many-coloured world, voluptuous yet enchanted, surrealistic.
The structure of these Books is much less apparent than that of
the earlier ones. But many of the episodes turn on the qualities of
contrasting women: the warrior Britomart, the tormented Amoret,
the timid, fleeing Florimell, the lecherous Hellenore. Britomart
is by general agreement Spenser's best 'character'; and however
anti-feminist may have been his official doctrines, it is clear that,
like his unfortunate Artegall, he is drawn to warrior women.
In Book V the tone changes again, to the world of the 'iron
man' Talus, Artegall's torturer and executioner, and his mission
of 'justice', and we have a glimpse of the hard side of Spenser
that we see in his prose dialogue on the state of Ireland. But
Book VI offers yet another metamorphosis. Here we are in the
world of Sidney's *Arcadia*, pastoral brought to life, so much more
than in *The Shepherd's Calender*, by the admixture of chivalrous
romance. Shakespeare seems to have drawn on this attractive
Book in his *The Winter's Tale*. The finest thing in the whole
Book, and perhaps in the poem, is the passage in which we are
shown a vision of the naked Graces dancing to the music of Colin
Clout – the poet himself. It has been thought that by introducing
himself in this way Spenser was saying farewell to his readers.

To convey the quality of so miscellaneous a work is not possible
in a short space, let alone to attempt to judge it. But perhaps the
essential question is this. Spenser's best modern critics agree on his
'undramatic' quality. We might take the story of Phedon (II.iv) as
an example. It is a Hero and Claudio story, of deceit and murder
and jealousy as cruel as the grave. It is crisply and vividly told. But
when it is told Guyon simply remarks:

> Squire, sore have ye beene diseasd;
> But all your hurts may soone through temperance be easd.

as if temperance were a patent medicine; while the Palmer
moralizes. The effect is to make the tragic events seem *not to have
happened*: the story becomes a mere cautionary tale, an *exemplum*.
What did Spenser intend here? It is hard to say. Why should he
have taken the 'drama' out of his own work? In the end the effect
on us is to produce a feeling of detachment: this is tapestry, not
flesh and blood. The question is whether this 'undramatic' quality
does not entail the omission of other potentialities that have usually

been held to be essential to great imaginative writing in any kind. Perhaps the conclusion must be drawn that Spenser's achievement in *The Faerie Queene* appeals to a very special taste, and does not convey at once that conviction that we are reading a great work which comes before 'understanding' and analysis. All that can be added to qualify this is that in every age, despite all the changes of taste since the 1590s, there have been a few readers who have felt the fascination of this problematic, enigmatic work, taken up its challenge to normal modes of perception, and come to terms with its elusive art.

Chapter 3
Paradise Lost:
Changing Interpretations and Controversy

Milton is such a towering figure in English literature that it is surprising to learn how little impression he seems to have made, as a poet, in his lifetime. The volume of 1645, which includes such famous poems as *Comus* and *Lycidas*, did not go into a second edition till 1673. And the three later poems on which Milton's international reputation rests — *Paradise Lost* (ten-book version 1667), *Paradise Regained* and *Samson Agonistes* (both 1671) — appear to have caused, at first, no great stir in the literary world. But before Milton's death in 1674 the mysterious forces by which poetic fame is created were already at work, and by the end of the century his main work, *Paradise Lost*, had already reached the position it was to occupy, virtually unchallenged, till the 1920s, as an established classic of English poetry, seeming to have been always 'there', part of the literary environment of every educated person.

Just how this momentous change in the status of Milton came about is hard to discover, and must remain largely a matter of guesswork. Scholars have suggested that political opinions played a part in it. During Milton's life his reputation as an inveterate pamphleteer and controversialist — in part, probably, a somewhat unsavoury reputation — may well have stood in the way of his recognition as a poet. The Roundhead ideologue that he had become eclipsed the scholar-aesthete and man of taste that he had been in his younger days (and indeed always remained). But in the years after the Restoration of Charles II in 1660, Milton's political views may have actually helped to strengthen his reputation among younger writers and intellectuals, growing more and more disillusioned about the Stuart monarchy and full of nostalgia for the days of Cromwell and the Good Old Cause. From the first, Milton's fame as a poet was bound up with his symbolic status as a defender of 'English liberty'.

However that may be, it is clear as a fact of literary history that the establishment of Milton's poetry at the centre of the canon of English literature was due to the 'wits' rather than the 'Puritans'. Paradoxically, it was in the 'age of Dryden' that Milton's greatness as a poet was acclaimed and his poetry became the potent influence on other English verse that it was to be until quite recent times. For by 1667 the poetic revolution inaugurated by Denham and Waller, and brought to consummation and consolidation by John Dryden, had been effected. An atmosphere of worldly wisdom, epigrammatic couplets and metropolitan urbanity now pervaded poetry, suggesting standards of taste and judgment very remote from the solitary, unworldly, unaccommodating visionary. Yet Dryden, the chief poet of the age and most active and influential of its men of letters, Dryden, most generous and catholic in taste of all the great English critics, admired Milton immensely. His mature verse bears splendid witness to the impact of Milton, in his Odes and in *Absalom and Achitophel* and elsewhere. Dryden was on friendly personal terms with Milton, who civilly gave him leave to 'tag' his verses – that is, to produce a rhymed dramatic version of *Paradise Lost* called *The State of Innocence*. And after Milton's death Dryden was to commemorate him in an epigram of 1688 which declares him to have combined the powers of Homer and Virgil. Dryden, then, takes his place in literary history as the first and not the least gifted member of the School of Milton which with only slight exaggeration, may be said to dominate English poetry for two centuries.

So it is tempting to see this meeting of the minds of Milton and Dryden, partial though it must have been, given the very different temperaments and poetic capacities of the two men, as a crucial factor in the establishment of *Paradise Lost* as the chief monument of the 'Augustan', post-Civil War culture. But some other, more general, considerations are also relevant. First, there was the contemporary concentration on *literary* works and interests, as shown by the flourishing of literary criticism, partly under French influence: no doubt a reaction against the political and religious obsessions of the Civil War and Commonwealth period. The richness of phrasing and verse-music of *Paradise Lost* provided an ample banquet for the scholarly wits and cultivated courtiers of Restoration days. Then there was the still active longing, which goes back as far as the Renaissance, for 'Christian epic': something which the poets of England, like the poets of continental Europe, had dreamed of for centuries. We might think of the Great American Novel as a comparable dream of later times. But while the Great American Novel has never appeared, the judgment of the generations following Milton's was that he actually had created a Christian epic. He alone had the combination of qualifications that were necessary, as the critics of the time saw it, for such a poem: the religious zeal and high spirituality, the command of all the arts and sciences, the reading in literatures ancient and modern, the capacity to make large-scale structures in verse while investing all the local details of the poem with poetic skill and feeling. Finally, and surely not least in importance, we must bear in mind the long-felt need for a great work of English literature, something that would be the equal, at least, of the great Greco-Roman classics. There had been some fine scholars in England since the Renaissance, and some major poets. But in Milton alone the new age saw the unique and happy fusion of the great scholar with the great poet.

Yet, even in the early days of Milton's poetic ascendancy, doubts and uncertainties began to emerge which were to break loose in the great twentieth-century questioning of his status, one day to be known as 'the Milton Controversy'. Had *Paradise Lost* after all really performed the miracle, which had defeated all other Christian poets, of harmoniously uniting the two norms of the culture which gave birth to it – the 'Christian' and the 'classical'? Some, at least, of the difficulties that have been found in the poem certainly arise from Milton's decision to treat the theme of the Fall of Man in a form based on the models of ancient epic. And this consideration suggests something deeply paradoxical and problematic about Milton's whole undertaking. He was the most learned of English poets, and perhaps the only one whose work is truly 'classical' in spirit. Yet for him much of what the pagan writers said was not only false, but pernicious. And in recent years scholars have come to see *Paradise Lost* as not so much an 'epic' as a radical *questioning*, a *criticism* (and at times an adverse criticism) of 'epic': in its treatment of norms of the Heroic, not so much a neo-classical homage to them, as almost a parody or an anti-epic. The early critics of Milton did not see the poem quite in this way. But even in the first published appreciation of *Paradise Lost*, Andrew Marvell's verses prefixed to the second edition of 1674, we seem to catch a note of misgiving about the congruity between its matter and its form. Having noted the vast scale of Milton's undertaking (Marvell sees the poem as not merely concerned with the incident of the Fall but with the whole of the fundamentals of Christianity):

> Messiah Crown'd, God's Reconcil'd Decree,
> Rebelling Angels, the Forbidden Tree,
> Heav'n, Hell, Earth, Chaos, All: . . .

Marvell says

> the Argument
> Held me a while misdoubting his Intent,
> That he would ruin (for I saw him strong)
> The sacred Truths to Fable and old Song,

Marvell of course goes on to say gracefully how, as he read, his doubts were overcome by Milton's mighty genius, But the impression still remains, amid all the admiration and respect (Marvell knew Milton personally), of a certain caution and reserve. Similarly we may see an anticipation of much later controversy in Dryden's remark in 1697 that *Paradise Lost* would have been more satisfactory as an epic 'if the Devil had not been his hero instead of Adam', Dryden's casual tone suggests that it was already a commonplace that Satan was the hero. Addison disagreed (*Spectator*, no. 297): 'it is certainly the Messiah who is the hero, both in the principal action, and the chief episodes'. Other critics were to suggest that Adam was the hero, or Adam and Eve together; or the seraph Abdiel, or Milton himself. In our own time the great scholar Sir Herbert Grierson was to rebuke a French writer for raising the question again; in this country, Grierson told him, it has been settled long ago. But has it been settled? Perhaps it has, more strictly speaking, been shelved.

Some of the other questions which early critics and editors brought up, most notably the question of the blank verse of *Paradise Lost*, Milton's innovation in using it for a narrative poem, its various peculiarities – is it a 'sport', or part of the mainstream of English versification? – were to recur later. But on the whole the eighteenth century was the time when the complete *success* of *Paradise Lost*, its total *adequacy* to the needs of the civilization it adorned, were the things that were most emphasized. Its standing as a work comparable in importance to the Classics and the Bible was reinforced by the enormously detailed commentary of Patrick Hume (1695).

But an established classic is not the same thing as a popular favourite. It was Steele in the *Tatler* (1709) and Addison in his *Spectator* papers of 1712 who seem to have brought Milton's poem home to the business and bosoms of ordinary English readers. In the twentieth century, when it is rarely read except by scholars and literary specialists, we are likely to forget how popular *Paradise Lost* once was. It stood on the shelves of every respectable household, beside the Bible and *The Pilgrim's Progress*. The whole literate community, with all shades of opinion from that of the pious John Wesley to that of the sceptical David Hume, paid homage to it. It is a safe guess that in the transmission of *Paradise Lost* to the general eighteenth-century culture the part played by the great educators, the *Tatler* and *Spectator*, was important.

Some continental European scholars have even maintained that Addison's *Spectator* papers really 'made' *Paradise Lost*. But this is probably not true. What Addison does seem to have done is to foster interest in the poem and widen its reading public. Addison's critique of *Paradise Lost* is not today much esteemed. Many would agree with Matthew Arnold that 'it is all based on convention'.

And like much else in Addison's writings it may be more distinguished for felicity of expression than for profundity of thought. Nevertheless Addison's critical achievement should not be minimized. It is true that he was very much a man of his time, and respected conventional opinion. He venerated Homer and Virgil, and deferred to 'the rules of Aristotle' as his age understood them. He opposed critics such as John Dennis, who tended to see Milton as an 'irregular' genius, like Shakespeare. He adopted a critical method of his time when he treated his subject under the four headings laid down by the French critic Bossu: fable, character, thought and expression. Addison, then, is 'dated'. But he was less the slave of classical precedents and authorities than most other critics of the day. He showed real independence of mind in judging that Milton at certain times is actually superior to Homer or Virgil, not merely a skilful follower. And he made a sustained attempt, as perhaps some other famous critics of *Paradise Lost* have not done, to capture the spirit of Milton's undertaking, to see the poem as the unique thing Milton meant it to be.

But the importance of Addison's criticism is today mainly historical. It is part of the evidence for the cult of Milton that began to pervade English literature. Milton's influence was now so vast and pervasive that it cannot be summarized. He was parodied, travestied, imitated, like an ancient. Eighteenth-century 'Miltonics' constitute a large proportion of the verse of the time – Thomson, Young, Akenside and the rest. Nor is it only the blank verse poets who are in his debt. The couplet poets draw on him as well. Pope, the chief poet of the age, carried out his own distinctive mutation of *Paradise Lost* in *The Rape of the Lock* and the *Dunciad*. In a single witty line he sums up what many readers have felt about certain speeches in Book III and elsewhere: 'And God the Father turns a School Divine.' Besides the intense and intelligent interest in Milton which Pope showed in his own verse, he made some valuable critical observations in prose. One of these is still very relevant, at a time when Milton has been much condemned as a bad influence on later poets. Pope points out the very *special* purpose of some of Milton's peculiarities of style, as ancillaries to the making of a world that had to be 'created', not 'copied'. He distinguishes Milton from his imitators, who, says Pope,

> like most other imitators, are not copies but caricatures of their original; they are a hundred times more obsolete and cramp than he, and equally so in all places; whereas it should have been observed of Milton, that he is not lavish of his exotic words and phrases every where alike, but employs them much more when the subject is marvellous, vast, and strange, as in the scenes of Heaven, Hell, Chaos, etc.[1]

Here Pope has put his finger on what was wrong with much in eighteenth-century Miltonics.

It should not be assumed that the admirers of Milton were so taken with the 'sublime' or 'tremendous' aspect of his genius that they neglected everything else. It is very notable how much Steele and Addison emphasize the 'tender' and the 'pathetic' elements in *Paradise Lost*. They see the treatment of Adam and Eve as contributing to the softening of manners and sentiment after the brutalities of the Restoration – 'melting passions of Humanity and Commiseration'. Milton is thus an important presence in eighteenth-century sentimentalism, as well as in the ambitions of the age to achieve epic grandeur.

The best evidence that *Paradise Lost* was read carefully in the eighteenth century, that the experience of it was not merely a matter of intoxicated self-indulgence in Milton's verbal orotundities and organ-like sonorities, is to be found in the editors and commentators whose work Christopher Ricks has skilfully used in his *Milton's Grand Style* (1963). Much clarification of Milton's way of writing, and illumination on points of detail, resulted from the controversy that arose over the notorious edition of *Paradise Lost* by the great classical scholar Richard Bentley (1732). (This controversy is amusingly discussed, if not with minute accuracy, by William Empson in *Some Versions of Pastoral*, 1935.) Zachary Pearce in 1733, and Thomas Newton in 1749, supply many detailed insights on which a modern scholar is glad to draw. But of these early eighteenth-century Miltonists it is Jonathan Richardson, 'Father and Son', whose 'Explanatory Notes' (1734) are most quoted today, especially the striking assertion that 'a reader of Milton must be always on duty; he is surrounded by sense, it rises in every line, every word is to the purpose; there are no lazy intervals, all has been considered, and demands and merits observation'. This stress on 'sense' is characteristic of the best eighteenth-century criticism of Milton. The prosaicism and literal-mindedness of Bentley are firmly resisted, but without the Romantics' tendency to resort to vague gestures about the 'beauty of sound' or 'magical effect' of this or that reading.

But as the century went on Romantic trends, in criticism as well as in poetry, become more and more evident, They are to be found, in relation to a Miltonic context, in Thomas Warton's edition of the minor poems (1785). It is against the background of this growing Romanticism, and anti-Augustanism, that we must view the most celebrated eighteenth-century critique of *Paradise Lost*, that of Samuel Johnson in his life of Milton (1779). This is one of the most remarkable critical essays ever written, and it has been very influential, probably more so in the twentieth century than in its own time. Johnson's attitude to Milton and his poetry is curious, and not easy to make out fully. It is not clear whether his critique, though memorably phrased, and locally always incisive, is coherent as a whole. In some ways Johnson's treatment of *Paradise Lost* represents the consolidation of the eighteenth-century position. No admirer of Milton could find anything wanting in Johnson's closing tribute, for it is plain that Johnson sees Milton as a great man as well as a great poet.

> He was naturally a thinker for himself. . . . From his contemporaries he neither courted nor received support; there is in his writings nothing by which the pride of other authors might be gratified, or favour gained; no exchange of praise, or solicitation of support. His great works were performed under discountenance, and in blindness, but difficulties vanished at his touch; he was born for whatever is arduous; and his work is not the greatest of heroick poems, only because it is not the first.

It would be easy to arrange quotations from the *Life* so as to make it appear the definitive 'classical' tribute to a great classical work. Johnson calls *Paradise Lost* 'a book of universal knowledge'. He has no fault to find with it on the score of religion or morals. 'Every line breathes sanctity of thought, and purity of manners.' As for the versification, Johnson's tribute to it is all the more impressive because he so strongly disapproves of blank verse outside the drama. He gives a long denigratory account of this verse-form, but then returns upon himself: 'whatever the advantages of rhyme, I cannot prevail on myself to wish that Milton had been a rhymer; for I cannot wish his work to be other than it is'. Nothing could better convey the sheer power of Milton's writing than this admission.

Yet most readers of the *Life* have felt, and surely rightly, that Johnson's endorsement of *Paradise Lost* is considerably less than total, and that it is not easy to make his remarks on it 'add up'. It is to be noted that where Milton's other poems are concerned Johnson is not enthusiastic. Perhaps he had in mind the Romantic trend soon exemplified in Warton's edition of the minor poems. At any rate, his castigation of *Lycidas*, a poem that has always been dear to Romantics, is notorious. 'The diction is harsh, the rhymes uncertain, and the numbers unpleasing. Its form is that of a pastoral, easy, vulgar, and therefore disgusting.' Even when this is decoded, as it has to be, the effect is of a severely adverse judgment. Johnson approves of *Comus*, but finds it 'inelegantly splendid, and tediously instructive'. The Sonnets 'deserve not any particular criticism; for of the best it can only be said, that they are not bad'. He thinks *Samson Agonistes* has been too much admired. Johnson, like other eighteenth-century critics, was interested in Milton's poetry, and wrote several studies of it outside the *Life*.[2] But his sympathy with it was clearly imperfect. And where Milton the man was concerned, Johnson's antipathy is hardly disguised. T.S. Eliot, who shared it, is probably right to put it down to political and ideological grounds. The English Civil War had not really ended in Johnson's mind and heart, and Milton had been on the wrong side. Johnson writes as a Tory and a High Churchman. The most unfortunate aspect of this prejudice is that it affected Johnson's approach as a biographer. Passing over the lives of Milton by people who knew him, and who presented him as pleasant and likeable, Johnson preferred inferior traditions which he found more in keeping with the 'acrimonious and surly republican' he believed Milton to have been.

Literary criticism is supposed to rise above personal prejudices. But it is difficult to write fairly about the work of a man you loathe. Perhaps this is the reason why Johnson's reservations about *Paradise Lost* have stuck in the minds of readers more than what he says in praise of it. Many of his criticisms, limiting, qualifying, or adverse, were to be taken up and developed in the nineteenth and twentieth centuries; a good deal of what, for instance, Eliot, Leavis or Waldock were to say is already anticipated in Johnson's remarks about Milton's 'faults'. Some of the points he makes are relatively minor in importance. He objects to the 'unskilful allegory' of Sin and Death. He finds the Paradise of Fools 'a fiction . . . too ludicrous for its place'. He queries the conduct of the action here and there; for instance, 'Satan is with great expectation brought before Gabriel in Paradise, and is suffered to go away unmolested'. Other criticisms are more radical. 'Milton's design,' he says, 'requires the description of what cannot be described, the agency of spirits', and he finds a 'confusion of spirit and matter' in the war in Heaven. C.S. Lewis in his *Preface to Paradise Lost* (1942) opposed Johnson on this point, referring to contemporary speculations about the possible materiality of angels; but A.J.A. Waldock's *Paradise Lost and its Critics* (1947) has plausibly argued that some of Johnson's objections still remain unanswered – and wonders if they can be. But Johnson's main criticisms of the poem strike deeper. They involve radical questioning both of subject and style. The plan of *Paradise Lost*, he says, 'comprises neither human actions nor human manners. The man and woman who act and suffer, are in a state which no other man or woman can ever know.' Granting Milton's soundness as a moral and religious teacher, Johnson observes that

> these truths are too important to be new; they have been taught to our infancy. They have mingled with our solitary thoughts and familiar conversation, and are habitually interwoven with the whole texture of life . . . the want of human interest is always felt . . . Its perusal is a duty rather than a pleasure.

Given the importance of 'human interest' and 'pleasure' among Johnson's literary criteria, it is difficult to reconcile these pronouncements with his general judgment:

> Such are the faults of that wonderful performance *Paradise Lost*, which he who can put in balance with its beauties must be considered not as nice but as dull, less to be censured for want of candour, than pitied for want of sensibility.

As for style, it is here that Johnson has been most influential; and it is here that he is most equivocal. Some of his censures had been anticipated by earlier critics: Addison had said that 'our language sunk under him'. But Johnson stated what was to become the Eliot-Leavis 'case' against Milton's handling of the English language in the most incisive and (seemingly) the most condemnatory way. Speaking of the 'uniform peculiarity of *Diction*' in Milton, he says: 'Both in prose and verse, he had formed his style by a perverse and pedantick principle. He was desirous to use English words with a foreign idiom.' Twentieth-century anti-Miltonists have been happy to enlist Johnson's support on this point, a central one for them. F.R. Leavis speaks of Milton's rejection of English idiom, and ascribes this to his addiction, over so many years, to polemics in Latin. Johnson, however, was inclined to ascribe the exoticism of Milton's style to Italian influence, anticipating the argument of F.T. Prince in our own day (*The Italian Element in Milton's Verse*, 1954). But the most important difference between Leavis and Johnson here is that for Leavis the supposedly unidiomatic quality of Milton's style is a matter for condemnation. Johnson is more equivocal. Having said that Milton 'was desirous to use English words with a foreign idiom', he goes on:

> This in all his prose is discovered and condemned; for there judgment operates freely, neither softened by the beauty, nor awed by the dignity of his thoughts; but such is the power of his poetry, that his call is obeyed without resistance, the reader feels himself in captivity to a higher and nobler mind, and criticism sinks in admiration.

On the face of it Johnson has made a big concession to the Romantics here. But how deep does it go? Is there not an oblique suggestion that the suitable reader of Milton's verse is under a sort of hypnotic spell?

It is easy to see, then, why Johnson's life of Milton was widely resented at the time. The poet Cowper, to whom Milton meant so much both as a poet and as a man, wrote that he would like to thrash Johnson's old jacket till his pension jingled in his pockets. Milton was already, as Leslie Stephen says, a taboo figure for criticism. In some ways Johnson can be taken to represent the typical eighteenth-century attitude to Milton, but in other ways he is more in tune with influential critics of the twentieth century.

For the moment literary opinion was not with him. A strong tide of Romanticism was running. And it is noteworthy that the Romantic movement, which attacked much that the eighteenth century admired, did not turn against Milton. On the contrary: Milton's fame was revived and refreshed by the poets of the new century. Wordsworth assailed the 'poetic diction' of the eighteenth century, much of which seems to the literary historian to derive from *Paradise Lost*. But as Wordsworth and Coleridge saw it, Pope was to blame for that, especially in his translations of Homer. Like Shakespeare, the other English idol of the eighteenth century, Milton was acclaimed by the Romantics as representing the true English poetry, in contrast with the artificiality and pseudo-poetry of the Augustans. The Romantics, both of the Wordsworth generation, and of the Keats/Shelley/Byron generation, were much more enthusiastic about Milton than the traditionalist critics, such as Jeffrey or Lockhart or Gifford.

The Romantic poets, of course, were very much individuals,

and Milton meant different things to them. To Wordsworth, Milton was a kind of spiritual father and forerunner. He admired Milton's personality: 'Thy soul was like a Star, and dwelt apart'. He saw Milton as patriotic, noble and responsible in a time, like Wordsworth's own, of conflict and national danger: 'England hath need of thee'. It was the reading of Milton's sonnets that inspired him to write his own. *The Prelude* is full of echoes of *Paradise Lost*, and indeed Wordsworth's whole undertaking in this long autobiographical poem can be regarded as a sort of Romantic 'answer' to Milton. The mode of *The Prelude* may be seen as a development of those beautiful personal passages with which Milton opens Books III, VII and IX of his poem. And Wordsworth, like Milton, admired Spenser and was influenced by his work, so that the 'line' Spenser-Milton-Wordsworth established for the history of poetry. Coleridge too greatly admired both Milton's poetry and his character. He had been a Miltonist before he became, under German influence, a Shakespearean; his earlier verse shows much Miltonic colour, both direct and through Gray and other 'Miltonic' poets of the eighteenth century.

The appreciation of Milton by Wordsworth and Coleridge may have been more intense than the Augustans'. But on the moral and religious side their attitude to *Paradise Lost* does not seem greatly different. Neither of them questions Milton's orthodoxy, any more than Johnson does. Johnson is typical of the eighteenth century in his untroubled assumption that the theology of *Paradise Lost* is in complete conformity with the mainstream of Christian tradition. But for the younger Romantics, who were themselves in revolt against Christianity, the possibility of an antinomian Milton, secretly subverting the official orthodoxy, was attractive. In this notion they may have been anticipated, though they did not know it, by an eighteenth-century thinker, William Blake. Blake wrote in his cryptic *Marriage of Heaven and Hell* (1793) that 'the reason Milton wrote in fetters when he wrote of Angels & God, and at liberty when of Devils & Hell, is because he was a true Poet and of the Devil's party without knowing it'. What exactly Blake meant by this can only be discovered by studying his own system of thought: Blake was, in his way, as complex and enigmatic a poet-mystic as Milton, and Denis Saurat is not the only modern scholar to draw attention to the affinities between them. If his remark is taken straightforwardly, the use of the phrase 'without knowing it' suggests that Blake's position was nearer to that of modern critics like E.M.W. Tillyard or A.J.A. Waldock, who argue that Milton made Satan a more attractive figure than he consciously meant to, than to the 'Satanists' of the Romantic period.

'Satanism' came to mean various things in the nineteenth century. But one thing all 'Satanists' have in common is the treatment of Satan as a character important in his own right, and the real centre of interest in the poem. It may be wondered whether they read much further than Book II of *Paradise Lost*: but of course it is open to a Satanist to reply that the first two Books are the only ones that really matter. At any rate, some of the Romantics saw the God of *Paradise Lost* as a tyrant and believed Satan's revolt against him to be justified. Shelley wrote in the *Defence of Poetry* (1821): 'Nothing can exceed the energy and magnificence of the character of Satan in *Paradise Lost*. It is a mistake to suppose that he could ever have been intended for the popular personification of evil.' Shelley described the wrongs of Satan as 'beyond measure'. His view of the poem has been developed fully in an extraordinarily brilliant and provocative book of our own time, William Empson's *Milton's God* (1961): 'The poem is so good,' says Empson, 'because it makes God so bad. . . . The poem is wonderful because it is an awful warning not against eating the apple but against worshipping that God.' This is, in essentials, the Shelleyan position. Byron agreed that Satan was the hero of the poem. And the 'Byronic hero' which was, for a time, to fascinate Europe, though of course largely based on elements of Byron's own personality, derives in part from the Satan of Romanticism, the villain-hero whose 'baleful' eyes have inspired a whole literary tradition from *Jane Eyre* to *Light in August*. It would seem that from the historical point of view this ambivalent symbol is the greatest of Milton's creations.

Coleridge did not see Milton's Satan as Byron and Shelley did. In his lecture of 1818 he holds a persuasive balance between moral condemnation and a positive imaginative response to the great figure of the fallen Archangel. 'The character of Satan is pride and sensual indulgence, finding in self the sole motive of action.' 'Sensual indulgence' is not very obvious in the poem, but perhaps Coleridge attached a special meaning to this expression. More persuasive is his account of Satan's 'restlessness, temerity and cunning which have marked the mighty hunters of mankind from Nimrod to Napoleon'. He speaks of Satan's 'intense selfishness, the alcohol of egotism'. But around this character Milton 'has thrown a singularity of daring, a grandeur of suffrance, and a ruined splendour'. This is 'the very height of poetic sublimity'. Coleridge's remarks suggest a more balanced view of Satan than Byron's or Shelley's, one based on a more complete induction, which takes into account the self-revelatory soliloquy in Book IV, and later stages of the story.

It is curious that while renewed attention was being given to the meaning of the poem, which the Augustans had tended to take for granted, little or no use was made by literary critics in this period of that astonishing treatise *De Doctrina Christiana*, which was discovered in 1823 and first published in translation, from Milton's Latin, in 1825. This is the most thorough and systematic exposition of Milton's theological views, and reveals him as a very original and in some ways very unorthodox religious thinker. Twentieth-century scholars have made much use of it in discussing the question whether or not *Paradise Lost* expresses Milton's private heresies. We may speculate whether the *De Doctrina* would have made more impact if it had been discovered earlier – perhaps for its advocacy of polygamy, if not for its views on the Trinity. But it does not seem to have influenced nineteenth-century ideas about Milton very greatly. It was discussed: the young Macaulay wrote his famous essay on Milton under the pretext of reviewing it, but we have the impression that the nineteenth century had really ceased to care much about Milton's thought, one way or another. His aim to 'justify the ways of God to men' received merely formal notice. Attention was more and more concentrated on the fictional and dramatic aspect of his work, together with his style (that 'magnificent invention', as Leavis calls it).

In some ways the attitude of Keats was to foreshadow much Victorian, Edwardian and modern criticism of Milton. Keats's view of *Paradise Lost* has different facets, and it is closely connected with his own problems as a poet. He wrote the beautiful, if puzzling, fragment *Hyperion* with the deliberate aim, it would seem, of cultivating a 'Miltonic' kind of art, but abandoned it in dissatisfaction. He found too many 'Miltonic inversions' in *Hyperion*, a want of 'the true voice of feeling'. It may have been unwise of twentieth-century critics like Middleton Murry and Herbert Read to generalize Keats's rejection of Milton ('Life to him would be death to me') into a wholesale condemnation of Milton's influence on any poetry. But in the same letter (of 21 September 1819) Keats describes *Paradise Lost* in terms which might have been accepted by many nineteenth-century readers, when he calls it 'a corruption of our language'. 'It should be kept as it is – unique – a curiosity – a beautiful and grand curiosity.' We may couple this with an earlier reference to Milton in a letter of 3 May 1818, in which Keats says: 'Wordsworth is deeper than Milton'. Milton 'did not think into the human heart, as Wordsworth has done'. (We must remember that Wordsworth 'spoke' to the nineteenth century as he does not speak to the twentieth.) For many in the Victorian age Milton remained on his pedestal as a master of language, a word-musician. But *Paradise Lost* was a kind of 'sport', a curiosity, essentially inimitable. Apart from his peculiar linguistic genius Milton was not interesting. His thought was a mere paraphrase of orthodox commonplaces; and his personality was unpleasant.

Such, at any rate, seems to have been the view of the leading Victorian critic, Matthew Arnold. Arnold did not question the traditional position of Milton, as second only to Shakespeare. But like Landor, De Quincey, and other nineteenth-century eulogists of Milton, he tended to base it mainly on stylistic grounds. For Arnold, Milton embodies in many ways the ideal of classicism which Arnold saw as a needed corrective in his own time: dignity, sanity, just subordination of detail, due adaptation of means to ends, the high respect of the craftsman for his craft and for himself. 'Milton,' he wrote in 1888, 'from one end of Paradise Lost to the other, is in his diction and rhythm constantly a great artist in the great style.' But this is very much the official Arnold, the champion of the Grand Style, the high decorum which he most decidedly did not find in England's supreme writer, Shakespeare. In another mood, discussing the iconoclastic views of the French critic Scherer, Arnold candidly admits that he finds the characters in *Paradise Lost* lacking in interest and coherence, and the theological speeches of God the Father repellent.[3] As Charles Williams was to say in 1940, late Victorian academic orthodoxy had established the notion of 'an august, solemn, proud, and (on the whole) unintelligent and uninteresting Milton'.[4]

The liveliest Victorian critic of Milton, Walter Bagehot, writing in 1859, was much more concerned than Arnold with what *Paradise Lost* actually *said*. Bagehot sees it as essentially a *political* poem; the whole action starts from a political 'job', God the Father's sudden exaltation of the Son, which touches off the revolt of the angels. Bagehot's witty, cynical tone is refreshing after the solemn moralizing of so many Victorian Miltonists, and his essay anticipates modern views. Thus like Tillyard he sees the balance of the poem as disturbed by the presentation of Satan, and like Waldock he notices Milton's habit of, so to speak, getting his poem back on course by authorial comments designed to rebuff or tone down what Satan says. Bagehot makes the poem seem challenging and enjoyable, but he does not consider it successful. 'So far from Milton having justified the ways of God to man, he has loaded the common theology with a new encumbrance' – Satan's heroism.

The more reverential Victorian Miltonists were ready to grant Milton, officially, more success in the handling of this theological theme. But it must be remembered that this was a time when the impact of Darwinism and Higher Criticism of the Bible, and the prestige of Victorian science, were doing much to empty it of substance. We get the impression from David Masson's monumental life of Milton (1858–81) that what really matters in *Paradise Lost* is not the argument but Milton's personality, the austere noble Puritan and champion of the Good Old Cause, a Great Man in the Carlylean mould.

The various trends of nineteenth-century thinking about *Paradise Lost* were assembled and consolidated in Walter Raleigh's witty handbook of 1900. It is clear from this critique that by the end of the century the poem still retained its high traditional standing, but that this standing was now very precarious. Raleigh treats Milton with great respect. He quotes Johnson on the poet's 'gigantick loftiness', and Landor's comparison of his verse with the music of Handel. But it is plain that *Paradise Lost* does not appeal deeply to his head or his heart. It is a wonderful *tour de force* of pure style; just trembling on the edge of absurdity, but saved by Milton's unfailing mastery of words. 'We find ourselves in a remote atmosphere. . . . All is power, and vagueness, and grandeur.' *Paradise Lost* retains its immortality, not because of any profound thought or rich humanity, but through sheer power of style. Otherwise, it is 'a monument to dead ideas'.

Perhaps a whole-hearted supporter of the aestheticism of that time would have had no difficulty in reconciling this view with the traditional acceptance of *Paradise Lost* as a great classic. But for Raleigh, a disciple of Johnson, this cannot have been so. In his book nineteenth-century academic orthodoxy is on the verge of collapse. It is only a short step from Raleigh's 'all is power, and vagueness, and grandeur' to Leavis's 'after the first two books . . . *Paradise Lost* . . . becomes dull and empty'. No one can sustain interest in so long a poem if it has, essentially, nothing to say.

But in the twentieth century scholars began to question the asssumption, so prevalent in the eighteenth and nineteenth centuries, that the meaning of *Paradise Lost* was simple and obvious. Until quite recent times few would have dissented from Addison's view: 'The great Moral . . . which reigns in Milton is the most universal and most useful that can be imagined: it is in short this, *that Obedience to the Will of God makes Men happy, and that Disobedience makes them miserable.*' But in our times book after book, essay after essay, has appeared to show that the thought of the poem is nothing like so straightforward as it looks. American scholarship led the way: Edwin Greenlaw's 1917 article in *Studies in Philology* is usually credited with launching the new Miltonism or as it came to be called, Christian Humanism. Greenlaw argued that the sin which led to the Fall was 'intemperance', and his investigation of what this meant to Milton led him back to Spenser and Book II of *The Faerie Queene*. Other Miltonists like Tillyard and C.S. Lewis disagreed with this interpretation; but they all concurred with other scholars, British, American, and continental European, in their preoccupation with Milton's handling of the Fall, and its moral and psychological subtleties. For Tillyard (1930), everything in *Paradise Lost* is subordinate to the human theme. Satan and the angels, God and his Son, are only of background interest: the real centre of the poem is the struggle in the minds of Adam and Eve. In contradiction of the vulgar belief about Milton's 'puritanism', these scholars emphasized Milton's fearless treatment of unfallen sexuality, his insistence that Adam and Eve had physical relations before the Fall, his rapturous picture of naked beauty unashamed. Indeed the upshot of the whole Christian Humanist movement was the denial that Milton was a 'Puritan' in any limiting sense. He should be seen as a Renaissance artist, essentially a humane writer, and one whose underlying thought and world outlook had less in common with the sectaries than with authors like Spenser or Shakespeare, Hooker or Bacon.

It is fair to say that twentieth-century Milton scholarship has been dominated by Christian Humanism, though there are still some, like Haller, who stress the older concept of Milton as a puritan, and others, like Saurat, who insist on the more unorthodox and antinomian aspects of his thinking. But a full account of all this flood of publication is impossible. What has to be said is that while Milton's thought, and the culture that underlies his work, his manifold sources, theological, scientific, and literary, were being studied as never before, the presence of Milton as a great poet and human force, a living part of English literature, was becoming more and more doubtful and ambiguous. We have now come to the 'Milton Controversy', the very influential movement, led by a number of twentieth-century poets and critics, to marginalize Milton's poetry, and in particular *Paradise Lost* (it was on that poem that the fire of the anti-Miltonists was concentrated).

Credit, or responsibility, for this questioning of Milton is usually assigned to the leading poet of the age, T.S. Eliot, together with the most provocative and controversial literary critic, F.R. Leavis. But there are many signs of indifference to or dislike of Milton in other circles which had no particular sympathy with twentieth-century trends in poetry. The decline of interest in verse generally, and in long poems in particular, and their supersession as the main literary form by the novel, have to be taken into account. Whatever the Christian Humanists might urge, there was a lack of interest in the Fall and Original Sin as providing, even in a symbolic way, any true interpretation of humanity's problems. There was a widespread assumption that Milton had been a gloomy, narrow-minded 'Puritan'. Above all, we must remember the virtual disappearance of the Classics and the Bible as effective parts of literary culture. Shakespeare, and most English authors before the twentieth century, are of course deeply in debt to the Classics in all sorts of ways. But Milton is in a unique position of disadvantage here, because he is the only English poet who even arguably succeeded with the classical forms of epic and drama. And

Biblicism pervades his three last poems in every detail. Like the Racine of *Athalie* and *Esther*, he was steeped in the Scriptures. But what was once a link between his work and ordinary readers has now become a barrier.

The Eliot/Leavis critique, then, came when the time for it was propitious. Other modern writers had already come out against Milton. Ezra Pound in 1914 called him 'the worst sort of poison'. In *Notes on Elizabethan Classicists* (1917) Pound denounced him for 'his asinine bigotry, his beastly hebraism, the coarseness of his mentality'. Ford Madox Ford, Middleton Murry, Herbert Read, all expressed dislike of Milton's stiff, unnatural, pompous style. Today none of these attacks seems particularly impressive or interesting. Only Eliot's two essays, of 1936 and 1947,[5] and Leavis's chapter in *Revaluation* (1936)[6] and his discussion of Eliot's second essay in *The Common Pursuit* (1952), are likely to be remembered, of all that was written in Great Britain and the United States in the course of the controversy.

To the reader who comes to Eliot and Leavis with some knowledge of previous Milton criticism there does not appear to be much that is new in what they say; both of them, indeed, cite Johnson in support of it. Both critics work within 'formalistic' assumptions; that is, they profess to be concerned solely with Milton's poetry 'as poetry', The discussion, then, turns on style, on the handling of words, although both critics do not conceal their distaste for Milton's subject-matter and attitude: Eliot has 'a glimpse of a theology that I find in large part repellent, expressed through a mythology which would have been better left in the Book of Genesis, upon which Milton has not improved'; Leavis considers that the 'myth' of *Paradise Lost* 'suffers from deficiencies related to those of the verse'. But the main point of the attack is Milton's style. Eliot writes as a practising poet, concerned to explain why Milton had been a bad influence on poetry, and could only be a bad influence. He thinks that Milton's sensuousness was withered by his book-learning, and that his blindness led to an overdevelopment of aural effects in his verse to the exclusion of all others. For Eliot there is little to visualize in *Paradise Lost*. There is nothing much but 'mazes of sound', which Milton delights in for their own sake, at the expense of any concern for conveying his meaning. Leavis's remarkable depreciation begins by calling in Eliot for support, since he thought that Milton's 'dislodgment' was really due to Eliot's 'creative achievement' as a poet, which had placed the history of English poetry in a new perspective.

The essence of Leavis's case is that the 'pattern' of Milton's verse, 'the stylized gesture and movement', 'has no particular expressive work to do, but functions by rote, of its own momentum, in the manner of a ritual'. Unusually good passages, like that on Mulciber (I. 740–46), where the verse-movement really is expressive, only show how external and mechanical it is elsewhere; such exceptions prove the rule. Leavis sees Milton's Grand Style as having 'renounced the English language'. He finds a 'sensuous poverty' in the description of the Garden of Eden in Book IV, a lack of 'sharp, concrete realization'. Though Leavis refers to the poetry of Donne as a standard for expressiveness, it is clear that the main contrast is with Shakespeare. 'Even in the most lively books of *Paradise Lost* the verse, brilliant as it is, has to the ear that appreciates Shakespeare a wearying deadness about it.'

There have been many attempts to rebut Leavis's account, some rejecting the criteria he works with, others accepting them but trying to show that Milton's verse does actually comply with them. Probably the most dubious aspect of Leavis's argument is its conception of a Miltonic 'average' or norm of style; many readers of *Paradise Lost* are doubtful whether it has *one* style that can be adequately represented, and dealt with critically, on the basis of a few selected passages. But the chapter of *Revaluation* raises so many issues of literary criticism, literary history and literary theory, not to speak of more fundamental educational and moral questions, that it cannot be discussed briefly. Eliot's second essay, which some have seen as an attempt to dissociate his position from Leavis's, does not advance the question much further. It would seem that at present attention has shifted away from the argument about style to the broader questions of Milton's handling of his story, his 'myth'.

It is here that A.J.A. Waldock's *Paradise Lost and its Critics* (1947), hailed by Leavis as bringing support to his own case, has been the critical storm-centre. Waldock, like Bagehot before him, finds all sorts of inconsistencies, emotional disharmonies in the poem. He considers that, at what he calls the 'crisis' of the poem when Adam decides to disobey God and defy death because of his passionate love for Eve, *Paradise Lost* 'breaks': the reader is being asked to react in incompatible ways, to feel with the full force of his mind that Adam acted rightly, and that he acted wrongly. Waldock considers that Milton got into this dilemma because he had not sufficiently pondered the problems he was bound to encounter in enlarging the cryptic story in Genesis to the proportions of a vast epic.

These debates go on. At present Ricks's *Milton's Grand Style* (1963) is widely regarded as the most effective treatment of the problems raised by Leavis and Eliot; while of the many attempts to show that, contrary to Waldock's opinion, Milton did indeed succeed in writing the poem he meant to write, D.H. Burden's *The Logical Epic* (1967) seems the best. Meanwhile, as Bernard Wright says in his book on *Milton* (1962), *Paradise Lost* 'is not nowadays widely read or highly regarded'. W.R. Parker, whose life of Milton (1968) has superseded Masson's, says sadly that 'after having disliked Milton's ideas for three centuries, while admiring his poetry, the English have finally decided . . . that the poetry too is bad'. The great revival of interest in English Romantic poetry, fostered by leading American scholars like Harold Bloom, has encouraged a new appraisal of *Paradise Lost* as the Romantics may be imagined to have come to terms with it, in their efforts to contradict, absorb, or transcend what W.J. Bate sees as 'the burden of the past', the perennial challenge and problem for later English poets, of which Milton's poem is so memorable and potent an exemplar.

It is also possible that a new stimulus may come from the growing interest of contemporary radicals in their great predecessor. The historian Christopher Hill, in his 1977 study of Milton, declares that it is 'quite wrong to see Milton in relation to anything so vague and generalized as "the Christian tradition". He was a radical Protestant heretic.' He 'rejected the Trinity, infant baptism and most of the traditional ceremonies, including church marriage; he queried monogamy and believed that the soul died with the body'. Hill thinks that Milton's poetic reputation stands today as high as ever. But he has become 'the poet of scholars and academic critics' – no longer either a people's poet or a poet's poet. Whether we agree with Hill's point of view or not, it seems clear that nothing but good can come from the rejection of a restricting formalism and the return of Milton's poetry, and the analysis and appreciation of it, to the real historical world and the intellectual, moral and spiritual concerns of actual men and women.

Chapter 4
Text and Context: Pope's 'Coronation Epistle'

Pope is a problem to anthologists. He is rarely at his best in short poems. Of course there are many passages in his longer poems – *The Rape of the Lock*, *The Dunciad*, *An Epistle to Dr. Arbuthnot* – that appear again and again in anthologies. But the understanding and appreciation of Pope's poetry has often been harmed by the habit of excerpting from his work. Pope explained one of the principles on which he wrote when he told Tonson the reason why he was not willing to show him the 'character' of the Man of Ross until he had completed the whole poem in which it was to appear.

> To send you any of the particular verses will be much to the prejudice of the whole; which if it has any beauty, derives it from the manner in which it is *placed*, and the painterly *contrast* (as the painters call it) in which it stands, with the pompous figures of famous, or rich, or high-born men. (Sherburn, 1956, iii, p. 390.)

The best choice for selection in an anthology would be a poem in which this consciously 'painterly' quality of Pope's poetry (if not himself a first-rate painter, he had a keen and devoted interest in the practice of that art) can be shown as operative in the work as a whole.

An early poem from the sunniest period of Pope's poetic career – the period of *The Rape of the Lock* – the poem called for short the 'Coronation Epistle', displays this quality admirably, and should long ago have been added to the 'canon within the canon', the short poems or passages which until quite recently were 'household words', familiar to all lovers of English poetry. Victorian taste, however, was evidently unable to recognize it as a serious poem. It does not appear in either *The Golden Treasury* (1861) or Quiller-Couch's *Oxford Book of English Verse*

(1900). But with the great revival in Pope's popularity in this century the 'Coronation Epistle' is now widely recognized as one of the most beautiful of his poems. Even the most hostile twentieth-century critic of Pope, James Reeves (1976), has words of praise for it. This is remarkable; for on the whole it is the dark side of Pope, the surrealistic imagination of *The Dunciad*, the night world of dream-like complexities and metaphysical horror, that has captured the moderns: so much so that the sunlit world of Popean humanism, from *The Rape of the Lock* to the *Essay on Man*, while by no means neglected by scholars, does not seem to bulk large in the image of Pope as the poets of today receive it. (Once again the aesthetic significance of *contrast* has been neglected.) If so, the 'Coronation Epistle', in the form in which it appears in modern anthologies, e.g. Helen Gardner's *New Oxford Book of English Verse* (1972), or Roger Lonsdale's *New Oxford Book of Eighteenth Century Verse* (1984), is a timely reminder that it is possible to combine with the touch of realism favoured by modern taste the grace of art belonging to an age which still recognized the existence of artistic and moral ideals.

Here now is the poem as it appears in the one-volume edition of the Twickenham text, edited by John Butt (1965). I have made only one emendation ('delight' in line 23, for Butt's 'a delight'.)

> Epistle to Miss Blount, on her leaving the Town,
> after the Coronation
>
> As some fond virgin, whom her mother's care
> Drags from the town to wholsom country air,
> Just when she learns to roll a melting eye,
> And hear a spark, yet think no danger nigh;
> From the dear man unwilling she must sever,   5
> Yet take one kiss before she parts for ever:
> Thus from the world fair *Zephalinda* flew,
> Saw others happy, and with sighs withdrew;
> Not that their pleasures caus'd her discontent,
> She sigh'd not that They stay'd, but that She went.   10
>   She went, to plain-work, and to purling brooks,
> Old-fashion'd halls, dull aunts, and croaking rooks,
> She went from Op'ra, park, assembly, play,
> To morning walks, and pray'rs three hours a day;

To pass her time 'twixt reading and Bohea,   15
To muse, and spill her solitary Tea,
Or o'er cold coffee trifle with the spoon,
Count the slow clock, and dine exact at noon;
Divert her eyes with pictures in the fire,
Hum half a tune, tell stories to the squire;   20
Up to her godly garret after sev'n,
There starve and pray, for that's the way to heav'n.
    Some Squire, perhaps, you take delight to rack;
Whose game is Whisk, whose treat a toast in sack,
Who visits with a gun, presents you birds,   25
Then gives a smacking buss, and cries – No words!
Or with his hound comes hollowing from the stable,
Makes love with nods, and knees beneath a table;
Whose laughs are hearty, tho' his jests are coarse,
And loves you best of all things – but his horse.   30
    In some fair evening, on your elbow laid,
You dream of triumphs in the rural shade;
In pensive thought recall the fancy'd scene,
See Coronations rise on ev'ry green;
Before you pass th'imaginary sights   35
Of Lords, and Earls, and Dukes, and garter'd Knights;
While the spread Fan o'ershades your closing eyes;
Then give one flirt, and all the vision flies.
Thus vanish sceptres, coronets, and balls,
And leave you in lone woods, or empty walls.   40
    So when your slave, at some dear, idle time,
(Not plagu'd with headachs, or the want of rhime)
Stands in the streets, abstracted from the crew,
And while he seems to study, thinks of you:
Just when his fancy points your sprightly eyes,   45
Or sees the blush of soft *Parthenia* rise,
Gay pats my shoulder, and you vanish quite;
Streets, chairs, and coxcombs rush upon my sight;
Vext to be still in town, I knit my brow,
Look sow'r, and hum a tune – as you may now.   50

It takes no very profound analysis to perceive that the distinctive
pleasure given by this lively poem derives from a series of contrasts.

The poem consists of five sections or paragraphs, of approximately equal length (1–10, 11–22, 23–30, 31–40, 41–50), and it proceeds by showing a different picture in each: each piquantly different from its predecessor. A glimpse of 'fair *Zephalinda*', in flight from 'the world', is followed by the detailed evocation of quite another world, that of 'Old-fashion'd halls, dull aunts, and croaking rooks', with fast and prayers in her 'godly garret' after seven o'clock in the evening. Then broad comedy supervenes, with the innocent flirtation with the 'coarse' and 'hearty' Squire. The tone changes completely as we identify with the romantic girl dreaming of 'triumphs' and 'imaginary sights' picking up the reference in the title to the recent Coronation. The last turn in the emotional sequence introduces the poet himself. The implied sympathy with the girl which has pervaded the poem now emerges from the amused detachment of the narrative and is revealed as tender love and longing. The delicate playing to and fro between the real and the imaginary which characterizes this poem is illustrated in the simultaneous parallel and contrast between the girl and the poet. The parallel is drawn clearly. *She* indulges in day-dreams 'Of Lords, and Earls, and Dukes, and garter'd Knights' but she gives her fan a 'flirt', and reality breaks in. *He* 'stands in the streets', seeming to 'study', but really thinking of her, when corresponding to her 'flirt' of the fan, '*Gay* pats my shoulder . . .' and she disappears. But the contrast is equally firm. They are both dreamers, but while *he* is dreaming of *her*, *she* is not dreaming of *him*. *She* is in the country, longing to be back in Town - but not because she wants to be with him; *he* is in Town, but 'Vext' to be there, because he wants to be with *her*.

The aesthetic effect of simultaneous similarity and difference can be illustrated in the verse-movement. Everything, of course, is under the control of the regular Popean five-beat couplet; yet the changes of tempo dramatically mark out the changing of moods in this opalescent miniature. Opening with an *allegro con brio*, the epistle sweeps along, with one line that seems to contain no pause at all: 'Thus from the world fair *Zephalinda* flew', but in line 10 slows down drastically: 'She sigh'd not that They stay'd, but that She went.' The pause at 'She went' is enhanced by the repetition of the words at the opening of the next section (the comma here seems more appropriate than Lonsdale's omission of it in the text

in his *Oxford Book*.) The adagio of the second section is epitomized
in that line of nine words which seems interminable: 'Count the
slow clock, and dine exact at noon' (and the slow clock seems to
go on clacking in the second part of the hemistich.) 'That's the
way to heav'n' could have come appropriately as the resonant
end of a pious adjuration. But everything changes at once with
the immediately following scherzo of the Squire, with his gun
and birds, his 'smacking buss', 'hollowing' from the stable like his
hound: blunt monosyllables, emphatically masculine vocabulary; all
is 'coarse' (but amiable), down to the final joke (in line 3O).

If the epistle had ended here, its probable effect on the modern
reader who finds it appealing might be similar to the effect of the
passage in Sheridan's *School for Scandal* (1777), which it perhaps
suggested.

> *Sir Peter Teazle.*   Yes, yes, madam, you were then in a
> somewhat humbler style – the daughter of a plain country
> squire. Recollect, Lady Teazle, when I first saw you sitting at
> your tambour, in pretty figured linen gown, with a bunch of
> keys at your side, your hair combed smooth over a roll, and
> your apartment hung round with fruits in worsted, of your own
> working.
> *Lady Teazle.*   Oh yes! I remember it very well, and a curious
> life I led. My daily occupation to inspect the dairy, superintend
> the poultry, make extracts from the family receipt book, and
> comb my aunt Deborah's lap-dog. . . . And then, you know,
> my evening amusements! To draw patterns for ruffles, which I
> had not material to make: to play Pope Joan with the curate;
> to read a sermon to my aunt; or to be stuck down to an old
> spinet to strum my father to sleep after a fox-chase. [From Act
> II, Scene i.]

The charm of this for moderns may be greater than it was for
Sheridan's contemporaries: what for them may have sounded
symbolic of dullness and dreariness may to us seem pretty,
picturesque, and nostalgic. Similarly with Pope's evocation of a
milieu which alternates pietism and bucolic vulgarity: his verse
makes it seem attractive to us who live in Philip Larkin's world,
disjointed, unserious, yet not cheerful either. But surely the last
two sections of the epistle add something which goes deeper than

the first three, and shows the whole piece as the work of a major poet, quite un-portentous, but deeply engaged? The bringing in of the poet himself and his love for the girl internalize the narrative, and create a total effect which is not easy to sum up.

Why, after all, have twentieth-century readers been taken with this poem, and (implicitly) discriminated in its favour against other early poems that obviously are related to it, such as 'To Miss Blount, with the works of Voiture', or the Epistle to Jervas? It is notoriously difficult to say what makes a poem good, or outstanding (fault-finding is much easier.) But in all probability what has made *this* poem stand out is the vivid evocation of the Young Lady (as the recipient of the Epistle was called when it was first published in Pope's *Works* of 1717). Now since she is so fully 'there' the poem is self-sufficient (it might be said). There is no need to go beyond the fictional mode. If we need points of reference outside the poem, we need only think about some young 'Sloane' of our acquaintance, and imagine (or remember) what it is like to be her 'slave'.

If the reading of poetry is just a private pleasure, that is clearly all that needs to be said. There is a great deal in favour of the commonly expressed view that the reader of poetry is better off without academic rigmarole and scholarly commentary. The difficulty in the view that one should just enjoy poetry and not think about it comes when we realize that people who enjoy poetry sometimes want to *talk* about it. But in that case thinking about poetry (i.e. criticism, scholarship, etc.) comes back again, for surely it will not be held that it is possible to talk about poetry without thinking?

This is a general reflection which, if correct, holds good for all poems and works of art without exception. In the case of the 'Coronation Epistle', moreover, there are grounds for thinking that this is a poem which is not quite so self-sufficient as it seems. Apart from the bio-literary problem about the Young Lady (not identified as 'Miss Blount' until the 1735 edition of the *Works*) the very first word of the Epistle is an invitation to deconstructive unravelling, for here we have a simile that doesn't compare: 'As some fond virgin . . . etc.' down to 'Thus . . . ' (line 7). Of course, for most readers the 'As ' (i.e. the analogical status of what follows) is rapidly elided, and may well have been so for Pope himself. At any rate scholars who insist that the so-called 'suppressed lines'; of this poem (included by Butt under the title 'Epistle to a Lady' at his p. 308) could not have ever been an alternative ending or coda are apt to point out the impossible indecorum of their being addressed to the 'fond virgin' of the opening lines. But if the sustained comparison in the opening is to be taken seriously then the Young Lady is *not* a 'fond virgin.' In his discussion of Dryden's *Eleonora* Samuel Johnson says of the opening lines 'As, when some great and gracious monarch dies,' etc. that 'there is so much likeness in the initial comparison that there is no illustration. As a king would be lamented, Eleonora was lamented.' But here there is a question not merely of likeness, but of identity!

The problem about the tone of the poem which this raises, and its relation or lack of relation to the so-called 'suppressed lines', may now be approached from another side. Instead of taking the poem by itself and as it stands we may attempt to reconstruct something of its original 'setting in life' (*Sitz im Leben*). First there is the question of form. Although the 'Coronation Epistle' seems to have no analogue in Horace's poetry it cannot be doubted that, as in the other epistles to 'Miss Blount', and in the late 'Epistle to a Lady', Pope is writing in his own personal variation of Horace's satiric-epistolary mode (Cf. Brower, 1959, ch. VI). In this mode his view of women has always been the subject of controversy from his own time to ours, and hostile things have been said about it, for instance by James Reeves (1969): 'Pope's attitude to women is cynical, and breathes the all-male atmosphere of the clubs and coffee-houses.' (p. 89) But it may be that this does not take sufficient allowance of the realities of the society and culture in which Pope was writing his compliments, and his sermons, to women. As Pat Rogers puts it (1974), he is telling them 'how to succeed in a man's world' (p. 91), a world in which they were admired, respected, teased, patronized and cajoled by men, but not treated with intellectual respect. Pope can be seen not as reinforcing the constrictions of the polite code but showing, from the inside, how to defeat them.

However that may be, there appears to be a continuity in the 'Blount' poems which makes them immediately relevant to the interpretation of the 'Coronation Epistle'. They begin with the poem that was first entitled 'To a Young LADY, with the Works

of Voiture', included by Pope in his first miscellany of 1712. This
poem appeared in the first collected edition of Pope's *Works* (1717),
and was there directly associated with another epistle immediately
following it: 'To the same, On her leaving the Town after the
Coronation', i.e. the 'coronation Epistle'. On the face of it, then,
the Young Lady who was given the Works of Voiture is the same
person who left the Town after the Coronation. She remained
anonymous till the 1735 edition of the *Works*, when the title of
the first epistle was changed to 'To Miss Blount, with the Works
of Voiture'. The title of the second epistle was unaltered. All the
biographers of Pope record that he early made the acquaintance
of two sisters, Teresa and Martha Blount, grand-daughters of an
elderly neighbour, Anthony Eaglefield. The younger, Martha, was
to become Pope's dearest and lifelong friend. He quarrelled with
Teresa, and by 1735 there can be no doubt that in Pope's circle
'Miss Blount' would have been taken to mean Martha.

Certainly Martha Blount is the addressee of the late 'Epistle to
a Lady', which, as Maynard Mack (1985) puts it 'shows what
happens to the Belindas . . . when the rose is blowing or has
blown'. Mack calls it 'a guided tour of a gallery of female portraits,
made in company with Martha Blount' (p. 627). After the famous
and terrible passage that begins 'See how the world its Veterans
rewards' the two words that follow, says Mack, 'come like an
awakening from nightmare':

> Ah Friend! to dazzle let the Vain design,
> To raise the heart and thought and touch the Heart be
> thine!
> That Charm shall grow, while what fatigues the Ring
> Flaunts and goes down, an unregarded thing.
> So when the Sun's broad beam has tir'd the sight,
> All mild ascends the Moon's more sober light.
> Serene in Virgin Modesty she shines,
> And unobserv'd the glaring Orb declines.
>
> (lines 249–56).

This admonitory tone had already been heard in the portrait of
'Pamela' in the epistle 'with the Works of Voiture', where, in
accordance with Pope's usual method of contrast, it is the foil to
Voiture's trifling with life:

The Gods, to curse *Pamela* with her Pray'rs
Gave the gilt Coach and dappled *Flanders* mares.
The shining Robes, rich Jewels, Beds of State,
And to compleat her Bliss, a Fool for Mate.
She glares in *Balls, Front-boxes,* and the *Ring,*
A vain, unquiet, glitt'ring, wretched Thing!
Pride, Pomp, and State but reach her outward Part,
She sighs, and is no *Dutchess* at her Heart.
                                                    (lines 49–56).

We do not have a clear sense in the 'Voiture' epistle of the supposed auditress; she might be an ideal figure, or she might be the Martha Blount of the late poem. But no one supposes that Martha Blount is the Young Lady of the 'Coronation Epistle'. The general agreement of biographers today is that she is Teresa Blount – or else a purely fictitious person.

The evidence that she is Teresa Blount is not conclusive, but reasonably convincing. There is evidence that in the early MSS the seventh line of the Epistle originally was: 'So fair *Teresa* gave the town a view' or perhaps 'Thus from the world the fair *Teresa* flew.' Scholars have also traced the names 'Zephalinda' and 'Parthenia' to a correspondence between the Blount sisters and a man called Moor (or Moore), about 1713, in which Teresa is 'Zephalinda' and Martha 'Parthenissa' (*sic*). Pope knew this correspondence, and there is evidence that in the original MS in line 46 Martha was alluded to: 'Or see the blush of *Parthenissa* rise.' Martha was notorious for her shyness and blushing (see Mack, 1985, pp., 242–3). Later Pope changed the name, in subsequent editions, to 'fair Parthenia', so sparing her blushes.

But why bother who the Young Lady of the Coronation Epistle 'really' was? Isn't it just a matter for gossip, or antiquarianism? Certainly a reader of literary interests must feel some qualms about venturing near the quagmire of Pope's relationship with the Blount sisters. Mack says that 'so many of Pope's letters to them are undated and undatable that to go about mapping the ups and downs of their relationship is like walking through a minefield.' (p. 340) The only way, it seems, to preserve some kind of coherence in this series of poems is to treat 'Miss Blount' as a composite figure, 'Martha Teresa Blount', as in Jervas's portrait of 1716, where the two young women are side by side, one the virginal Parthenissa, holding the laurel associated with Apollo, the other holding a wreath of myrtle sacred to Venus.

No wonder Norman Ault (1949) complains of Pope's 'wilful mystification' (p. 49) about the Young Lady. Undoubtedly this was a trait in Pope's character. But the explanation for it may not be wholly psychological. It may have derived from the habitual necessities for various kinds of subterfuge, given the numerous legal, political and social restrictions on Catholics at this time, comparable to those imposed on Jews in Hitler's Germany. And as for the mystification about these poems, we may see in it Pope's way of vindicating the autonomy of poetry, the extraterritoriality of the imagination. He wanted to say something serious to, and about, women which the badinage of Voiture, etc. would not have permitted him to do; to suggest the presence of the real, particular, personal world out of which he wrote; but without being tied down to it.

If we decide to accept the composite status of the Young Lady it is possible, finally, to see the 'suppressed lines' in a somewhat different light. This is the text as given by Butt.

> Epistle to a Lady
>
> In this strange Town a different Course we take,
> Refine ourselves to Spirit, for your Sake.
> For Want of you, we spend our random Wit on
> The first we find with Needham, Brooks, or Briton.
> Hackney'd in Sin, we beat about the Town,
> And like sure Spaniels, at first Scent lie down,
> Were Virtue's self in Silks, – faith keep away!
> Or Virtue's Virtue scarce would last a Day.
>
> Thus, Madam, most Men talk, and some Men do:
> The rest is told you in a Line or Two.
> Some strangely wonder you're not fond to marry –
> A double Jest still pleases sweet Sir Harry –
> Small-Pox is rife, and *Gay* in dreadful fear –
> The good Priests whisper – Where's the Chevalier?
> Much, in your Absence B—'s Heart endures,
> And if poor *Pope* is cl—pt, the Fault is yours.

The Twickenham editors were not sure whether to accept these lines as the work of Pope, since few of his early editors had felt able to print them. But it is difficult to believe that any other poet of the time could have been capable of these incisive, balanced and compact comic lines. The last line is almost a signature! Yet as a conclusion to the 'Coronation Epistle' they seem quite incongruous. Ralph N. Maud (1958) admits that the lines are probably by Pope, but holds that they were never part of that poem but were part of some other poem. 'Zephalinda' of the Epistle and 'Madam' of the additional lines seem to him different people. Zephalinda has only begun to recognize her natural charms; her flirtation with the Squire is totally innocent. 'Madam' is a sophisticate, who is expected to enjoy *double-entendres*, and to take it as a compliment that her frustrated friends have to seek solace from such as 'Needham' (a brothel-keeper). Maud suggests that the world of the additional lines is the same as that of such MSS poems as 'A Farewell to London' (*c.* May 1715) and 'The Court Ballad' (December 1716). The lines could be the end of a verse-letter to one of the ladies-in-waiting. Pope knew Mary Bellenden and Mary (or Molly) Lepell intimately. The 'Coronation Epistle' is virtually self-sufficient in its fictional mode; whereas the additional lines are full of specific references and topical allusions. The *persona* of the poet is now that of the man–about–town, writing in a knowing jocular manner, quite unlike the 'slave' he has just portrayed.

These arguments have some force. And no one, if only on aesthetic grounds, is going to suggest that these lines should be printed in future as the authentic close of the 'Coronation Epistle'. But in taking that view it has to be recognized that it rests ultimately on an aesthetic, a critical, decision by *us*, i.e. modern readers or editors. If we take a non-biographical view of the 'Blount' poems they can be seen as illustrating the shifting moods and inconsistencies in the relations between men and women. Pope likes to dwell on the traditional theme of female mutability: taking his metaphors from painting, he exhorts himself to

> Come then, the colours and the ground prepare!
> Dip in the Rainbow, trick her off in Air,
> Chuse a firm Cloud, before it fall, and in it

Catch, ere she change, the Cynthia of this minute.
(Epistle II, To a Lady. Of the Characters of Women, lines 16–19).

But he also likes to expatiate on the inconsistencies of men, and himself in particular. 'What is Man altogether, but one mighty inconsistency,' he wrote to Caryll. In the 'Farewell to London. In the Year 1715' he paradoxically depicts himself as

> Still idle, with a busy Air,
> Deep Whimsies to contrive;
> The gayest Valetudinaire,
> Most thinking Rake alive.

It seems impossible to rule out the suggestion that the 'suppressed lines' continue the sequence of contrasts in which the canonical version of the 'Coronation Epistle' consists. Wise as Pope may have been to finally exclude them, they serve a purpose in reminding us that cynicism as well as idealization, matters of fact and artifices, *all* belong to 'reality'. Protesting against the analytical tradition in Anglo-American philosophy in his *Limited Inc.* (1977), Jacques Derrida exclaims: 'As though literature, theater, deceit, infidelity, hypocrisy, infelicity, parasitism, and the simulation of real life were not part of real life!' We might think of these words when, now and then, we read through the 'Coronation Epistle' – and add its 'coda'.

Chapter 5
Johnson as a Poet

Johnson's poetry appears to be little read or discussed, even by Johnsonians (I mean readers who know him through his writings as well as the records of his conversation.) There are, I think, two reasons for this.

1. The Dryden-Addison-Pope style in poetry is still widely disliked, in spite of helpful discussions like Sutherland's and Rachel Trickett's. The discrediting of this style was one of the lasting achievements of the Romantics. During the Anti-Romantic movement of the twentieth century there was a gesture at reviving it, but, as an American scholar has said, many of T.S. Eliot's followers professed to admire Dryden not because they really cared about him but in order to show that they did not consider themselves Romantics. Now that the Romantics are back in favour, sailing under new colours as what Harold Bloom calls the Visionary Company, there is even less chance that eighteenth century poetry will ever again be generally enjoyed. In any case, few would deny that Johnson is a lesser master than Dryden or Pope. Even in his best verse there is nothing quite so dazzling as Dryden on Achitophel or Pope on Timon's Villa.

2. There is a common feeling that Johnson both in his theory and his practice deviated from the main tradition of English poetry in the interests of a transient 'Augustanism'. In his wide-ranging survey of the development of English poetry Philip Hobsbaum does not even mention him. The main charge against his verse is that it lacks particularity and lively metaphor. These ideas, usually in association, have been for many years very influential in the teaching of poetry in schools and colleges. There is a strong conviction that English poetry requires such qualities to be effective, though they may not be needed in Latin or French; a line of Racine, wholly 'abstract', may have as much force as a

'concrete' line of English poetry. But English, it is held, requires the particular, the specific, the boldly metaphorical. On the other hand Johnson believed in 'the grandeur of generality'. His poetry has been thought to be abstract, colourless, conventional. It is marmoreal and inscriptional, unlike his lively talk. He is thought to have regarded poetry as the application from outside of melody and pattern to thoughts that could as well (and therefore could better) have been expressed in prose.

This account of Johnson the poet is still current in textbooks. I believe it to be quite false. It has inhibited the recognition of the great poems Johnson wrote as part of the central tradition of English poetry. I think it is a complete misrepresentation of Johnson to say that he did not favour the concrete and particular, and the vividly metaphorical, in his writing. It would be obviously absurd to say this of his conversation. Any random instance will furnish a counter-example: when Johnson was asked how he felt after the failure of *Irene* he replied: 'Like the Monument'. Some critics however (like Macaulay) while granting that Johnson *spoke* vigorously, have held that he *wrote* ponderously, in polysyllabic 'Johnsonese'. But others who knew Johnson personally testified that his talk and his writing were very similar. It is unfortunate that in an influential essay the late W.K. Wimsatt insisted on the abstractness of Johnson's prose style. To take just one example: think of the exuberant passage in the *Preface to Shakespeare* in which Johnson sighs over Shakespeare's quibbles. It is a positive firework display of similes and images, obviously taking an amused pleasure in doing the same sort of thing as Shakespeare. Even in less colourful passages the pressure of concrete reality is always felt behind his phrases. I am speaking here of Johnson's prose. Anyone who has read in it at all widely will know how absurd it is to use the term 'abstract' of it, in a pejorative sense. If that term is to be used, in that sense, it would be more appropriate for lacklustre Victorian prose, or even more for modern cloudlands of structuralese than for Johnson's pungent shipshape eighteenth century sentences. The question of his verse is more complex, but the same considerations apply to it, as the discussions by F.R. Leavis and Christopher Ricks have shown. As for 'the grandeur of generality', it has nothing to do with polysyllabic abstractions. Some such expression as 'human centrality' would be a better rendering of what Johnson meant.

In a short discussion I have to speak categorically. I hope the passages from Johnson's poetry that I shall be quoting presently will bear out my assertions. If these are over-emphatic, my excuse must be that the Romantic tradition about it is still prevalent, and according to that tradition Johnson was not a poet at all, except in the minimal sense given in his Dictionary: 'an inventor; an author of fiction; a writer of poems'. I disagree with this and believe that Johnson was essentially a poet. This is proved by the brilliance of his conversation, the best in the language. It is full of proliferating imagery, bold imaginative flights, unexpected but happy analogies, all tokens of the poet, just as the wit and weightiness are tokens of the wise and strange man. As for formal verse, there are many signs that Johnson as poet was 'born', not 'made'. His best poetry came to him easily. He was a master of improvisation. Some of his impromptus were no more than light society verse, but even here he is a poet and not merely a versifier. And other examples of his quickly composed verse are serious and noble.

Further evidence of Johnson's poethood is amply available to those who know him as a critic of English poetry. His range is here far wider, his taste more catholic, than is commonly supposed. As is usual with real poets he loved to discuss technical questions. He can discourse happily for pages on elision and caesura, the use of the Alexandrine in triplets, the preferability of rhyme or blank verse for long poems, etc. But he did not believe in recipes for writing poetry. He believed in 'inspiration' and 'originality' as much as any Romantic, in 'inwardness' and 'authenticity' as much as any Modern, though the words he used for these ideas were different. His theory of poetry was anti-intellectualist. As for imagery, so much stressed by twentieth-century criticism, he regarded it as of paramount importance. He again and again objected to its subordination to the conceptual. To give just one example: in his *Life of Cowley* he says in depreciation of this poet that he 'gives inferences instead of images, and shews not what may be supposed to have been seen, but what thoughts the sight might have suggested.' Johnson favoured what the Moderns call 'immediacy'.

Was Johnson a major poet? His contemporaries thought so, but the twentieth century has not agreed with them. Even those who take the view that I have outlined have to admit that his best poetry is small in quantity and mostly occasional. Not that these admissions are very damning. Some famous poets, far more voluminous than Johnson, have written less great poetry. And most genuine poetry has been occasional. Still, I cannot forget Arnold's reason for ranking Wordsworth so high, 'the great and ample body of powerful work' which Arnold thought remained when the inferior work was cleared away. This could not truly be said of Johnson as poet. But why not?

Since Johnson was a personal poet, not gifted for drama or narrative, biographical considerations cannot be avoided here. Johnson was very neurotic, but he hated 'whining'. We know mostly from others about his titanic struggle against mental and bodily suffering. He himself kept quiet about it. He did not record intimate experience in verse; or if he did, it was in Latin, a second language to Johnson, (We might think here of two twentieth-century Latin poets, W.R. Inge and A.E. Housman.) One of the few passages that refer directly to his own life occurs in the touching Latin poem in which he mentions his father teaching him how to swim. (Partially paralysed people are often happy in water, which supports the body.) Another Latin poem, with a Greek title, 'Gnōthi Seauton', (Know Thyself) was composed when Johnson had completed the arduous task of the fourth revision of the Dictionary: it is a salute, at once wry and sombre, to a great predecessor, Scaliger, and it is the most personally revealing of his poems. His lively friend Arthur Murphy turned it into a passable imitation of his English verse, but it is impossible to imagine Johnson writing such a poem in English. No one had better earned the right to say with Whitman 'I am the man. I suffered. I was there', and with Frost 'I have been one acquainted with the night.' But Johnson could express such thoughts only as a human being, not as a poet.

I believe that the main reason why Johnson's poetic output was so small is the problem that sincerity presented to him as a poet. Some modern critics dismiss the question of a poet's sincerity as irrelevant, or naive. Lionel Trilling smiles at the 'engagingly archaic' quality of F.R. Leavis's attempt to discriminate in Eliot's poetry between the more and less sincere. Trilling may be right, but it doesn't matter, since Johnson believed that poets should be sincere. But this involved him in a difficulty. Poetry required artifice, fiction, and Johnson defined 'fiction' in his Dictionary as 'the art of feigning or invention; the thing feigned or invented; a falsehood; a lye.' No other meanings are given. We remember his objection to the mingling of fiction with 'awful truths' in *Lycidas*, and his doubts about the possibility of satisfactory devotional poetry.

In attempting to be rid of the 'sincerity' problem modern criticism has made much of the *dramatic* quality of poetry (and not only in plays). But we do not need to look at *Irene* to realize that Johnson could rarely personate successfully. His masks in *The Rambler* are often transparent. All the characters in *Rasselas* speak alike: the dialogue is stylized. This is not a fault, for it has made the book a classic of the world. But we do not want all drama or fiction to be like *Rasselas*. Some have accused Johnson of lack of imagination, but the truth seems to be that far from being deficient in that 'licentious and vagrant faculty' he had too much of it, and it frightened him. It 'preyed upon life'. Sober, factual truth was something he had to hold on to. Johnson was not completely in sympathy with the anti-Romantic movement of Hobbes (who assimilated imagination to madness) and Locke. (No real poet could be, whole-heartedly.) But formality of style, the iron curtain of the eighteenth-century manner, was evidently a defence he needed. We know that at the time his mother was dying, he wrote *The Idler* no. 41, a dissertation on the death of a friend, full of dignity and philosophic calm and adult feeling, in majestic Johnsonian periods; yet at the same moment he was pouring out letters to Lucy Porter which are full of the grief and confusion of an anguished child.

In what he wrote for a public, Johnson does not display what he called 'the wounds of the mind'. But he was a direct, open, candid writer. In *Rasselas*, in *The Vision of Theodore*, in the *Life of Boerhaave*, the feeling is heartfelt. Everyone knows how formidable he was in person, the Colossus of Literature, as Boswell called him, the Great Cham, Ursa Major; yet he was amazingly ingenuous and ready to confide in even slight acquaintances. Boswell (sometimes for dramatic purposes) can appear naive, but he was psychologically devious; Johnson was not. This straightforwardness is what makes his Prayers appealing beyond anyone else's with their shortness and simplicity and the deep seriousness of Johnson's repeated appeals for grace to amend his life. But how far did Johnson achieve this personal quality, this stamp of experience, in his poetry?

To read through Johnson's poems in J.D. Fleeman's admirable edition is to have some surprises. Johnson's youthful work includes some pieces which suggest very different directions which his talent might have taken. The earliest poem of his to be preserved is on a daffodil! His view of the poetic art may have debarred him from minute descriptions ('numbering the streaks of the tulip'), yet there is evidence that he shared Wordsworth's feeling about nature and associated it with childhood and a sense of boundless freedom in a lost paradise. But while Wordsworth expressed this in poems such as *Tintern Abbey* Johnson reserved its expression for prose.

Another unexpected aspect of the young poet is disclosed in 'On the Feast of St. Simon and St. Jude'. This is an example of what was then called 'enthusiasm', a pejorative word. Christopher Smart could have written it: it is in the stanza of his *Song to David*.

> Where Atlas was believ'd to bear
> The weight of ev'ry rolling sphere,
>   Where sev'nmouth'd Nilus roars,
> Where the Darkvisag'd Natives fry,
> And scarce can breath th'infected sky,
>   But bless the Northern shoars.

In later years Johnson deprecated these youthful ecstasies to Boswell, but we know from Burney's memoirs that even as an older man he was subject to fits of 'enthusiasm' which obliged him to wave his arms in the air. Johnson may have belonged to the Age of Reason, but he also belonged to the Age of Sensibility. He wept over the *Dies Irae*; he wept over his 'young Enthusiast' in *The Vanity of Human Wishes*.

Some of Johnson's most accomplished poems are ostensibly inspired by music (ladies playing on the spinet or harpsichord). These have been assumed to be frigid exercises, because he was notoriously unmusical. But when not teasing he would admit that in failing to appreciate music he lacked something essential. Not six months before his death he asked Burney to teach him 'the Scale of Musick'. 'Teach me your language.' Music had to be for him a purely notional value, and in the 'Stella' poems he uses this art, together with the art of painting, as an evocative symbol for the ideal conduct of life.

> Mark, when the diff'rent Notes agree
> In friendly Contrariety;
> How Passion's well-accorded Strife
> Gives all the Harmony of Life:
> Thy Pictures shall thy Conduct frame,
> Consistent still; tho' not the same;
> Thy Musick teach the nobler art,
> To tune the regulated heart.

Here Johnson is close to the graceful side of Swift's verse, as in 'Cadenus and Vanessa', and to poems like Marvell's 'The Fair Singer'. As a poet Johnson descended from the Metaphysicals, to whom he gave that name.

The most beautiful of Johnson's poems in honour of music is his 'Epitaph on Claudy Phillips, a Musician', which he is said to have composed while stirring his tea.

> Phillips, whose touch harmonious could remove
> The pangs of guilty pow'r, and hapless love,
> Rest here distress'd by poverty no more,
> Find here that calm, thou gav'st so oft before.
> Sleep, undisturb'd, within this peaceful shrine,
> Till angels wake thee, with a note like thine.

Christopher Ricks draws attention to the word 'touch' here. We should think not only of its meaning as a musical term but of Queen Anne touching the child Samuel Johnson (without success) for scrofula. There is a religious-magical suggestion, so that the 'angels' at the end do not appear merely to clinch a gracious eulogy. These poems on music should be read in the light of Dryden's great poem 'Alexander's Feast', to which Johnson alludes in 'To Miss Hickman'. In 'Alexander's Feast' the tribute to music is implicitly a tribute to the power of art generally, to the power of poetry, so that the poem celebrates itself. Johnson writes in that tradition.

It was on the strength of *Irene*, *London*, and *The Vanity of Human Wishes* that Johnson's reputation as a major poet was based in his own time. Everyone agrees that *Irene* is a failure both as drama and as poetry. It lacks 'the Johnsonian aether'; its only atmosphere is that of Drury Lane. How ironical that Johnson failed to achieve formal tragedy! The writer of *The Vanity of Human Wishes* and

Rasselas and the *Life of Swift*, perhaps uniquely in the eighteenth century, had what Unamuno called the tragic sense of life. Yet *Irene* is dead. It was slowly and painfully elaborated, unlike Johnson's successful poems; except for an occasional cry from the heart, there was no place in it for the author's tortured feelings. It is hardly worth mentioning that there are no memorable characters and the theme is not conceived and presented dramatically; worse still, it is not even a good poem. The blank verse is that of a couplet writer who has dropped the rhymes and added from time to time an extra syllable or 'feminine ending', by which he gains nothing, and loses the opportunity for writing witty epigrams or clinching his effects. *Irene* can be read with interest for its serious political and moral reflections, but as a tragedy it is cold. Yet its author's state of mind was quite otherwise.

I . . . delayed my departure for a time to finish the performance by which I was to draw the first notice of mankind upon me. When it was completed I hurried to London, and considered every month that passed before its publication, as lost in a kind of neutral existence, and cut off from the golden hours of happiness and fame. (*The Rambler*, no. 163).

But the patentee of Drury Lane was more interested in pantomimes than in classic drama, and Johnson turned to writing for the *Gentleman's Magazine*. (Thanks to Garrick he did in the end see *Irene* staged.)

London and *The Vanity of Human Wishes* are much livelier poems, but they present readers of today with some problems. They are both 'imitations' of poems by the Roman writer Juvenal – Decimus Iunius Iuuenalis (*c*.AD 60– *c*.AD 130.). This mode of writing was fashionable in the seventeenth and eighteenth centuries, but came to be suspect on the ground that an English poet is lamed by having to follow in the footsteps of his Latin original. In recent times, however, the notion of updating an ancient poem by way of 'homage' has become current through Ezra Pound and his followers. Still, Roman Satire does not appeal to English tastes. It seems a meandering diatribe. The great English satires owe nothing to it; in works such as *Gulliver's Travels*, *The Dunciad*, *Erewhon*, *Animal Farm*, our writers have created their own form.

But something must be said about the relation between *London* and Juvenal's third poem. That poem is hard to interpret. Juvenal's intentions remain a subject for scholarly controversy. He has been seen as like Isaiah, scourging the sins of the Roman Babylon. On the other hand H.W. Garrod (in 1912) dismissed his poetry as 'rhetoric of rancour' and excluded him from the *Oxford Book of Latin Verse*. And a more recent critic, H.A. Mason (in 1963) denies Juvenal any claim to moral seriousness, though ranking him high as a poet because he is 'a supreme manipulator of the Latin language'. One of Johnson's predecessors in the 'imitation' of this poem, the French poet Boileau (1636–1711), was evidently so puzzled by its tone that in transferring its action to the Paris he knew he had to divide it into two poems. One of these introduces the character of 'surly Virtue' which Johnson took over for his *London*, and it is a serious treatment of political and moral scandals. The other is a hilarious extravaganza in which the 'je' of the poem is a Jacques Tati figure, swept half-demented through scenes of funeral and scenes of farce, losing his hat. The English reader is reminded of Byron's *Don Juan*. Johnson, mostly through his mouthpiece 'injur'd Thales' – sometimes thought to be modelled on his friend Richard Savage – tries to maintain a tone of angry seriousness throughout. His poem is bitterly partisan. It is a scathing attack on the regime of Sir Robert Walpole for domestic corruption and appeasement of Spain. But it engages only the hard and noisy side of Johnson the political publicist, not the melancholy sceptic about 'laws and kings'. In other ways it has a very strange effect. The use of the Juvenal material, so full of burlesque and extravaganza, for serious polemical purposes leads to incongruities.

> Here falling Houses thunder on your Head,
> And here a female Atheist talks you dead.

It is hard to know just how to take this kind of thing. A bit of Juvenal plus a bit of real life?

London is an anomaly among Johnson's poems. Alone among them it raises the problem of sincerity. T.S. Eliot says bluntly that it fails because it is insincere. It is a diatribe against London by someone who did not really mean it. In real life Johnson would have been the very first person to want to 'change the rocks of Scotland for the Strand'. I am not wholly convinced by this judgment. We all know that Johnson said that 'he who is tired

of London is tired of life' and 'the high tide of existence is at
Charing Cross', but that was when he was well settled in London.
As a struggling young provincial in the great heartless city he might
quite probably have felt what the Shropshire Lad felt in the next
century.

> Homespun collars, homespun hearts,
> Wear to rags in foreign parts.
> Mine at least's as good as done,
> And I must get a London one.

Eliot also criticizes the references to the countryside in *London*
as weak and unconvincing.

> Some pleasing Bank where verdant Osiers play,
> Some peaceful Vale with Nature's paintings gay;

Or

> There ev'ry Bush with Nature's Music rings,
> There ev'ry Breeze bears Health upon its Wings;

But I don't think they are perfunctory or insincere, as Juvenal's
probably are. Moving water always fascinated Johnson (see Mary
Lascelles's essay 'Johnson and Juvenal' in *New Light on Dr. Johnson*,
ed. F.W. Hilles (1959)) and his feelings about the Trent were real.
He remembered Lichfield, a small country town built round a confluence of streams and springs which feed the river. His allusions to
his memories of home might be compared to those invocations of
another order of existence which suddenly illuminate the confused
modern world in Eliot's *Coriolan* poems.

> O hidden under the dove's wing, hidden in the turtle's breast,
> Under the palmtree at noon, under the running water
> At the still point of the turning world. O hidden.

I suspect that the 'country' references are part of the political
code of the poem. They are associated with 'rebellious Virtue', as in
Pope's epistle to Bolingbroke (published 1738), in which Virtue is
associated with the values of the landed interest, the Country Party.
They are to be taken as nostalgic contrasts to the England of the
Walpole regime, as are the references to vanished Plantagenet and
Tudor glories. In this patriotic appeal to the past Johnson is drawing

on another previous imitator of Juvenal, John Oldham (1653–83), best known as the subject of Dryden's fine elegy. It may well be to Oldham that he owes the stimulus for the liveliest passage in *London* (the Yale editors have missed this) on the 'drunken Scourers'.

Prepare for Death, if here at Night you roam,
And sign your Will before you sup from Home.
Some fiery Fop, with new Commission vain,
Who sleeps on Brambles till he kills his Man;
Some frolick Drunkard, reeling from a Feast,
Provokes a Broil, and stabs you for a Jest.
Yet ev'n these Heroes, mischievously gay,
Lords of the Street, and Terrors of the Way;
Flush'd as they are with Folly, Youth and Wine,
Their prudent Insults to the Poor confine;
Afar they mark the Flambeau's bright Approach,
And shun the shining Train, and golden Coach.

What made Eliot uncomfortable about the poem is the constant hyperbole. 'Thales' says, for example, that there are so many executions that the navy is suffering from a hemp shortage. This exuberance can be explained as the expression of youthful high spirits; as Aristotle says in his *Rhetoric*, 'there is something youthful about hyperboles'. I am afraid, however, that the obvious dull explanation is correct. Johnson was writing for readers who had enjoyed the witty preposterousness of Juvenal and were pleased to see it in modern dress. Thus, wanting an equivalent for Juvenal's supple Greek, he was content to lampoon the French.

But this does not clear up all the puzzles of *London*. I wonder if the curious tone of the poem has something to do with Johnson's ambivalent feeling towards his mother. 'She was always recounting the glories of the city. . . . By these narratives I was fired with the splendour and dignity of London.' (*The Rambler*, no. 116). It may not be entirely fanciful to recall that London is the 'Metropolis' (the word is used in the poem), the mother-city.

The Vanity of Human Wishes is also an 'imitation' of Juvenal (the tenth poem) but now Johnson has found the right form for his matter. With the aid of Shakespeare he achieves the tragic note he had failed to produce in *Irene*. The Wolsey passage (lines 99–129) shows the depth of his poetic relationship to Shakespeare. Macaulay thought Juvenal did better in making us visualize the fall of Sejanus, but Johnson creates a drama of the mind. After 'At length his Sov'reign frowns' we see everything through Wolsey's eyes. For Eliot 'Swedish Charles' was the greatest passage (192–222). Charles XII was a much discussed figure in Johnson's day, and the career Johnson describes was historically portentous; its catastrophe was the battle of Poltava (1709) which was to make Russia a great European power, as Stalingrad (1943) made her a world power. Johnson rises to the historic occasion with splendid solemnity and grand irony. Much has been said also in praise of the 'young Enthusiast' of Oxford, the best-known passage of Johnson's poetry and a fine example of his power to invest a commonplace with reality and poignancy.

> Yet hope not Life from Grief or Danger free,
> Nor think the Doom of Man revers'd for thee.

Equal strength is shown in the contrasting Maupassant-like portrait of the old man (lines 256–90). My own favourite is the last of the little dramas of the poem, less often quoted; a witty sermon to the 'Nymphs of rosy Lips and radiant Eyes'.

> Against your Fame with Fondness Hate combines,
> The Rival batters, and the Lover mines.
> With distant voice neglected Virtue calls,
> Less heard, and less the faint Remonstrance falls;
> Tir'd with Contempt, she quits the slipp'ry Reign,
> And Pride and Prudence take her seat in vain.
> In croud at once, where none the Pass defend,
> The harmless Freedom, and the private Friend.
> The Guardians yield, by Force superior ply'd;
> To Int'rest, Prudence; and to Flatt'ry, Pride.
> Here Beauty falls betray'd, despis'd, distress'd,
> And hissing Infamy proclaims the rest.

Boileau's tenth satire may have helped Johnson here to paint that lively miniature of fashionable society. Here as elsewhere in the poem his abstractions translate readily into individuals, such as Pope gives us in his tale of Sir Balaam, or Crabbe in his versified short stories. The total effect (unlike Robert Lowell's imitation of the source-poem) is of magnanimity.

The Vanity of Human Wishes contains some of Johnson's best poetry. But often it is too declamatory and too 'tinny': the ghost of Roman Satire still haunts it. I feel that a successful satirist must be something of a buffoon; a *grave* satirist, such as Johnson, is almost a contradiction in terms. *Rasselas* remains his real masterpiece on this subject.

I think Johnson's best poems are the Prologues: 'Drury Lane', the prologue to Goldsmith's *The Good-Natur'd Man*, and above all the prologues to *Comus* and to Hugh Kelly's *A Word to the Wise*. Johnson has found the attitude to the audience that suited what he wanted to say to them. His contempt for them is balanced by his respect for literary and moral decency. We hear the voice of the great Johnson of the Preface to the Dictionary. Personal bitterness comes through, but so too does largeness of soul and, in the end, Christian humility. The prologue to *A Word to the Wise* is the greatest of these poems. Here the Johnsonian generality was an asset. He could not say anything about the play itself because he did not admire Kelly, so he appeals for English fair play and asks the audience to make a beautiful and ceremonious occasion out of a performance of something which in itself may have lacked merit. We hear Johnson's moral authority:

> To wit, reviving from its author's dust,
> Be kind, ye judges, or at least be just:
> Let no resentful petulance invade
> Th'oblivious grave's inviolable shade,
> Let one great payment every claim appease,
> And him who cannot hurt, allow to please,

Most of Johnson's later poetry is light verse, the bagatelles and throw-offs preserved by Mrs Thrale. Her character and her relationship with Johnson cannot be described briefly, On his side it appears to have been what psychoanalysts call a 'transference' relationship, and it may well have saved his life and sanity. The literary results were also happy. In his early poems Johnson had no Muse and he found it hard to create a convincing *persona*. Democritus, invoked in *The Vanity of Human Wishes*, the man who laughs at everything, would not really do, for Johnson was a Tchehovian character, tragic as well as comic. But in his later poetry his Mistress was his Muse, and his *persona* is convincing:

the gregarious Johnson, Johnson without his wig, who could be at home with topers as with fashionable ladies, with profligates as with scholars, a figure of Shakespearean largeness, humour, and charity. This later verse consists mostly of what Johnson called 'Easy Poetry', one of his critical terms which, unlike 'Metaphysical Poets', has never been taken up. He defines it thus: 'Easy poetry is that in which natural thoughts are expressed without violence to the language. The discriminating character of ease consists principally in the diction, for all true poetry requires that the sentiments be natural.' I have found no discussion of Johnson's essay on Easy Poetry (*The Idler*, 77, 1759), but I believe it to be crucial for the understanding of his later work. He was to say of the revolution in English poetry effected by Dryden that Dryden 'found it brick and left it marble', but here he seems to prefer 'brick'. He praises the directness of Cowley, an aspect of that poet at variance with the Metaphysical, fanciful aspect which Johnson deprecated. Johnson's conception of this kind of poetry resembles what W.H. Auden called Light Verse. It will be seen that Johnson's view of this genre allows for its accommodation of the serious and even tragic.

Johnson had ceased to be a formal satirist by now, and we should think of him as an *improvisatore*. His finest poem of this kind is his 'Reply to Impromptu Verses by Baretti'.

> At sight of sparkling Bowls or beauteous Dames
> When fondness melts me, or when wine inflames,
> I too can feel the rapture fierce and strong
> I too can pour the extemporary song;
> But though the number for a moment please,
> Though musick thrills, or sudden sallies seize,
> Yet lay the Sonnet for an hour aside,
> Its charms are fled and all its power destroy'd:
> What soon is perfect, soon alike is past:
> That slowly grows which must for ever last.

Something could be said here of Johnson's relations with Baretti, the volatile Italian, once tried for murder, the most disliked figure (with the exception of Hawkins) in the Johnson circle. But the poem does not require biographical comment. Its mode, like that of Ben Jonson's 'fit of rhyme against rhyme', is paradox: in the form of an impromptu the poet exalts the product of slow and deliberate creation as alone imperishable.

The 'Short Song of Congratulation', sardonic and Housman-like, gains by a biographical gloss: its message was well suited to the future husband of Letty Lade, ex-mistress of the highwayman Sixteen-string Jack. But it stands well by itself as an indulgence of the 'Restoration' side of Johnson's temperament. The best-known of these personal poems is 'On the Death of Dr. Robert Levet'. It is perhaps less immediately appealing; it is formal rather than 'easy'. It is deeply moving for those who know Levet, the man 'obscurely wise and coarsely kind', the companion of Johnson's solitary mornings, who, Johnson said, was the only man he knew who got drunk from motives of prudence (his patients could only pay him in gin), whose manners were brutal, but not his mind. But to students attending only to the words on the page it has seemed chilly and artificial. Perhaps the moral is that Johnson's poems, like Cowper's, but unlike Blake's, require us to conjure up the intimate world they came out of. Only then can we appreciate the pathos of a line like: 'Our social comforts drop away.'

Chapter 6
Romantic Narrative Verse:
The Autobiographical Element

There is something surprising about the great outburst of English narrative poetry at the beginning of the nineteenth century. We think of the typical eighteenth-century poem as descriptive and reflective: Thomson's *Seasons*, Gray's *Elegy*, Goldsmith's *Deserted Village*. None of these has a story to tell. So it is remarkable that at the end of the eighteenth century not only did various kinds of narrative poetry suddenly flourish, but they achieved a commercial as well as critical success. Some of them were bestsellers to a degree that English poetry has not known before or since.

How did this happen? Even before 1800 there were signs that writers were becoming aware of an emerging market for this kind of poetry. The 1790s saw the production of a number of epic poems. The only ones that anyone now reads are the visionary poems of William Blake, and Blake ignored market considerations, and his contemporaries ignored him. But even the epics that were written to please the public did not win lasting popularity. They were too long, too difficult to read, too emotionally unengaging.

A kind of narrative poetry that had a more direct appeal was the revival of a very old kind of poetry, the ballad. The *Lyrical Ballads* of Wordsworth and Coleridge (1798) are the best-remembered examples, though there were other balladists who were more popular. But they did not conform to the influential critical doctrine of the day which held that great poetry had to be on a large scale. What was needed to please both critical and popular opinion was something which had epic qualities as the eighteenth century understood them, yet was vivid and readable like the ballad, direct and emotionally appealing. The poet who achieved this style was Walter Scott. His *Lay of the Last Minstrel* (1805) sold over 20,000 copies in five years, and was followed in 1808 by the even more popular *Marmion*. Scott was thought a great poet by his contemporaries – even by critics who deplored his slapdash style and over-emphasis. He gave both the public and the critics what they liked. But Scott was not fully committed to the kind of poetry he wrote, and profited by. He was in many ways a typical late eighteenth-century man of letters, scholarly, urbane, unemotional. The poets he admired most were the English Augustans. His favourite poet was Samuel Johnson, and he brought out an edition of John Dryden's works in the hope that it would revive interest in the father of Augustan poetry. 'I can with honest truth exculpate myself from having been at any time a partisan of my own poetry,' he wrote in 1830. But from a purely commercial point of view Scott had hit on the right formula. It was he who created the vogue for the tale of adventure and exciting incident. I have already mentioned *Marmion*. Its hero-villain is the forerunner of the type that became known as the 'Byronic hero'. Byron took over Scott's kind of verse romance and made it even more sensationally popular. 'Byron beat me', sighed Scott; and turned his energies to the writing of prose fiction.

Byron was already known for his descriptive and reflective poem, *Childe Harold's Pilgrimage*: the first two cantos appeared in 1812. The verse-romance which followed it in 1813, *The Giaour*, was an instant success; and it was quickly followed by the *Bride of Abydos* (also 1813), by *Lara* in 1814, *The Siege of Corinth* in 1816, and other romances. Byron's popularity soon surpassed Scott's.

One reason for this was probably that Byron's tales are much shorter and faster-moving. And then Byron had the advantage of being able to develop a taste which Scott had already established; casting glamour on figures remote in place or time from his readers. Byron gave his tales a spicier flavour. He writes of Corsairs, Italian bandits, Levantine pirates. There is a great deal of action and violence. Extreme physical and emotional states are written up with much emphasis. But perhaps the main reason for Byron's eclipse of Scott was 'the Byronic Hero'. Innumerable thrilled readers were tempted to identify this strange, guilt-stricken, ambivalent figure with the poet himself, the reckless aristocrat with the hints of scandal and mystery about him, 'mad, bad and dangerous to know', as Lady Caroline Lamb called Byron. But Caroline Lamb was an unbalanced woman who knew little of Byron. The people who knew Byron well did not think he was at all like the Byronic hero. And this suggests another curious point. Byron, like Scott, did not care for the sort of poetry he wrote himself with such popular success. Like Scott, his taste in poetry was for the Augustans: his favourite poet was Alexander Pope. As with Scott, but more acutely, there was a division in Byron between 'the poet' and 'the man'. For example: Byron was famous in his time for his power of describing nature. But in real life he had no interest in nature whatever. While passing through picturesque landscapes he drew down the blinds of his carriage. It was in his later work, and particularly *Don Juan*, that the 'poet' and the 'man' drew more closely together.

But *Don Juan* is largely a comic poem; and it was the impassioned poetry of Byron that conquered Europe. And there can be little doubt that his success was due to his readers' feeling that they were experiencing the poet's actual personality. There was a sense of direct contact between poet and reader which had been lacking in the poets of the 1790s. Here once again Scott is the forerunner of Byron. I am thinking of such things as the introduction to Canto III of *Marmion*, dedicated to his friend William Erskine. It gives us at the same time a pleasant glimpse of the author in boyhood and a modest apologia for his informal manner of writing.

> Thus while I ape the measure wild
> Of tales that charm'd me as a child,
> Rude though they be, still with the chime
> Return the thoughts of early time;
> And feelings, rous'd in life's first day,
> Glow in the line, and prompt the lay.
> Then rise those crags, that mountain tower
> Which charm'd my fancy's wakening hour.
> Though no broad river swept along,
> To claim, perchance, heroic song;
> Though sigh'd no groves in summer gale,
> To prompt of love a softer tale;
> Though scarce a puny streamlet's speed
> Claim'd homage from a shepherd's reed;
> Yet was poetic impulse given
> By the green hill and clear blue heaven . . .

And ever, by the winter hearth,
Old tales I heard of woe or mirth,
Of lovers' slights, of ladies' charms,
Of witches' spells, of warriors' arms . . .
While stretch'd at length upon the floor,
Again I fought each combat o'er,
Pebbles and shells, in order laid,
The mimic ranks of war display'd;
And onward still the Scottish Lion bore,
And still the scatter'd Southron fled before . . .

For me, thus nurtur'd, dost thou ask,
The classic poet's well-conn'd task?
Nay, Erskine, nay; on the wild hill
Let the wild heath bell flourish still;
Cherish the tulip, prune the vine,
But freely let the woodbine twine,
And leave untrimm'd the eglantine . . .
Though wild as cloud, as stream, as gale,
Flow forth, flow unrestrain'd, my Tale!
(*Marmion*, introduction to Canto Third
To William Erskine, Esq.)

Scott was prepared to tell his readers about himself what he thought they should be permitted to know, but no more. This is partly because he wanted to preserve the dignified reticence of an eighteenth-century gentleman. But there were other reasons. We should remember that Scott was a very complex person. We hear of men leading double lives, but Sir Walter Scott led a treble and even quadruple life. A Border laird and a well-known figure in Edinburgh society, a scholar and antiquary, he was also in private a businessman, and a world-famous novelist, the anonymous 'Author of *Waverley*', the Great Unknown. Most secret of all was an inward imaginative and emotional life which he carefully kept from the knowledge of the world. So that although in his autobiographical publications Scott speaks to his readers with manly frankness, he is never intimate. Byron deliberately exploited a fictional version of his personality. In part his motive was literary: to establish the dominant manner of his masterpiece, the long unfinished quasi-autobiographical and *sui generis* poem *Don Juan*. Where Scott had put in a modest claim for his art as a 'wild flower', contrasting it with 'The classic poet's well-conn'd task', Byron openly derides the epic pretensions of his contemporaries. In place of their fabrications he promises the real thing. 'My poem's epic . . .' (he says):

> There's only one slight difference between
> Me and my epic brethren gone before,
> . . . They so embellish, that 'tis quite a bore
> Their labyrinth of fables to thread through,
> Whereas this story's actually true.
>
> (*Don Juan*, canto I, stanza CC and stanza CCII)

Byron's autobiographical manner is more casual and unbuttoned than Scott's.

> As boy, I thought myself a clever fellow,
> And wished that others held the same opinion;
> They took it up when my days grew more mellow,
> And other minds acknowledge my dominion:
> Now my sere fancy 'falls into the yellow
> Leaf', and Imagination droops her pinion,
> And the sad truth which hovers o'er my desk
> Turns what was once romantic to burlesque.
>
> (*Don Juan*, canto IV, stanza iii)

> I perch upon a humbler promontory,
> Amidst life's infinite variety:
> With no great care for what is nicknamed glory,
> But speculating as I cast my eye
> On what may suit or may not suit my story,
> And never straining hard to versify,
> I rattle on exactly as I'd talk
> With anybody in a ride or walk.
>
> (*Don Juan*, canto XV, stanza xix)

But for English readers the standard of poetic autobiography has been finally set by Wordsworth in *The Prelude*. Scott's use of autobiography in his poems had been casual. Byron, in *Don Juan*, had used it as a literary instrument, a means to establish the genre of his writing. But we cannot imagine Scott or Byron pondering the problems of the autobiographical poet, the writing of psychological narrative or subjective epic, as Wordsworth did (just as we cannot imagine him writing, as they did, a kind of poetry which the poet himself does not deeply believe in). He worked on *The Prelude*, version after version, throughout most of his long poetic career. Why did he have so much difficulty in putting the story of his life before the world? One reason is that Wordsworth regarded *The Prelude* as merely a subordinate part of his great philosophical work, *The Recluse*. He was quite firm that there could be no question of publishing it until *The Recluse* had been completed; and it never was. So *The Prelude* lay in manuscript until after his death in 1850, known only to his family and closest friends. It had not even a title: Wordsworth himself usually speaks of it as 'the poem to Coleridge'. (The title *The Prelude* was suggested by the poet's widow.) There may have been a deeper reason for the delay. For Wordsworth autobiography was a problematic thing. It is, he wrote to Sir George Beaumont in 1805, 'a thing unprecedented in literary history that a man should talk so much about himself.' Surely Wordsworth was right to feel that autobiography is provocative as a literary form? In our own time Jean-Paul Sartre has defended the autobiographer by saying that in subjectivity one discovers other people as well as oneself. That may be so: but the fact remains that the autobiographer is asking a large number of men and women whom he does not know to take an interest in his personal affairs.

Some autobiographers have drawn attention to their own frankness. Baudelaire wrote a prose work called 'My heart laid bare' (*Mon coeur mis à nu*). *The Prelude* is not this kind of work. It is not 'confessional'. It was left to modern research to unearth the story of his love affair in France with Annette Vallon and the birth of their child out of wedlock. The poem does indeed allude to it (in the Vaudracour and Julia episode), but so indirectly that no reader unfamiliar with the secret could know what was being referred to; and compared with Byron, and even with Scott, Wordsworth does not adopt an air of frankness.

The quality that he does achieve, and which they do not, is inwardness, intimacy. In the finest passages of *The Prelude* Wordsworth conveys, not outward facts, but a vision. He is the greatest spiritual autobiographer in English. It is easy to understand why in his own time he could not compete with the more superficial attractions of Scott's or Byron's poetry.

But he speaks out of regions of the spirit which they never entered.

I have quoted Scott and Byron recalling youthful memories. Here is Wordsworth recreating one of those moments which he called 'spots of time', recollected from his childhood, which were to him of deep but almost incommunicable significance: the Girl with the Pitcher.

> I left the spot
> And reascending the bare slope I saw
> A naked pool that lay beneath the hills,
> The beacon on the summit, and more near
> A girl who bore a pitcher on her head
> And seemed with difficult steps to force her way
> Against the blowing wind. It was in truth
> An ordinary sight, but I should need
> Colours and words that are unknown to man
> To paint the visionary dreariness
> Which, while I looked all round for my lost guide,
> Did at that time invest the naked pool,
> The beacon on the lonely eminence,
> The woman and her garments vexed and tossed
> By the strong wind.

The effect of this picture on me is one which I am sure many other readers share. I am awed by it; but at the same time puzzled. How can something so extraordinary be made out of something on the face of it so ordinary? and by such simple means?

The Prelude has other things to offer besides these moments. It is an invaluable document for students of Wordsworth's life and times. But much of it is prosy and boring. Struggling with the duller parts, I find myself recovering the early nineteenth-century taste for the lively movement of Scott, and, even more, of Byron.

> I rattle on exactly as I'd talk
> With anybody in a ride or walk.

But if we feel like this it is only fair to Wordsworth to recall things like the Girl with the Pitcher. Even if in the end, all *The Prelude* has to offer the lover of poetry is the evocation of a few moments in a life, isn't that enough? Of how many of the billions of human beings who have lived and died can it be said that we have the kind of inward knowledge that, in its great places, *The Prelude* gives us of one man's soul?

Chapter 7
Tennyson and Victorian Balladry

Could Tennyson write good ballads? To answer this question we must first decide what is meant by 'ballad.' The word has been applied to various kinds of verse, but they all have a family resemblance. For English-speaking readers the Border Ballads represent the prototype. In this kind of poetry the intention is to tell a story, and at the same time to arouse the emotions appropriate to it. Poetic 'beauties' are sometimes present but always seem incidental, even unintentional: the attention of the reader or hearer is directed to the story and the characters. The verse-form is short rhymed stanzas. The metre is simple and does not call attention to itself, though repetitions and refrains may create an effect of incantation. There are no complications of rhythm corresponding to subtleties of feeling that cannot be taken in at the first hearing. Some ballad verse is old and it can be regarded as a primitive form, but it has not been superseded: the ballad has persisted, it has developed in its own way, it has its own history. T.S. Eliot, however, thinks that it is difficult to write in the conditions of present-day society, pointing out that the greatest of modern balladists, Rudyard Kipling, had an advantage over more recent poets of this kind because he still had the living music-hall behind him.

There is still no agreement among scholars about the origin of ballads. But about one of their qualities there is no dispute. They are impersonal. It is not merely that the poets' names are unknown: the absence of the poet is, so to speak, a requirement of the form. If 'poem', as it surely does, implies 'poet' (*das Volk dichtet* cannot be literally true) a ballad must have had an author. But, as G.L. Kittredge said, it has the effect of appearing to tell itself, without the instrumentality of a conscious speaker. 'The style is the man' does not apply here. The teller of the tale has no role in it. Unlike other songs, it does not purport to give utterance to the feelings of the speaker. The first person does not occur, except in the speeches of the characters. The narrator offers no comments or reflections, does not analyse the characters psychologically. Nor does he take sides for or against any of them. He merely tells what happened, and what people said. The dialogue is confined to its simplest and most inevitable elements. The story exists for its own sake.

This kind of popular poetry, impersonal and enigmatic, has often appealed to sophisticated poets, but, as Albert B. Friedmann shows in *The Ballad Revival* (1961), they have found it tricky to handle. Friedmann's last chapter is, significantly, entitled 'The Difficulties of Imitation.' It tells the story of the ballad revival, starting from Percy's *Reliques of Ancient English Poetry* (1765), and it makes clear the uneasiness of many poets with the ballad and the problem that both the early and the late Romantics and the Pre-Raphaelites encountered when they tried to assimilate it into their personal styles. Sir Walter Scott, the great collector of ballads, noted that a good many readers did not find them attractive in their original form. Sometimes they were so crude and harsh as to be repellent. His own solution was to cross them with romance. Scott is often credited with initiating this confluence. But he had been anticipated by Percy. Some of the best known and most influential ballads in Percy's collection, like 'The Hermit of Warkworth', were largely fabricated by him. W.J. Mickle's ballads, with their Spenserian locutions and archaic spellings, have a similar manufactured quality. So do the romance-ballads fathered by Thomas Chatterton on 'Rowley', though the completeness of Chatterton's delusion gives a charm to the pseudo-antique style which is merely tiresome in Mickle.

And so it came about that two of the traditions of medieval storytelling were given a new life by the Romantic movement. 'The penetration of the Ballad by Romance' is an appropriate formula for the wave of nineteenth-century poetry launched by Scott's *Lay of the Last Minstrel* (1805) and other poems by him and by other poets, Coleridge, Southey, Wordsworth, Keats. These poets do not always mingle the two traditions. Southey was well versed in chivalry and studied the metrical romances, but he did not draw on this knowledge when he was writing his ballads. Wordsworth explicitly renounces romance at the beginning of

Peter Bell (written 1798), though it is still plausible to argue, as Hugh Sykes Davies did, that Wordsworth is a greater master of the eerie and strange than Coleridge or Keats or Shelley. In other poems he shows a continued liking for romance. His 'Song at the Feast at Brougham Castle' is, stylistically, a curious mixture. The minstrel, expressing warlike emotions, speaks in Scott's manner, in the short rhymed couplets of a romance, but Clifford's response is made in long meditative lines and sounds a more characteristically Wordsworthian note of thoughtfulness and limpid gravity:

> The silence that is in the starry sky,
> The sleep that is among the lonely hills.

The romances are not an important source for Coleridge in his 'Ancient Mariner.' His most famous romance-ballad is 'Christabel' (1797), influenced by Percy's 'Sir Cauline'. But 'Christabel' is much more romance than ballad. If literary historians still call it a ballad, this is perhaps on account of its sensationalism about snakes, which links it with 'Gothic' ballads, or because of its metre, which derives from Coleridge's study of the irregularities of the older ballad verse. A poem of this period that exhibits a more balanced blend of romance and ballad is Keats's 'La Belle Dame Sans Merci' (1819). Keats loved the old ballads for their dramatic effect and air of mystery. In this respect his poem is a distillation of the ballad spirit. It is written in a modified form of the ballad stanza, opens abruptly as they do, with the ballad formality of the query: 'O what can ail thee, knight-at-arms . . .' and uses dialogue as the means of revelation. But unlike the ballads 'La Belle Dame Sans Merci' is not a tale of action. It is more like an allegorical episode in a romance. As Albert Friedmann says, the lady is more like Spenser's Phaedria or Duessa than like the Queen of Elfland. The effect of the poem is the evocation of a state of strange undefinable anguish. The situation, unlike those in the ballads, remains unresolved. The poem is like the ballads in being concentrated and elliptical, but the setting, weird and desolate, and the languid, dream-like atmosphere are properties of a suggestive, subjective kind of poetry, not of old balladry.

So many poems were written in this tradition – for example by Tennyson, Gabriel and Christina Rossetti, Swinburne, Morris, and Yeats – that it looks like the main line in Victorian balladry.

So atmospheric, so centred on mood rather than action are some of Tennyson's poems in this manner that Eliot in 1932 said that he could not tell a story. Whether this is true of the whole of Tennyson's balladry is a question I shall return to . Certainly the story is only hinted at in 'Mariana' and 'Oriana', for example, and it is hardly the main interest in 'The Lady of Shalott'. But there is some Victorian balladry which, though suffused with romantic colouring, manages to tell a story.

An example is the once very well known poem of Jean Ingelow, first published in 1863, 'The High Tide on the Coast of Lincolnshire, 1571'. Born at Boston, Lincolnshire, Jean Ingelow (1820–97) belonged to Tennyson's native region and had some personal acquaintance with him (he expressed mild approval of some of her poetry, while deploring 'cockneyisms' in her rhymes). The 'High Tide' is a 'period' narrative, with suggestions of Elizabethan spelling and diction, but it is not primarily a pastiche but obviously a nineteenth-century poem, with Scott and the Romantics and the Pre-Raphaelites behind it. (Jean Ingelow in her time was a more popular practitioner of Pre-Raphaelite poetry than Christina Rossetti, as Christina ruefully noted.) The poem opens with the promise of a gripping narrative.

> The old mayor climb'd the belfry tower,
> The ringers ran by two, by three;
> 'Pull, if we never pull'd before;
> Good ringers, pull your best,' quoth he.
> 'Play uppe, play uppe, O Boston bells;
> Ply all your charges, all your swells,
>   Play uppe "The Brides of Enderby".'

I used to wonder just how the farmers, as they struck out with stout breast-strokes, were helped by being informed that there was a flood: perhaps it was some sort of early warning system. Anyway, that brisk start is in the ballad manner. But the 'High Tide' makes no attempt at a 'Border' starkness of style. There is an emotionally involved narrator, the heroine's mother-in-law, and the tone of the poem soon becomes elegiac and pathetic: the refrain, the calling of the cows by 'my son's wife Elizabeth' has the effect of a lament. The power of the poem comes from the evocation of the flood:

> For lo! along the river's bed
> A mighty eygre reared his crest.
> And uppe the Lindis raging sped.
> It swept with thunderous noises loud;
> Shaped like a curling snow-white cloud,
> Or like a demon in a shroud.
>
> So farre, so fast the eygre drave,
>   The heart had hardly time to beat,
> Before a shallow seething wave
>   Sobbed in the grasses at oure feet:
> The feet had hardly time to flee
> Before it brake against the knee,
> And all the world was in the sea.

'Sobbed' is a well chosen and thrilling word here, but a traditional ballad would have been more literal. The details are rendered from within the subjective experience of the human beings concerned: again, not in the manner of the old ballads.

Victorian debate about modernizing the Ballads was sharpened by Swinburne's review (in the *Fortnightly Review*, May 1870) of Rossetti's first volume of original poetry. Swinburne laid down the requirements for sound balladry. The form demands from a poet, he says, 'narrative power, lyrical, and dramatic', and all three at once. It must condense the loose fluency of romantic tale-telling into tight and intense brevity. It must give 'as in summary' the result and the essence of events and emotions, without the exhibition of their gradual changes and growth which 'a romance of the older or the newer type' must lay open to us in order. There must be no pause in a ballad, no excess, no 'waste of a word or a minute in the course of its rapid and fiery motion.' Swinburne thought Rossetti had reproduced these qualities of the old ballads.

Andrew Lang disagreed. He was probably right. But he may have been unfair to Rossetti. Faithful imitation of the old ballads was not Rossetti's purpose, which he disclosed when he described his very remarkable narrative poem 'Stratton Water' as 'a modern antique'. A 'modern' element is present in all his balladry, revealing itself in a sophisticated psychological interest, and a romantic antiquarianism, which are both alien to the ballad spirit. He was an excellent storyteller in 'The King's Tragedy' and 'The Bride's Prelude', but they are purely romances.

How far Swinburne's own specialist connoisseuring of the ballads influenced his own poetry is not an easy question to answer. It seems at any rate to be agreed that he did not do his best work in the poems of his that can strictly be described as ballads. I have come across no ballad by Swinburne that can compare with the tense grimness and mounting horror of Kipling's ballad 'Heriot's Ford', the one that ends with the line 'You've finished with the flesh, my Lord.'

Gerard Manley Hopkins achieves an urgent and stark horror in his unfinished poem 'Margaret Clitheroe', but it is not in the ballad manner. His ballad 'The Queen's Crowning' has a mainly decorative effect: Rossetti could have written it.

More real affinity with the Border Ballads is to be found in some of William Morris's poems, such as 'The Haystack in the Floods', or 'Sir Peter Harpsdon's End'. Morris's medievalism belongs to a different ethos from that of 'La Belle Dame Sans Merci' or 'The Lady of Shalott'. Interested as he is in the picturesque details of medieval life, he uses them, not as Rossetti does for romantic antiquarianism, but to convince modern readers of the human realities (often very harsh ones) of medieval life. His stories themselves may belong to romance, bu the hard-bitten style in which he tells them surely owes much to the Border Ballads.

But Morris is also the poet of 'The Nymph's Song to Hylas' and 'The Blue Closet', preoccupied, as Eliot said, with the creation of a dream world. He is also part of the tradition of Victorian balladry we have been considering, the line that runs from Coleridge and Keats through Tennyson to the Pre-Raphaelites and Yeats: introverted poetry, foregrounding the individual poet's reactions to what he describes or evokes. It is time to look now at a more outward-looking, publicly orientated kind of nineteenth-century balladry, playing for a communal rather than an individual response, and more concerned with external action, events that are exciting in themselves, than with the poet's moods or reveries.

Of this realm Walter Scott was for long the king. Then Byron's verse romances stole the affections of the reading public, and Scott turned to prose fiction. The supremacy in narrative verse passed eventually to Thomas Babington Macaulay (1800–59), with his *Lays of Ancient Rome* (1842). Macaulay was influenced by Scott. His praise of Scott in his early essay on 'History' is a salute to Scott's power in the imaginative recreation of the past. In his youthful poem 'The Battle of Bosworth Field' he plunges into Scott's own domain, the world of chivalry. But though the great Whig owed much to the great Tory he was more at home in a different country of the mind: Ancient Rome as he imagined it. And this suggests another influence. In his preface to the *Lays*, while acknowledging his debt 'to our own old ballads', and his larger debt to Scott, 'the great restorer of our ballad poetry,' , Macaulay adds: 'To the *Iliad* still greater obligations are due.' We touch here on the fringe of an extensive subtext of Victorian poetry, the struggle for the mantle of Homer. It was widely believed that the *Iliad* and the *Odyssey* were based on primitive lays, and probably Macaulay was offering, in a modern English version, a suggestion of what they might have been like. The *Lays of Ancient Rome* were very popular. Published in 1842, the year of Tennyson's *Poems* and Browning's *Dramatic Lyrics*, they outstripped all competitors and had reached the 100,000 mark by 1875. Why was this? Many other collections of historical ballads were published in those days. The explanation perhaps is that Macaulay's imagination was not so much historical as contemporary. The world he wrote about was an immediate reality to him, and he brought to it the zeal of a political partisan. 'Horatius' and 'Lake Regillus' are about the struggle of liberated peoples to prevent the reimposition of alien rule.

> 'Hear, Senators and people
>   Of the good town of Rome,
> The Thirty Cities charge you
>   To bring the Tarquins home:
> And if ye still be stubborn
>   To work the Tarquins wrong,
> The Thirty Cities warn you,
>   Look that your walls be strong.'
>   (from 'Lake Regillus')

Kingsley Amis included 'Horatius' entire in his *Faber Popular Reciter* (1978). He aptly suggests the quality of this splendid poem when he notes that its Rome has the appeal of a golden-age England (though there are English ideas in the ranks of Tuscany also). Yet, he adds, 'there is something unreal, something almost ritualized about ['Horatius'], not vulgar or sentimental as these words are normally applied, something not of pretence but of let's-pretend. The brave days of old belong to a time when all the world was young.' This is well said. But Macaulay's partisan fervour is at least as prominent as his nostalgia. In the preface to 'Virginia' he extends his partisanship into the Class War. He points out that the heroic warriors of the two preceding Lays were all members of the dominant order. 'A poet singing their praises, whatever his own political opinions might be, would naturally abstain from insulting the class to which they belonged, and from reflecting on the system which had placed such men at the head of the legions of the Commonwealth.' 'Virginia' is to be seen as one of a group of compositions that attacked the privileged families by relating the bitter contest between the great houses and the commonalty, 'whose position bore some resemblance to that of the Irish Catholics during the interval between the year 1792 and the year 1829.' The villain, Appius Claudius, represents unbridled government authority:

> He stalked along the Forum like King Tarquin in his pride.
> . . . .
> For never was there Claudius yet but wished the Commons ill.

The plebeians dared not oppose his seizure of the lovely Virginia:

> For then there was no Tribune to speak the word of might,
> Which makes the rich man tremble, and guards the poor man's
>   right . . .
> But all the city, in great fear, obeyed the wicked Ten.

Macaulay's exclusive concentration on the political issue means the extinction of Virginia as a character. As a youthful reader of the poem I used to wonder whether the fate Appius Claudius had in store for her really was worse than death, and even so, whether she might not have been allowed to find out for herself. Virginius was one of the stern Roman fathers I had already learned to dislike in Corneille. Virginia is not allowed to say or do anything in the poem, and to her mercy-killing by her father her betrothed

Icilius responds not with swift and terrible anger but with a long revolutionary speech about freedom. This has been thought an artistic mistake, yet in a sense it is the point of the poem: the child Virginia has no significance except as a symbolic focus for the patrician/plebeian opposition. The subtlety of historical perspective of which a Lay of Ancient Rome is capable is illustrated here. The implicit author, i.e. Macaulay himself, is using the *persona* of a propagandist of Catholic Emancipation in the 1820s looking back at an Ancient Roman narrator who is himself looking back, from a fiercely anti-Claudian point of view, at a legendary past.

The other Victorian master of this kind of poetry was William Edmundstoune Aytoun (1813–65), with his *Lays of the Scottish Cavaliers* (1849). Mark Weinstein in *W.E. Aytoun and the Spasmodic Controversy* (1968), to which I am much indebted, calls it a Victorian bestseller. In 15 years there were 15 British editions, and 32 editions in 32 years. Blackwood and Sons sold over 60,000 copies in the Victorian period alone; including foreign editions, the final total approached 100,000. The greatest vogue of these Lays was in Scotland, where selections from them were included in students' reading books. Aytoun's model was Scott. Scott had changed the nature of the old Ballad, lengthened it to a Lay, removed its 'coarseness', and glamorized the life and manners of olden times. He had innumerable imitators, but none so successful in his own day as Aytoun. Aytoun also owed much to Macaulay, and his Lays can be seen as a Tory answer to Macaulay's. He was fixated on the Stuarts: six of the eight Lays deal with the fortunes of that family. Obviously this put him in opposition to Macaulay's reading of British history. But the situation is complicated by the fact that Macaulay himself had some sympathy – imaginatively if not politically – with the defeated side; especially when they were brave and loyal Englishmen, as in 'A Jacobite's Epitaph'. This motif, marginal in Macaulay, is central in Aytoun. He had a personal devotion to the defeated royal house. His use of the ballad form is centred on the Scottish cavalier, seen as a romantic figure, always in defeat, killed, like James IV, Montrose, Dundee, or the Old Scottish Cavalier, bereaved, like the Widow of Glencoe, or in exile, like Charles Edward and Dundee's Scottish regiment. Aytoun's emphasis on defeat may explain why his ballads so often end on a religious note, invoking the peace and calm of Heaven.

This is as alien to the ballad tradition, which is this-worldly,as it is to Macaulay's *Lays*. Aytoun is like Macaulay, and unlike the old ballads, in making the narrator often an active participant. And like Macaulay he is a partisan. The soldier who narrates Dundee's conduct and death in 'The Burial March of Dundee' makes the greatness of Claverhouse more real to us by relaying it through his account of its effect on him.

As a champion of the ballad, Aytoun, from his professorial chair in Edinburgh, was engaging both in academic power-politics and in current literary controversy. The contradictory tendencies of the Romantic movement were thrown into relief by the ballad revival. Both in theory and practice Aytoun stood for action in poetry and the expression of strong simple passions; for the Scott tradition, as against Wordsworthian autobiography (*The Prelude* was published in 1850). In opposition to the Wordsworth who favoured meditation, sentiment, and a concern with modern subjects he extolled Homer and Greek tragedy and the ballads, because of what he thought their universal appeal. This makes his critical position look like that of Matthew Arnold, in the Preface to his *Poems* (1853), in which Arnold deprecated modern introversion and called for a return to the objectivity of the old masters. But Arnold thought poorly of the traditional ballad. In his lectures on translating Homer (1861, 1862) he discouraged the use of the ballad style for that purpose, making game of the *Homeric Ballads* of Maginn (which were to have a successor in our own time in Robert Graves's translation of the *Iliad*). He spoke of Macaulay's *Lays* as 'pinchbeck', and he said of these lines in 'Horatius':

> Then out spake brave Horatius,
> The captain of the gate:
> 'To all men living on this earth
> Death cometh soon or late.'

that they were 'hard to read without a cry of pain'. In contrast, in his lectures of 1853, Aytoun drew a distinction between the 'minstrel', whose poetry is read aloud to a group, and the 'poet', whose works are perused by the individual in solitude. Aytoun ranks the minstrel above the poet, because of his more general appeal.

In doing so he was taking sides in a dispute which has flared up from time to time down to the present day: the opposition, sometimes bitter, on the part of readers and critics to the trend of withdrawal in poetry: the abandonment of that 'common world' which Wordsworth, whatever his own subjectivism, had called 'the place where in the end/We find our happiness, or not at all!' Aytoun exalted the ballad in his lectures in England and Scotland. He may have formed the taste of a generation of students; or perhaps he was merely responding to it.in reviews and articles on contemporary poetry in the *North Review* he constantly returned to the topic of balladry. Aytoun in Edinburgh had the practical advantage over Arnold in Oxford of knowing whom he was addressing (i.e. undergraduates studying English and Scottish Literature). Arnold, twice Professor of Poetry at Oxford, had no such definable audience: the Chair of Poetry had no connection with any distinct 'English' course. He himself was the first Professor of Poetry to lecture in English (rather than Latin), and most of his examples were drawn from outside the English tradition. In later years, when the possibility of establishing a School of English at Oxford was mooted, Arnold refused to support it, on the ground that it would endanger the supremacy of Classics. It is ironical that Aytoun is now almost forgotten, while Arnold is revered as a pioneer of English Literature. But in his day the conflict between his supporters and the Arnoldians gave an edge to the growing debate about 'English', and it can be seen now and then to impinge on the concerns of Tennyson.

Aytoun's sympathies with the common world and the common reader brought him into the great Victorian flowering of parody and burlesque. With Theodore Martin he published *A Book of Ballads* (1845) under the pseudonym 'Bon Gaultier', parodying various poets and styles of the time. They were very popular, and both Saintsbury and Mark Weinstein, a modern authority on Aytoun, speak highly of them, but they have not outlasted their century: their targets have dated, and their humour, while agreeable enough, is at the same time too gentle and too broad for our tastes. In view of Aytoun's ballad sympathies it is noteworthy that the old ballads are parodied in 'The Queen in France' (Queen Victoria had recently visited France). Tennyson provides one of the targets, with the exaggerated sensibility of 'The May Queen'. The parody ends: 'Draw me a pot of beer, mother, and mother, draw it mild.' The young man of 'Locksley Hall' is also parodied, and it may be noted that he is an anticipation of the (unnamed) hero of *Maud* (1855), round whom the 'Spasmodic' controversy was to simmer. Aytoun owes his own niche in literary history to his satire on the Spasmodics in *Firmilian*; its imaginary author, T. Percy Jones, is clearly a literary descendant of Bon Gaultier.

I now leave the literary and academic cross-currents round Tennysonian balladry for the poems themselves. The tradition of languid *Angst* associates several of his ballads with 'La Belle Dame Sans Merci'. Deserted lovers, hopeless passion, beautifully described settings, and self-absorbed sad music, are pervasive in 'Mariana', 'The Lady of Shalott', and 'Oriana'. The first two of these are agreed to be among Tennyson's best poems in this kind. The mood is skilfully conveyed by the refrains, linking 'aweary' and 'dreary' in 'Mariana', while in 'The Lady of Shalott', written in the tail-rhyme of the romances, the tags in each stanza alternately join together and separate Camelot and Shalott, the poles on which the poem turns. It would be an exaggeration to say that folk ballads never use atmospheric effects, but they are never the main point, as they are here. The action consists of little more than vague gestures, indicative of inner suffering. The description of battle in 'Oriana' is not there for its own sake but as a pretext for grief.

The interest centres on the teller, not the tale. The poem suffers from Tennyson's characteristic fault of overdoing it. 'Oriana' is metrically coarser than the other two. If Robert Graves has destroyed this poem by his suggestion that we should substitute 'Bottom upwards' for 'Oriana' every time the refrain occurs, Tennyson had invited vandalism by making the speaker repeat it so often. 'St. Agnes Eve' has an austere simplicity of diction which is like the ballads, and there is some vigour in the writing ('He lifts me to the golden doors', etc). But it is too introspective, too lacking in narrative, to be really like a ballad. In most poems it was romance that suited Tennyson better, with his slow movement, his involved sentences, his habit of pausing to paint verbal pictures. His liking for the old metrical romances is especially clear in the Arthurian poems he wrote in preparation for the *Idylls of the King*. 'Sir Galahad' begins like a ballad but soon settles down to a more sedate pace as the hero's bravado is subdued to his sense of religious dedication. In 'Morte d'Arthur' the poet looks beyond romance to epic, but his doubts are unconcealed in the prefatory poem:

> Why take the style of those heroic times?
> For nature brings not back the Mastodon,
> Nor we those times; and why should any man
> Remodel models?
>
> (from 'The Epic', 1842)

In 'Morte d'Arthur' the epic style is muffled by decoration: jewellery, white samite, sumptuous materials. Malory has prevailed over Homer. It looks as if Tennyson's doubts about the possibility of epic extended to the ballad, for the poems of his that come nearest to that model lack conviction. 'Lady Clare' with its anti-snobbery overtone, comes nearer to a middle-class homily like 'Lady Clara Vere de Vere' than to the high tragedy and the elemental simplicities of the old ballads.

'The Sisters' repays special attention. It has never been regarded as one of Tennyson's best poems: it is mostly ignored by critics, or disparaged in passing. Yet it is not easy to say just why.

The Sisters

> We were two daughters of one race:
> She was the fairest in the face:
>   The wind is blowing in turret and tree.
> They were together, and she fell;
> Therefore revenge became me well.
>   O the Earl was fair to see!
>
> She died: she went to burning flame:
> She mix'd her ancient blood with shame.
>   The wind is howling in turret and tree.
> Whole weeks and months, and early and late,
> To win his love I lay in wait:
>   O the Earl was fair to see!
>
> I made a feast; I bade him come;
> I won his love, I brought him home.
>   The wind is roaring in turret and tree.
> And after supper, on a bed,
> Upon my lap he laid his head:

O the Earl was fair to see!

I kiss'd his eyelids into rest:
His ruddy cheek upon my breast.
   The wind is raging in turret and tree.
I hated him with the hate of hell,
But I loved his beauty passing well.
   O the Earl was fair to see!

I rose up in the silent night:
I made my dagger sharp and bright.
   The wind is raving in turret and tree.
As half-asleep his breath he drew,
Three times I stabb'd him thro' and thro'.
   O the Earl was fair to see!

I curl'd and comb'd his comely head,
He look'd so grand when he was dead.
   The wind is blowing in turret and tree.
I wrapt his body in the sheet,
And laid him at his mother's feet.
   O the Earl was fair to see!

Tennyson adopts here the laconic manner of the old ballads. The use of the two refrains which bind the poem together is ingenious. The second refrain, identical throughout, keeps the beauty of the Earl before us right to the end, when he has been killed and become an erotic-aesthetic object to his murderess. The first refrain cleverly dramatizes the emotional curve of the action through the changes in the verb used to describe the wind: 'blowing', 'howling', 'roaring', 'raging', 'raving' – the climax – and then back to 'blowing' again, when the story is over. This is the kind of stylistic effect not found in the old ballads, but that is not a sufficient reason for condemning it. 'The Sisters' could still have been an effective poem. But the judgment of readers and critics, if we may infer it from their collective silence, is that it is not. Perhaps this is because the story is gruesome and sensational: it is a 'Gothic ballad'. But these were written competently by Victorian poets: Rossetti and Morris succeeded with similar stories. They may not greatly appeal to twentieth-century readers, but they do not seem silly, as Tennyson does here. The only explanation I can suggest is that the terse manner has misfired.

> They were together, and she fell.

'So what?' is the natural reaction. How much better the line sounds when Eliot adapts it for the demure gaiety of 'Burbank with a Baedeker:. Bleistein with a Cigar'.

> Burbank crossed a little bridge,
> Descending at a small hotel.
> Princess Volupine arrived,
> They were together, and he fell.

The telegraphic manner makes for comedy, whereas in 'The Sisters' we feel that the poet has not given himself enough time to create a thrilling atmosphere.

It is time now to look at Tennyson's performance in a different kind of Victorian balladry, the popular or demotic. The decline of poetry as a public art has long been lamented by people who care about such things. America's first-ever Poet Laureate, Robert Penn Warren, was quoted in 1986 as regretting that schools today provide no general education in poetry, and students are not exposed to it. Whether as a cause or effect of this situation, or both, many modern poets seem to ignore the origins of poetry in song, riddle and proverb, and to discard its ancient devices of rhyme, metre and cadence. There has been a constant emphasis on the world of private experience, on the isolated 'image', and a manifest diminution of emotional and intellectual force, and of substance, in the work of poets. They reject general truths and common experience in favour of a purely personal reality. Old-fashioned talk of 'pleasing the ear' and 'stirring the blood' is scorned. The appeal to ancient communal or 'stock' responses, physical, emotional or social, is rejected as vulgarity. The result has been that poetry is not read or taken account of by the generality of human beings. It plays no part in their lives. The chasm between the artist and the public continues to widen. Evidence seems continually to mount against the truth of Vico's saying, made current by Croce, that poetry is 'the primary activity of the human mind'. Yet some of us go on feeling that this is not just the sort of thing that is said on suitable public occasions, with no expectation that anyone will take it seriously, but that in some mysterious way it is *true*. And while that feeling persists there may be still hope for poetry.

Its future turns on the survival of what Kingsley Amis calls 'reciter' verse and I have referred to as balladry. George Orwell made current the description of this kind of verse as 'good bad poems'. This expression is obviously unsatisfactory, but it seems to have stuck. It refers to poems which the current critical orthodoxy disapproves of, or professes not to take seriously, yet shrinks from calling bad (it is indeed hard to see in what possible sense Byron's 'So We'll Go No More A-Roving', or Belloc's 'Ha'nacker Mill', could be judged bad). Orwell called a good bad poem 'a graceful monument to the obvious'. It records, in memorable form, some emotion which nearly every normal human being can share. It is a kind of rhyming proverb, founded on values which are straightforward and unchallenged. Leslie Fiedler, speaking of the old anthology favourites of American poetry, calls them the Lovely Commonplaces. Kingsley Amis thinks that in Britain this whole genre disappeared during the 1930s. The great themes of popular verse had been the nation and the Church. Today these, together with such minor themes as the desire for a simple rustic existence, have disappeared. To see why this is so we need only refer to the title of one of Philip Larkin's poems, 'MCMXIV', the year when the Great War broke out: 'Never such innocence again'. Yet it would be wrong to suppose that since the 1930s there have been no poets who could have written good balladry. Auden wrote 'Victor'; Empson (so often abstruse and esoteric) wrote his 'Chinese Ballad'; Graves wrote 'The General Elliott'; Betjeman wrote 'The Arrest of Oscar Wilde at the Cadogan Hotel'. But all these have a jocular or ironic or oblique quality alien to the good bad poem. As for serious or tragic balladry, it seems to have vanished altogether.

In the nineteenth century it was abundant: Wordsworth, Coleridge, Scott, Mrs Hemans, Campbell, Southey, Longfellow, Whittier, Kingsley and others, all wrote that kind of poetry, and some of their pieces survive in anthologies and in ordinary speech. But a question mark hangs over the name of Tennyson. Some of his good bad poems are remembered, but not with affection. They are disliked, or ridiculed. Nor do they have a McGonagall sort of reputation. As we should expect from Tennyson, they are very competent technically. If they are bad, it is not because they fail to be good, but because they do successfully something that critics don't like. To many of Tennyson's admirers they are merely an embarrassment. And as no one today thinks they are his best poems it might be asked why they should be discussed at all. I do not dispute that parts of *In Memoriam*, and some of the personal lyrics, represent Tennyson's poetry at its supreme height. But there are many areas of his work that need reappraisal. There has been a great increase in literary scholarship devoted to Tennyson, and much new information has come out about him, but there is no influential modern critique. I have the impression that Harold Nicolson's study of 1923 is still a potent influence. In some ways this is not a bad thing. Nicolson's book is enjoyable and elegantly written. Like his master Lytton Strachey in *Queen Victoria* (1921) Nicolson may have begun with the intention of debunking, but then came to feel both affection and respect for his subject. I finished the book with the conviction (clearly shared by the biographer) that in spite of all Tennyson's pettinesses and pettishness and absurdities he was a great man. But much has changed in English literature since 1923, and the image of Tennyson needs adjustment. To explore the *Collected Works* is to be immersed in Victoriana, some morbid, some mawkish, some quaint, some positively bizarre, some endearing. And now and then there is the poetry that speaks to us directly, requiring no extenuation. I suggest that some poems in the extroverted part of Tennyson's work need to be looked at again, without either the preconceptions of Tennyson's own time, or of the 1920s and 'Modernism'. Nicolson himself, while deprecating the 'Laureate' work (the 'Farringford period') had already praised some of the demotic poems. This is the poetry I will now look into.

Among the various kinds of popular poetry Tennyson wrote I will refer to three: the homiletic; the celebratory; and the dramatic monologues of common life.

The homilies include some poems which dramatize the hostility between the bourgeois and the aristocrat, always from an anti-aristocratic point of view. This links them with *Maud*. One of them is 'Lady Clara Vere de Vere'. The speaker, a 'yeoman' , exhorts the tease Lady Clara to remember that

> Kind hearts are more than coronets,
> And simple faith than Norman blood.

'School-miss Alfred' is not far enough away here. Good advice has a harder thrust in Tennyson when it is shrewdly prudential and delivered in a regional accent:

> An' thou'll be his Curate here, but, if iver tha means to git 'igher,
> Tha mun tackle the sins o' the wo'ld, and not the faults of the Squire.
>
> (from 'The Church-warden and the Curate')

The celebratory poems are more problematic to-day.

> A voice by the cedar tree
> In the meadow under the Hall!
> She is singing an air that is known to me,
> A passionate ballad gallant and gay,
> A martial song like a trumpet's call!
> Singing alone in the morning of life,
> In the happy morning of life and of May,
> Singing of men that in battle array,
> Ready in heart and ready in hand,
> March with banner and bugle and fife
> To the death, for their native land.
>
> (from *Maud*)

This beautiful description of Maud singing arouses mixed feelings. We are exhilarated by the springiness of the versification, but we fear that the song itself would have been Tennyson at his worst. He could be bellicose, even bloodthirsty, and he certainly did what he could to get us into war with Napoleon III. But he also wrote 'The Voyage of Maeldune', years later, expressing the futility of hatred and the value of forgiveness.

Tennyson's most famous military poem was topical, 'The Charge of the Light Brigade'. Technically it is superb. The ominous opening ('Half a league, half a league . . .') puts us at once in the midst of things. Jerome McCann has analysed the use in the poem of battle stereotypes, like the paintings of Meissonier. But, though distributed on broadsheets to the troops in the Crimea, the 'Charge' remains a Home Front poem, even if the troops naturally relished the line 'Someone had blunder'd'. What seems to have gone wrong is not technique but the poet's attitude: 'Forward the Light Brigade! Was there a man dismayed?' Yes; 600 were.

To get the point of view of the soldier is always difficult for a civilian poet, as Lord Wavell pointed out in his introduction to *Other Men's Flowers* (1944). On the other hand, popular songs and street ballads, which might be expected to strike a note of greater reality, usually fail through lack of technical skill. Perhaps the only possible form of dignified patriotic-military utterance was found by Thomas Campbell (1777–1844) in 'Ye Mariners of England'. Campbell, a Scotsman, was a master of poetic decorum, finding the right note (heroic) for the English (or 'British'), plaintive for the Irish. The non-combatant does not purport to speak as himself a 'Mariner.'

Tennyson's masterpiece in patriotic poetry is 'The Revenge'. Here the event commemorated is far away and long ago, already a legend, which is just as well, for whether we take the view of Sir Richard Grenville which A.L. Rowse takes in his 1937 book on him, or accept Hilaire Belloc's description of Grenville as 'that nasty fellow', Grenville is not a sympathetic character, and to appreciate Tennyson's ballad fully we have to de-sensitize our historical imagination and see Grenville as a fictional figure, merely a symbol of reckless English courage. This is a little chilling. And the first person (the 'we') of the poem arouses misgivings. Some of the best lines in the poem would be hard to imagine as spoken by a sailor-participant:

So Lord Howard past away with five ships of war that day,
Till he melted like a cloud in the silent summer heaven
. . .

But who could complain about such lines? It is that sense of over-arching spaciousness that makes the poem so memorable. It is all 'seen', not as if it were a memory of something in real life, but as if it were a great nineteenth-century historical painting:

> Thousands of their soldiers looked down from their decks and
>   laughed,
> Thousands of their seamen made mock at the mad little
>   craft
> Running on and on, till delayed
> By their mountain-like San Philip that, of fifteen hundred
>   tons,
> And up-shadowing high above us with her yawning tiers
>   of guns,
> Took the breath from our sails, and we stayed.

In its mastery of metre and rhythm the poem is rivalled in the
Victorian age only by Hopkins's *The Wreck of the Deutschland*
and Francis Thompson's 'The Hound of Heaven.' The free-
ranging movement of the lines is from time to time set off
against rallentando moments of serenity: 'And the sun went
down, and the stars came out far over the summer sea'. There
are two rhythmic principles at work in the poem, one energetic and staccato, one retarded and gracious, and at the end
they come together, when all the rhythmic power is gathered
up in the 14th stanza as the wind rises and the great wave
breaks and the 'Revenge' goes down, 'to be lost evermore in
the main'.

   In the history of poetic forms 'The Revenge' belongs to the
period after the vogue of the Lays which we have noted with
reference to Scott and Macaulay and Aytoun. It may be that
the element of democratic aspiration in them proved to be
their undoing as a genre. They were too exalted, had too
much literary dignity, to compete with street ballads for the
attention of the general public. Historical ballads now moved
slightly downmarket, became less ambitious in scope than the
Lays, as sophisticated poets used them in an attempt to capture
the note of popular feeling. Browning did this in 'Hervé Riel',
and Tennyson in 'The Revenge'. Tennyson was well placed to
write 'The Revenge' because his own attitude to foreigners seems
to have been the same as that of Sir Richard Grenville in the poem;
the same as that of the protagonist of Kingsley Amis's novel *I Like
It Here* (1958):

But he tells 'em '*Obrigado*',
Full of courtly foreign grace,*
'Cos he's got his homeward voucher
Safely locked up in his case.
* A phrase from 'The Revenge'.

But there was still too wide a gap in historical ballads between the popular tones and rhythms that were used and the poet's own dignity and lofty historical point of view. It is now time to consider how far Tennyson overcame this difficulty in his monologues of common life. An example is 'In the Children's Hospital.' Some readers have thought it unpleasant and sentimental, but it is powerful. The mawkish nurse who is the narrator, and the sadistic doctor, with his traditional red hair (cf. Hugh Walpole's novel *Portrait of a Man With Red Hair*, 1925) are plausible as well as nightmarish. The contemporary reality behind the poem can be verified. Martin Goldman in *Lister Ward* (1987) says 'Hospitals at that time were places to be killed in, rather than cured. . . . So many bacteria were there to make surgical wounds turn septic that the diseases they caused were known collectively as "hospitalism".' Tennyson's poem, though written round about 1880, seems to belong to the pre-chloroform period. George Orwell in 'How the Poor Die' (1946) relates how it became, long after it was written, a living actuality for him when he lay ill in a French hospital.

> As a child I had had it read aloud by a sick-nurse whose working life might have stretched back to the time when Tennyson wrote the poem. The horrors and sufferings of the old-style hospitals were a vivid memory to her. We had shuddered over the poem together, and then seemingly I had forgotten it. Even its name would probably have recalled nothing to me. But the first glimpse of the ill-lit murmurous room [at the Hospital X] with the beds so close together, suddenly roused the train of thought to which it belonged, and in the night that followed I found myself remembering the whole story and atmosphere of the poem, with many of its lines complete.

In 'In the Children's Hospital' Tennyson has adopted the manner of George R. Sims, 'It was Christmas Day in the Workhouse', and there may be a slightly falsetto effect. More congenial today are the poems in dialect, and some of the versifications of anecdotes he was told, or scraps from newspapers or magazines. It was once thought that his avid search for subjects was a sign of his failing inspiration, but it now seems clear that Tennyson was always by temperament not so much a writer with a 'message' as a *bricoleur*, delighting to apply his skill to the most miscellaneous topics. In this region of his poetry the chauvinist-military tone is rarely heard. Nor is there much of the Laureate in his singing robes. The attitudes behind the popular poems and versified tales are quite different. They are often written from the point of view of a woman, whereas, as the pacifist C.K. Ogden pointed out many years ago, there is a strong misogynistic element in militarism. Some of these poems have the human warmth and the unsqueamish tenderness, the freedom from all forms of humbug, which Tennyson is often supposed to lack. Insight into personal, social and regional characteristics is shown in 'The Northern Farmer', 'The Northern Cobbler' and 'The Village Wife.' There is something deep, as well as odd, about that monologue by a village spinster who has rejected all her suitors because she thinks they are only after her money, but names her cats after them. ['The Spinster's Sweet-Arts'] Down to earth, matter-of-fact, heterogeneous, unpredictable, Tennyson in this vein is more like Hardy than any other Victorian poet.

'Rizpah' seems to me the most notable of these monologues of common life and one of the best of Tennyson's poems of any period. Swinburne eulogised it in the same essay in which he made some cutting criticisms of the *Idylls* and their 'blameless King'. He cites 'Rizpah' as a proof that all great poets are bisexual, making much of the phrase 'the bones had moved in my side' as getting the inwardness of the old woman's point of view. Along with the oddity there is something psychologically convincing in the deranged legalism of the speaker: the bones she had taken down from the gibbet, her son's bones, had been nourished from her own body, they were her property, whatever the law might say (and she hates lawyers). The rights to property in a corpse are from a legal point of view, a controversial subject, and the question has some interest for students of Tennyson's poem. But for the most part 'Rizpah' is a study in dementia, raised to a sombre, tragic height by the hint of something ultimate and universal in the situation: it

is an elemental evocation of the maternal. By entitling the poem
'Rizpah' (not the name of the speaker) the poet depersonalizes and
universalizes her. The passage about Rizpah in II Samuel 21, 10-11,
brief and cryptic, sounds like a summary of an Antigone-type
tragedy:

> And Rizpah the daughter of Aiah took sackcloth, and spread it
> for her upon the rock, from the beginning of harvest until water
> dropped upon them [the bones] out of heaven, and suffered
> neither the birds of the air to rest on them by day, nor the
> beasts of the field by night. (Authorised Version.)

The political edge to the poem is sharpened by the presence as
auditor of the supercilious lady, the District Visitor, whom the old
woman denounces; there is a link here with 'Lady Clara Vere de
Vere' and other poems in that category. But there seems to be
another interest at work in the poem, something more personal
and subjective. Dr Susan Shatto, the editor of *Maud*, drew my
attention to the many echoes of the earlier poem (with which
we know Tennyson was always obsessed) in 'Rizpah': the touches
of paranoia of the protagonist of Part I of *Maud*, the similar
cadences and phrases in both poems, the mad scene in *Maud*
II.5. The preoccupation with bones is characteristic of both
poems. I learn from Christopher Ricks's edition that 'Rizpah' was
recited as 'Bones' on 5 June 1879. There are of course differences
between the two poems. In *Maud* the narrator is a troubled young
intellectual of the 1850s, not a simple, half-crazed old woman in the
eighteenth century. And 'Rizpah' shows a concern with Christian
motifs not found in *Maud*: election, salvation, sin and punishment
and repentance, the after-life, the resurrection of the body. But the
later poem can plausibly be regarded as a variation on themes from
Maud. Perhaps we may come to regard this poem, neglected by
critics, as in resonance with the Tennyson who matters to us.

   Just what that is will be a matter for the hoped-for late twentieth
or twenty-first century critique. It is doubtful whether we can
now look to Tennyson for guidance in philosophical and religious
thought. What he says is not uninteresting but it belongs to his
time rather than ours. The mystical element is more tantalizing
and puzzling than illuminating. In his prettier poems the men and
women and children have a waxwork quality. We are uneasy with

the Arthurian properties and the classical mythology, and not so thrilled as the Victorians were with the indefatigable onomatopoeia and the delicate colourings of the nature notes. The Tennyson who still fascinates us is the poet of 'black blood', aware of the divisions and dissociations that are among the possibilities of the human mind, the poet of 'madness', of the 'weird seizures' in *The Princess*, and the visions and dreams and nightmares of *In Memoriam* and *Maud*:the poet who not only perhaps reveals his own psychological conflicts, but can bring intelligence and insight to bear on them. The road to understanding here is through the study of Tennyson's use of language, with which modern scholarship has helped us. We may be now in a better position to make sense of Eliot's puzzling judgment that Tennyson's surface, his 'technical accomplishment', is 'intimate with his depths'; to ponder more closely the association between sound and feeling that gives their haunting quality to 'The splendour falls' or 'To Virgil'. But today, as I hope to have shown, there is matter of great interest in the study of Tennyson as a poet writing for a public: the things in his poetry that move between the surface and the depths.

Chapter 8
Reality and Cosiness in Nicholas Nickleby

Nicholas Nickleby is quite different from those later novels of Dickens which are now so high in critical favour. Certainly there is the memorable scathing paragraph on the horrors of Dotheboys Hall – what the 'young noblemen' were really like – but the horrors are soon switched off and we go on directly to Mrs Squeers dishing out brimstone and treacle. Gissing points out the moment at which the presentation changes:

> And yet this scene, painful as it was, had its grotesque features, which, in a less interested observer than Nicholas, might have provoked a smile. (ch. 8)

Quite in keeping is Dickens's letter[1] to a five-year-old member of his public, promising to distribute more adequate rewards and penalties:

> Nicholas had his roast lamb, as you said he was to, but he could not eat it all, and says if you do not mind his doing so he should like to have the rest rehashed to-morrow with some greens, which he is very fond of, and so am I.

Honest John Browdie in the novel itself reacts in the proper way.

> Nicholas told them all, and never was there a story which awakened so many emotions in the breasts of two eager listeners. At one time honest John groaned in sympathy, and at another roared with joy; at one time he vowed to go up to London on purpose to get a sight of the Brothers Cheeryble; at another, swore that Tim Linkinwater should receive such a ham by coach, and carriage free, as mortal knife had never carved. (ch. 64)

So we should read, or re-read, 'with the same spirit that its

author writ'. What is most attractive about Nicholas Nickleby is
the trait above all others that he shared with his young creator:
'when there's a will there's a way'. This is reflected in the manly
vigorous stride of the narrative down to the encounter with the
Brothers Cheeryble.

But the book is in some ways uncharacteristic of Dickens. There
is no poetry: with one exception. Ralph when poetic is like
Marlowe (in the mode of 'Sometimes I go about and poison wells').
There are other affinities with specifically Elizabethan drama, in
a book so permeated with the theatre, containing Crummles and
his troupe, and dedicated to Macready: I think of the neighbours
wondering what's happened to Peg Sliderskew.

> Some of the neighbours threw up their windows, and called
> across the street to each other that old Gride's housekeeper must
> have dropped down dead. Others collected round the coach,
> and gave vent to various surmises; some held that she had fallen
> asleep; some, that she had burnt herself to death; some, that she
> had got drunk; one very fat man, that she had seen something
> to eat, which had frightened her so much (not being used to it)
> that she had fallen into a fit. (ch. 56)

This reminds me of Ben Jonson, especially of the scene at the
beginning of Act V of *The Alchemist*, when Lovewit returns and
questions the neighbours about what's happened to 'Jeremy butler'
('pray God he be not made away,' says the Sixth Neighbour, and
later, in what *must* have been a high piping voice, '. . . About/Some
three weeks since, I heard a doleful cry/As I sat up a-mending my
wife's stockings.') But it is not usually the *poetic* side of Elizabethan
drama that is recalled in *Nicholas Nickleby*.

Nor is there any of Dickens's characteristic poetry.

> Old Time heaved a mouldy sigh from tomb and arch and vault;
> and gloomy shadows began to deepen in corners; and damps
> began to rise from green patches of stone; and jewels, cast upon
> the pavement of the nave from stained glass by the declining sun,
> began to perish. (From *Edwin Drood*)

Such things do not occur in *Nicholas Nickleby*. The book has
little *atmosphere*. The Yorkshire scenes don't give much feeling
of Yorkshire, or the Portsmouth scenes of Portsmouth. Most of

the book is set in London; but this is not the powerfully evoked London of the opening of *Bleak House*, nor the bad dream of *Oliver Twist*, nor the fascinating-sinister London whose impact is so curiously different on the young David Copperfield and the young Pip of *Great Expectations*. The London of *Nickleby* is the garish crude 'emporium' which is the London of *The Prelude*, but seen through the more friendly Dickensian eyes. But on the whole it's just 'London', the place where 'everyone' lives. Golden Square, Cadogan Place, Eel-Pie Island, and other localities, all have their characteristic parts to play in the story; but they are in contexts of shrewd prosaic analysis rather than poetic evocation. Though Newgate is mentioned occasionally (it is near Squeers' London headquarters, and Smike, before he is recaptured by Squeers, 'has a look' at it), it has no thematic force.

There is no poetry. There is melodrama. How deep is it? Dickens can use melodrama for serious purposes: think of Fagin, or Dr. Manette. And there is, I think, a phantasmal stirring of deeper life around the 'family' theme in *Nicholas Nickleby*, which is part of the melodrama.

> As the brother and sister stood side by side, with a gallant bearing which became them well, a close likeness between them was apparent, which many, had they only seen them apart, might have failed to remark. The air, carriage, and very look and expression of the brother were all reflected in the sister, but softened and refined to the nicest limit of feminine delicacy and attraction. More striking still, was some indefinable resemblance in the face of Ralph, to both. (ch. 54)

But the development of the 'family' plot, with its phantasma-goric reminiscence of the Oedipus legend – Ralph's discovery that Smike is his son, the part played by Brooker – none of this convinces me that Dickens has recaptured much of the spirit of Greek tragedy. There are themes here that Dickens in his best work could quicken to deeper life, but here they are not essentially different from the things that most of us find jarring, the business of Madeline Bray and Gride and so on. The best melodrama is the duel fought by Sir Mulberry Hawk, recalling, in some good and bad points alike, the duel in *Maud*. This supplies the only example in the book of a comic character turning into a serious character: a consummation rare, and rarely successful in Dickens. We note that Lord Frederick Verisopht's silly name is hardly mentioned when he becomes a serious character, and his fatuous manner of speech disappears. But none of this is very striking.

Finally, there is no moving pathos (as there had been in *Pickwick*, in the two quite different, but equally touching deaths, the Chancery prisoner's and Mrs Weller's: both so much better than Little Nell). This is strange, since Dickens's story, as everyone knows, has a good deal to do with the suffering of children. But, except for a few touches after the break-up of Dotheboys Hall, there is nothing to compare in excellence with the workhouse scenes in *Oliver Twist*.

I am thinking particularly of something that is often frowned on: the exalted poetry given to some of the wretched anonymous inmates of the workhouse. Dickens does not recapture this, perhaps does not wish to; *Oliver Twist* had been his immediately previous book. But Dickens *does* want a powerfully pathetic effect with Smike, and Smike is the notorious example of how Dickens' pathos in *Nickleby* jars on us. The child-theme is relevant here. Smike remains a child in mind; his tragedy is that he has never been loved and finds the experience of love too overwhelming to bear. Dickens' art is more unwholesome – and stronger – here. We are disturbed rather than moved by the strength of feeling in the closing paragraph. (It seems to draw on Pope's 'Elegy to the memory of an unfortunate lady').

> The grass was green above the dead boy's grave, and trodden by feet so small and light, that not a daisy drooped its head beneath their pressure. Through all the spring and summer-time, garlands of fresh flowers, wreathed by infant hands, rested on the stone; and, when the children came there to change them lest they should wither and be pleasant to him no longer, their eyes filled with tears, and they spoke low and softly of their poor dead cousin. (ch. 65)

The disturbance about Smike, which prompts the familiar charge of 'sentimentality', is, I think, due mainly to the unconscious insincerity of Dickens. Only in his comedy was the young Dickens capable of diagnosing unconscious insincerity – the insincerity that has become ingrown habit.

Squeers covered his rascality, even at home, with a spice of his habitual deceit; as if he really had a notion of some day or other being able to take himself in, and persuade his own mind that he was a very good fellow. (ch. 7)

But such insights do not occur when Dickens is getting emotional relief through pathos; neither Dickens nor Nicholas Nickleby seems aware that the relief we feel at Smike's passing is not only the relief that he has been freed from tragic suffering, it is Nicholas's relief at getting rid of Smike, who – embarrassingly fixated on Kate – has become a nuisance. Tolstoy would not have missed that.

Smike, then, is a jarring note, and so is Ralph Nickleby. As for Kate, she is merely the stock 'shrinking' novelette heroine. The sympathetic contemporary reader no doubt filled in for himself the outline that is all Dickens offers. We are inclined to sympathise with him when the villain Sir Mulberry begs her to be 'more natural', but she has no nature to be natural out of. Dickens could have done something more with her apparently continuous anxiety-state:

the warm young heart palpitated with a thousand anxieties and apprehensions (ch. 10)

It is typical of her that right at the end she is 'shrinking' from Mantalini, in the rather harsh finale provided for this character. She should have felt his absurdity, even if she doesn't, understandably, delight in it as much as the reader does.

The Cheerybles occupy a good deal of space, and much has been said about Dickens's favourite early fantasy-figure of the good rich man, the reformed Scrooge or old Fezziwig, '*Carol* philosophy'. Some of the benevolence in Dickens is not disagreeable, and is even moving. Here it is fairytale. Yet in the same book he gives us the superb *parody* of benevolence exhibited by Squeers and Snawley (ch. 38). And it is a minor irritant when Miss La Creevy, who *is* real (if only with the special Dickensian brand of reality) is drawn into the Cheeryble orbit, the unreal cosiness, by Dickens' generous heart – and his professional novelist's instinct – which must find a mate for her.

Newman Noggs is rather taking when he is a puzzling grotesque:

'But what's the matter – are you ill?' said Nicholas, suddenly breaking off, as his companion, after throwing himself into a variety of uncouth attitudes, thrust his hands under the stool, and cracked his finger-joints as if he were snapping all the bones in his hands.

Newman Noggs made no reply, but went on shrugging his shoulders, and cracking his finger-joints; smiling horribly all the time, and looking steadfastly at nothing out of the tops of his eyes, in the most ghastly manner. (ch. 4)

But he is a 'ruined gentleman', and this was still a danger-area for the son of John Dickens; his humour and pathos (see, for example, his letter to Nicholas in chapter 7) are somewhat trying, and we do not yet see the insights that go to the making of a Micawber or a William Dorrit. But the character repays study.

Nicholas himself, as Dickens points out in the preface, is not meant to be a conventionally perfect hero. We certainly feel for Mrs. Nickleby when she complains, in an unusually lucid moment: 'Why in the name of wonder should Nicholas go about the world, forbidding people's banns?' But his addiction to assault and battery is dramatically justifiable in each instance. Hugh Kingsmill seems wrong to say that Nicholas just assaults people and doesn't fight: he may be said to have 'fought' Sir Mulberry Hawk. And his aggressive manner in his first interview with Ralph, which has also been censured, has enough provocation in Ralph's brutal heartlessness. Where he is most abnormal, and most like the young Dickens of whom he is an idealized self-portrait is in a way that the young Dickens would probably have regarded as normal: his colossal want of tact in the Fanny Squeers affair, his extraordinarily and unnecessarily violent repudiation of her at the showdown; the language he uses:

'Stop,' cried Nicholas hurriedly, 'pray hear me. This is the grossest and wildest delusion, the completest and most signal mistake, that ever human being laboured under, or committed.' (ch. 13)

sounds remarkably like the vehement language used by Dickens himself, much older, in the statement he printed in *Household Words*, at the break-up of his marriage, to upbraid the scandalmongers who were sullying the sacred name of Georgina (or was it Ellen?). Dickens probably put more of himself into Nicholas than he knew.

One remembers Nicholas as merely there to hold the book together, an amiable stock type. Certainly there is little in Orwell's point that, although the plot is largely concerned with the jobs taken by Nicholas and Kate in their struggle towards the social rehabilitation of their family, neither Dickens nor the Nicklebys show any interest in jobs as such; when Nicholas becomes prosperous through the help of the Cheerybles he immediately retires into Devonshire and an incestuous large-family atmosphere and – apart from breeding a family – does nothing. The obvious comment on this is that Nicholas is not the centre of interest and we don't care much what he does. But there is still something worth saying about him. He is Dickens's first attempt at a self-portrait. He is less inwardly studied than David Copperfield, much more an early Victorian adaptation of the standard eighteenth-century picaresque hero, like Roderick Random. But he does show some interesting traits: his intense and wholly unconscious egotism, and his slowness on the uptake about people's feelings, as with Fanny Squeers, or Smike's love for Kate.

The most obvious characteristic of Nicholas, however, is his staginess, his theatricality. Vincent Crummles noticed it:

> 'There's genteel comedy in your walk and manner, juvenile tragedy in your eye, and touch-and-go farce in your laugh. (ch. 22)

He is conceived largely in theatrical terms. His speech idiom lapses into early Victorian melodrama at moments of excitement:

> ''Tis false!' cried Ralph, shrinking back.
> ''Tis true, and you shall find it so.' (ch. 54)

He is very much a 'walking gentleman' of the 'Dickens theatre' (to use Robert Garis's phrase). And this may explain what otherwise is his queerest characteristic, his passivity for so long in face of Squeers's cruelty, and especially the cruelty to Smike, who suffers on his behalf:

Squeers was jealous of the influence which his man had so soon acquired, and his family hated him, and Smike paid for both. Nicholas saw it . . . But what did he do? He merely . . . ground his teeth at every repetition of the savage and cowardly attack.

The explanation seems to be that he is waiting for his 'big scene' – when he thrashes Squeers.

But it might well be said that all this merely illustrates the sort of thing that makes many people, to this day, dismiss Dickens as merely 'good family reading' – and perhaps for families of a now-bygone age. And even some of the characters who more assuredly will 'do', such as Fanny Squeers – one can forgive much for her glorious letter 'I am screaming out loud all the time I write', – cannot be said to illustrate a particularly fine or subtle art. They resemble the art of *Sketches by Boz* rather than that of Jane Austen – not to speak of many lesser artists. *Nicholas Nickleby* might be regarded, by people who don't care for Dickens, as the 'typical Dickens novel', full of humour, melodrama, pathos, and a topical 'social purpose'. All these remain, including the 'social purpose'. The cheap schools are gone, but the spirit that produced them has not – in England. Dotheboys Hall will never, alas, be wholly 'dated'. But does this make *Nicholas Nickleby* a distinguished work of art?

Certainly it would be odd to judge it as a masterpiece in which every touch is significant. It is padded out by things which are only there because Dickens's inspiration failed and time pressed. (For example, the two interpolated stories on the journey to York.) And even some of the better things are not 'organic'. We can enjoy the United Metropolitan Hot Muffin and Crumpet Baking and Punctual Delivery Company (ch. 2) without thinking it particularly relevant to the Ralph theme; Ralph's main function is that of an old-fashioned 'usurer', not a capitalist. And we can explain Nicholas's outburst (totally irrelevant to the story) about dramatists who purloin the work of industrious novelists, only as the author letting off steam; as an utterance of Nicholas himself it comes with a particularly bad grace from one who has had no scruple, on Crummles's advice, about 'borrowing' a French play. Clearly it would be absurd to prove at laborious length that *Nicholas Nickleby* is not a well-organized novel. Yet

some modern critics talk as if it were. No one can accuse Mr
Steven Marcus of insensitiveness to the work of Dickens –
rather, I feel that the objection to his procedure in *Dickens
from Pickwick to Dombey* is that his readings are too close, too
coherent, too comprehensive: they make the reader feel a little
cramped. We want to have room for our own interpretations,
our own changes of mind and changes of mood about novels,
our own more fragmentary, intermittent perceptions. A looser,
freer approach would be desirable. At any rate, Mr Marcus almost
convinces us when we are reading him that *Nicholas Nickleby* is
organized as a peculiarly Dickensian treatment of the theme of
Prudence versus Imprudence. He almost convinces us – till we
go back to the book, and reflect on the final and total impression
it leaves. And this impression is not of a book that would satisfy
the demands of modern critics of the novel, any more than Mr
Curdle's:

> 'a kind of universal dovetailedness with regard to place and time
> – a sort of general oneness, if I may be allowed to use so strong
> an expression.' (ch. 24)

It is better to go back to the view held by Chesterton. The
book is part of a rich and varied commodity. Those who love
Dickens will eat it all, good, bad and indifferent, some will be
more discriminating, and some will be so put off by the bad
parts that they can't stomach the good. Belonging to the first
category, I will take the opportunity which the book certainly does
afford for talking about the quality in which it excels – Dickens's
humour.

Everyone agrees that Dickens is a great humorist. All the
contributors to a recent collection, *Dickens and the Twentieth
Century* (edited by John Gross), agree about this. They agree
about little else: they offer an incongruous variety of Dickenses.
All the essayists agree about the 'humour'. But they all find
it difficult to talk about. Bernard Bergonzi, in his essay on
Nicholas Nickleby, observes acutely that it is just those things –
humour and 'character' – which the Victorian reader enjoyed
so much, and which probably modern readers would admit
enjoying too if they are candid, that modern critics find difficult
to talk about.

Well, I will not attempt to succeed where they have failed. I will certainly not try to 'illustrate' Dickens's humour in *Nicholas Nickleby*. Dickens's humour is inseparable from his repetitiveness, his accumulation, and his movement. But I will try to draw attention to a curious, if obvious, feature of Dickens's art as a humorist: not to analyse or explain it, but to urge others to analyse and explain where I cannot.

The feature I am thinking of is apparent in a quality of the book as a whole which youthful as well as adult readings bear witness to: its pleasantness. This pleasantness is a paradoxical quality. *Nicholas Nickleby* gives us a picture of middle-class life which, by and large, is *not* pleasant. Quite apart from the obviously painful or lurid or spectacularly unpleasant things – the evil of Ralph, the cruelty of Squeers, the agony of Smike, the senile lust of the miser Gride – quite apart from such things, there are the petty spite of Miss Knag, the snobbery, vanity and jealousy of Mrs Wititterly, the weakness and pliability of Mrs Nickleby, the officious vanity of Lillyvick, the mercenariness of the Kenwigs. And these things, unlike the spectacular evils, are felt to be *typical* of this middle-class world. For it is middle class: the poor (unlike *Oliver Twist*) are on the periphery in this novel, the upper classes are present only as bounders:

> 'What do you call it, when Lords break off doorknockers and beat policemen, and play at coaches with other people's money, and all that sort of thing?'
> 'Aristocratic?' suggested the collector.
> 'Ah! aristocratic,' replied Miss Petowker, 'something very aristocratic about him, isn't there?' (ch. 15)

But society in the wider sense – in this novel, middle-class society – is not very attractive either. There is a pointed irony in Squeers's tribute to his wife:

> 'Oh Lor!' said Squeers, heaving a sigh, and nodding his head a great many times, 'what a member of society that woman is!' (ch. 34)

It is bourgeois pieties of family-feeling that are mimicked in Squeers's cant, and we do not have to look very far behind these pieties to find utter selfishness, anxious greed for status, and a sort of social atomism. When these egos are not simply uncommunicating, as in the hilariously solipsistic 'conversation' between Mrs Nickleby and Mrs Wititterly 'about' Shakespeare, they are competing for dominance of their imaginary worlds.

Yet in this novel things that would be unpleasant, or even horrible in real life become amusing without losing their reality. Squeers is a famous example; his patter is invariably captivating (it is notable that he keeps it up even in soliloquy):

> 'If there's a screw loose in a heavenly body, that's philosophy; and if there's a screw loose in an earthly body, that's philosophy too; or it may be that sometimes there's a little metaphysics in it, but that's not often.' (ch. 57)

And episodes like Squeers thrashing Smike in the coach, which Julien Green found so horrible, are surely rather different in effect, when we remember Squeers's comment:

> 'I never thrashed a boy in a hackney-coach before,' said Mr Squeers, when he stopped to rest. 'There's inconveniency in it, but the novelty gives it a sort of relish, too!'

However, it might be said that the basis of all humour lies in cruelty. But this hardly seems to fit the general character of Dickens's humour in this book, in which Dickens uses the *method* of satire to produce an effect which is not aptly summed up as satirical. Miss Knag is spiteful; but what are we to think when we hear her proud explanation of her brother's eccentricities?

> 'The fact is, that he did find so much in the books he read, applicable to his own misfortunes, and did find himself in every respect so much like the heroes – because of course he was conscious of his own superiority, as we all are, and very naturally – that he took to scorning everything, and became a genius.' (ch. 18)

Mrs Wititterly is vain; but what do we think of her when we hear her husband's boast – in which she complacently concurs?

'Mrs. Wititterly,' said her husband, 'is Sir Tumley Snuffim's favourite patient. I believe I may venture to say that Mrs. Wititterly is the first person who took the new medicine which is supposed to have destroyed a family at Kensington Gravel Pits.' (ch. 28)

We do not *like* Miss Knag or Mrs. Wititterly any better, but we feel differently about them in some way. How is this? Or take the scene where Lillyvick is reconciled with the Kenwigs (ch. 52). Everyone in this reconciliation is insincere, and they all know that they are, and that the others are. Kenwigs, like so many characters in *Nicholas Nickleby*, on the stage or off, is always theatrical (and compare the account of his tempestuous wooing: '"Mother," she says, "I love him!" "What do I hear?" cries her mother; and instantly falls into strong conwulsions.') And his theatricality reaches an appropriate climax when he composes a final tableau of reconciliation:

'When I see that man,' said Mr. Kenwigs, with one hand round Mrs. Kenwigs's waist: his other hand supporting his pipe (which made him wink and cough very much, for he was no smoker). (ch. 52)

But the others too are putting on an act. And yet the total effect is of something genial and *genuine* – a genuine cosiness. How can this be?

The problem of Dickens's humour – the problem for those who are not simply content to enjoy it – is inseparably connected with the problem of his own attitude towards his comic characters (the characters who matter in *Nicholas Nickleby*). It seems to be a more general form of Nicholas's attitude towards the theatrical people he is thrown among. Nicholas feels them as comic characters, people he can't identify with or take seriously; if he *did* take them seriously, his own status as a 'serious' character would somehow be undermined. This, like many other problems in Dickens, has to do with class-uneasiness. The comic characters are either lower-middle class, or of uncertain status within the middle class. But it is not *merely* a class question. Dickens's attitude to his comic characters in general is a complex matter, which it would take much time to sort out. In *Nicholas Nickleby* his attitude, amused but a little Olympian, a little patronizing, is also a little ungrateful; one feels ungrateful because it is often the contact with comic characters that gives the serious characters what life they have: for example, after Ralph with some difficulty has got out a few 'benevolent' platitudes:

> If an iron door could be supposed to quarrel with its hinges, and to make a firm resolution to open with slow obstinacy, and grind them to powder in the process, it would emit a pleasanter sound than did these words in the rough and bitter voice in which they were uttered by Ralph. Even Mr. Mantalini felt their influence, and turning affrighted round, exclaimed: 'What a demd horrid croaking!' (ch.10)

Here the touch of comedy gives a little retroactive reality to Ralph; we hear his voice. On the other hand, the comic characters, as often in Dickens, can suffer through being forced into the idiom which the plot requires: even Squeers loses his natural voice at one point:

> 'I've got it! Hurrah! The plan was a good one though the chance was desperate, and the day's our own at last!' (ch. 57)

Reality and comedy are closely associated in *Nicholas Nickleby*.

But it is a curious reality. The characters who have it are neither very convincing, nor, as a rule, very sympathetic: we don't identify with them, we don't take them very seriously because we know the author is not taking them seriously: such pearls of wisdom and insight as they let fall are, we know, accidental, because they don't think, they only talk. And yet we are not 'outside' the characters, with the irritated amusement we find in a writer like Wyndham Lewis.

Nicholas Nickleby seems to violate the conditions for a serious art of the novel. It is not 'true to life'; but through a peculiarity of the art which I have failed to explain, it manages to convince us, in its most amusing scenes, that life is like this: life isn't 'true to life'.

Chapter 9
The Choir Master and the Single Buffer

'I call my book the Mystery, not the History, of Edwin Drood', Dickens is said to have told inquirers after the fate of Edwin, and it is natural that most criticism of his unfinished last novel should have been occupied with guesses about how it was to have ended. And this essay is no exception. But *Edwin Drood* contains much good reading apart from the Mystery. Not all of it is Dickens at his best. Few readers, I imagine, have been greatly interested in the eponymous hero, or the heroine, who seem little more than structural properties of the genre (mid-Victorian sensational fiction). And the novel is less exuberant than some of Dickens's earlier books. There is a cloistral mellowness about it. But this has its own charm, and there are many glimpses of the old Dickens magic, the dream-like transitions between fairytale and what Northrop Frye calls 'low mimesis', the inimitable comic extravagance of Mr Sapsea's epitaph for his reverential Ethelinda, the brilliant little fantasia of the immovable waiter and the flying waiter. There is a touch of satire there, and more than a touch in Mr Honeythunder ('That this assembled Body of Professing Philanthropists views, with indignant scorn and contempt, not unmixed with utter detestation and loathing abhorrence') whom I seem to recognize in the 'protest' movements of our own day. Other figures who live on in the memory when the book is over include Angular Mr Grewgious, Miss Twinkleton of the Young Ladies' Seminary, Durdles the drinking stonemason with that practice of searching out hidden tombs which so intrigues Mr Jasper – and not forgetting the incorrigible Deputy for whom he says he is providing 'a sort of a – scheme of a – National Education'.

Memorable too is Cloisterham where most of the action takes place, 'an ancient city . . . a drowsy city . . . a city of another and a bygone time', with the peacefulness of Minor Canon Corner, the Weir, place for solitary moonlight walks and views of the sea, and the crypt of the Cathedral, resting-place for the bones of long-dead local worthies. At the heart of Cloisterham stands the Cathedral, the 'evocative para-symbol' which gives a poetic dimension to the novel.

> 'Dear me,' said Mr. Grewgious, peeping in, 'it's like looking down the throat of Old Time.'
>
> Old Time heaved a mouldy sigh from tomb and arch and vault; and gloomy shadows began to deepen in corners; and damps began to rise from green patches of stone; and jewels, cast upon the pavement of the nave from stained glass by the declining sun, began to perish.

The Cathedral is a focus for contrasting associations. It gives dignity to life and death; its services are a reminder of the holy things that are a standing reproach to sin and wickedness. Yet it is old and crumbling, the embodiment of an ancient faith that has lost its vitality; and the sense of this is quickened by the evocation of the warm stirring of present-day life around it. In the closing pages 'a brilliant morning shines on the old city'.

> Changes of glorious light from moving boughs, songs of birds, scent from gardens, woods, and fields – or rather, from the one great garden of the whole cultivated island in its yielding time – penetrate into the Cathedral, subdue its earthy odour, and preach the Resurrection and the Life. The cold stone tombs of centuries ago grow warm.

But the Cathedral is also sinister, the scene of murder perhaps, and mystery, shunned after dark. In the silence pervading the venerable monument of a dying faith, its cloisters and its churchyard, Cloisterham people feel 'the innate shrinking of dust with the breath of life in it from dust out of which the breath of life has passed.' John Forster, Dickens's biographer, in his only comment on *Edwin Drood*, remarked that it was quite free from 'the biting social criticism' characteristic of Dickens's later work. But it is hard to imagine anything more 'biting' than the stress laid on the rottenness and decay – in the human heart as much as in the stonework – associated with the central religious symbol of the civilization Dickens knew.

Cloisterham is based in part on Dickens's memories of Rochester, and a real event that happened there is believed to have provided him with the idea for his story (see Hughes, 1891). It was a place of personal significance to him. 'At Rochester,' says Gissing, 'begin the adventurous travels of Mr. Pickwick; near Rochester stands the house of Gadshill; and it was Rochester that he chose for the scene of his last story.' (It may be added that Ellen Ternan was born in Rochester.) Gissing found it touching 'to read that final chapter, which must have brought back to the writer's mind the days long past, when, a little boy, he read and dreamt amid the scenes he was describing.' Passages like the opening of chapter 13 give us, in Frank Kermode's phrase, 'the sense of an ending'.

Christmas Eve in Cloisterham. A few strange faces in the streets; a few other faces, half strange and half familiar, once the faces of Cloisterham children, now the faces of men and women who come back from the outer world at long intervals to find the city wonderfully shrunken in size, as if it had not washed by any means well in the meanwhile. To these, the striking of the Cathedral clock, and the cawing of the rooks from the Cathedral towers are like voices of their nursery time. To such as these, it has happened in their dying hours afar off, that they have imagined their chamber floor to be strewn with the autumnal leaves fallen from the elm trees in the Close: so have the rustling sounds and fresh scents of their earliest impressions revived when the circle of their lives was very nearly traced, and the beginning and the end were drawing close together.

In the setting of this old cathedral town is placed the main character of the novel and the centre of the Mystery, John Jasper the Choir Master. His part in the story has been a matter for controversy ever since Dickens died leaving the novel without its denouement. Jasper is a man with a secret life, his time divided between his duties in the Cathedral and the opium den. 'Religion,' said Karl Marx, 'is the sigh of the oppressed creature, the soul of soulless circumstance, the heart of a heartless world. It is the opium of the poor.' But this opium has ceased to work for the Choir Master, and he has turned to the literal variety as an escape from ennui. He tells Edwin:

The echoes of my own voice among the arches seem to mock me with my daily drudging round. No wretched monk who droned his life away in that gloomy place, before me, can have been more tired of it than I am. He could take for relief (and did take) to carving demons out of the stalls and seats and desks. What shall I do? Must I take to carving them out of my heart?

The mystery of Jasper is heightened by the external way in which he is (usually) presented.

Jasper turned that perplexed face to the fire. Mr. Crisparkle continuing to observe it, found it even more perplexing than before, inasmuch as it seemed to denote (which could hardly be) some close internal calculation.

He bears a family resemblance to Bradley Headstone, the school-master in *Our Mutual Friend*.

in his decent black coat and waistcoat, and decent white shirt, and decent formal black tie, and decent pantaloons of pepper and salt, with his decent silver watch in his pocket and its decent hair-guard round his neck, looks a thoroughly decent young man.

Compare this with the description of Jasper in chapter 2.

a dark man of some six-and-twenty, with thick, lustrous, well-arranged black hair and whiskers. He looks older than he is, as dark men often do. His voice is deep and good, his face and figure are good, his manner is a little sombre. His room is a little sombre, and may have had its influence in forming his character. It is mostly in shadow.

G.K. Chesterton remarks on the effective 'piece of artistic mystery' of the fact that Jasper always keeps his eyes fixed on his nephew's face with a dark and watchful tenderness. 'The thing is so told that at first we really take it as only indicating something morbid in the affection; it is only afterwards that the frightful fancy breaks upon us that it is not morbid affection but morbid antagonism.' The likeness to Bradley Headstone is very marked in the melodramatic chapter 19, when Jasper reveals to Rosa his passion for her – perhaps an artistic mistake, unless Felix Aylmer is right in thinking that it is a deliberate parody of Headstone. Aylmer believes in Jasper's innocence, but the references to *Macbeth* in the novel have been often noticed, and in chapter 14, significantly entitled, in a near-quotation from that play, 'When Shall These Three Meet Again?', there are *Macbeth*-like ironies; for example we hear that Jasper

> is early among the shopkeepers, ordering little table luxuries that his nephew likes. His nephew will not be with him long, he tells his provision-dealers, and so must be petted and made much of.

Compare Lady Macbeth's 'He that's coming/Must be provided for.' We hear that

> Mr. Jasper is in beautiful voice this day. His nervous temperament is occasionally prone to take difficult music a little too quickly; to-day, his time is perfect.

Mr Crisparkle, noticing a change in him, says:

> 'One would think, Jasper, you had been trying a new medicine for that occasional indisposition of yours.'
> 'No, really? That's well observed; for I have.'
> 'Then stick to it, my dear fellow,' says Mr. Crisparkle, clapping him on the shoulder with friendly encouragement, 'stick to it.'
> 'I will.'

Richard M. Baker suggests that the 'new medicine' is the opium, but he had taken that before. Is it not likely that it is the decision to murder Edwin?

> In his opium dreams he had often done the murder.
> 'I did it over and over again. I have done it hundreds of thousands of times in this room.'
> 'It's to be hoped it was pleasant to do, deary.'
> 'It *was* pleasant to do!' . . .
> '. . . I did it so often, and through such vast expanses of time, that when it was really done, it seemed not worth the doing, it was done so soon . . . '
> 'No struggle, no consciousness of peril, no entreaty – and yet I never saw *that* before.'

Baker may be right to interpret this as meaning that in his dreams before the murder he could not visualize the actual appearance of a dead body.

> 'Look at it! Look what a poor, mean, miserable thing it is! *That* must be real. It's over.'

There is a suggestive parallel with another novel of Dickens. When the Dean and Minor Canon Crisparkle and the rest look towards Jasper's window

> a fire shines out upon the fast-darkening scene, involving in shadow the pendent masses of ivy and creeper covering the building's front.

On the Christmas Eve when Drood disappears

> . . . the red light burns steadily all the evening on the margin of the tide of busy life.

Through the terrible wind storm the red light in Jasper's window burns on steadily. The parallel is with Mrs Clennam, another victim of suppressed passion, and *her* windows, in *Little Dorrit*.

> The varying light of fire and candle in Mrs. Clennam's room made the greatest change that ever broke the dead monotony of the spot. In her two long narrow windows, the fire shone sullenly all day, and sullenly all night. On rare occasions, it flashed up passionately, as she did; but for the most part it was suppressed, like her, and preyed upon itself evenly and slowly. Strange, if the little sickroom fire were in effect a beacon fire, summoning someone, and that the most unlikely someone in the world, to the spot that *must* be come to.

Mrs Clennam's windows summon Rigaud to his death; did Jasper's do the same for Edwin?

The final tableau in the Cathedral gives a glimpse of the demons that Jasper has carved out of his heart, as Mr Datchery and Deputy watch the Princess Puffer watching Jasper.

> She is behind a pillar, carefully withdrawn from the Choir Master's view, but regards him with the closest attention. All unconscious of her presence, he chants and sings. She grins when

he is most musically fervid, and – yes, Mr. Datchery sees her do it! – shakes her fist at him behind the pillar's friendly shelter. Mr. Datchery looks again to convince himself. Yes, again! As ugly and withered as one of the fantastic carvings on the under brackets of the stall seats, as malignant as the Evil One, as hard as the big brass eagle holding the sacred books upon his wings (and, according to the sculptor's presentation of his ferocious attributes, not at all converted by them) she hugs herself in her lean arms, and then shakes both fists at the leader of the choir.

And at that moment, outside the grated door of the choir, having eluded the vigilance of Mr. Tope by shifty resources in which he is an adept, Deputy peeps, sharp-eyed, through the bars, and stares astounded from the threatener to the threatened.

If we assume the guilt of Jasper it is possible to trace plausibly the development of the story down to the point where *The Mystery of Edwin Drood* breaks off. The case against Jasper is clear. He has a motive in his jealousy of Edwin over Rosa. There is his warning – is it a threat? – to Edwin (ch. 2). Why is he so polite to Sapsea? (No doubt for the same reason why Datchery is, later on; they both want to use him.) Why does Jasper take up Durdles, and why is he interested in his keys? (ch. 4). He overhears Edwin and Neville quarrel in the street, revives the quarrel, drugs the wine. The way he looks from one to the other suggests that he knows that the presence of a third person will aggravate the quarrel (ch. 8). He tells Crisparkle that night about the quarrel and tells Mrs. Crisparkle next day, apparently in case Crisparkle kept it from her. There is his peculiar choice of words, insisted on: 'God *save* them both!' (ch. 9). Jasper wants everyone to know of Neville's animosity towards Edwin. He is at first perplexed by the proposal that he should make peace between Edwin and Neville, but agrees to it, realizing that a meeting at his house could be to his advantage. He shows his diary entry to Crisparkle (ch. 10).

Then there is the matter of the quicklime. How much did Jasper (or Dickens) know about quicklime? Did they both 'entertain the common but entirely erroneous belief that quicklime was capable of completely destroying a body'? (Baker, 1951). Compare Forster's account of the plot as Dickens sketched it to him, which refers to 'a gold ring which had resisted the corrosive effects of the lime.' And here I will cite a passage I have not seen referred to, from *Great Expectations* (ch. 53), when Orlick says to Pip:

> I won't have a rag of you, I won't have none of you, left on earth. I'll put your body in the kiln – I'd carry two such to it, on my shoulders – and, let people suppose what they may of you, they should never know nothing.

On the other hand, as Saunders (1914) points out, Dickens lived near the Medway cement works and might well have known that quicklime (without water) would not destroy a body. Could it be that, while *Dickens* knew that, *Jasper* did not, and the discovery of the murder was to depend on it?

But this is to anticipate a part of the novel that was never written. Returning to the actual story, we read of Jasper's 'Night with Durdles' (ch. 12). He apparently drugs Durdles into a long sleep till 12 a.m. His rage at Deputy seems to be due to his not wanting a witness. Then there is the business of the ring, clearly to be important. (Edwin did not mention it to Rosa.) Their parting kiss, really a brother-and-sister farewell, is mistaken by Jasper ('He saw us as we took leave of each other,' says Edwin) for a lovers' parting. From then on Edwin is doomed (ch. 13). Jasper makes much of his affection for Edwin to shopkeepers, and prejudices Sapsea against Neville, but tells Crisparkle he has overcome his fear of Neville and will burn this year's diary at the year's end – the purpose of this being to prevent the Minor Canon from suspecting Jasper (ch. 14).

What happened on the night of Edwin's disappearance? We are not told, but the obvious inference is that Jasper drugged Edwin and then strangled him with 'that great black scarf'. How did he dispose of the body? Again we do not know. The crypt is not indicated, for Durdles delights in making discoveries there. But Durdles always carries his dinner bundle, and on one occasion it contained the key to Mrs Sapsea's tomb. Perhaps it does on this occasion. Jasper may have substituted another key for it. The tomb would not be opened till Mr Sapsea's death, and by then he thought all traces of Edwin's body would have disappeared. His activities covered by the wild stormy night, he put the body in the tomb, went to the Weir and saw to it that the watch-chain was caught in the interstices of the timbers, and flung the shirt-pin into the water. It was his scheme to bring about that Crisparkle should find the watch, so that he becomes a chief witness against Neville.

None of this was suspected. What drew suspicion to Jasper was his collapse at Grewgious's news, in a sort of proleptic hanging (ch. 15).

> Mr. Grewgious heard a terrible shriek, and saw no ghastly figure, sitting or standing; saw nothing but a heap of torn and miry clothes upon the floor.

Compare Fagin's meditations on hanging in *Oliver Twist*, chapter 52.

> With what a rattling noise the drop went down; and how suddenly they changed from strong and vigorous men to dangling heaps of clothes.

How was Jasper brought to justice? Datchery, an enigmatic character, appears to be playing the part of a detective watching Jasper. (Perhaps he is employed by Grewgious.) We note his look of interest when Deputy points to part of the gate-house and says 'That's Jarsper'. Like Jasper he is excessively polite to Sapsea. His white hair is unusually thick and ample, and he has black eyebrows (ch. 18).

More than half a year passes. Jasper reveals to Rosa his love for her, admitting that but for his affection for Edwin he would have swept him from his path. Rosa suspects Jasper, but she hides her suspicion. Neville and Helena may suspect Jasper, but they say nothing, and the open and frank Crisparkle suspects no one. Grewgious admits he dislikes Jasper, but nothing more.

As the extant story draws to a close there are signs that Jasper will be brought to justice. We see him again in the opium den. Her Royal Highness the Princess Puffer had overheard his broken sentences, devoted herself to learning his secret. She had tracked him that Christmas Eve and warned Edwin of his danger.

When Jasper leaves her house she exclaims: 'I'll not miss ye twice!' She follows Jasper to Cloisterham and falls in with Datchery, who extracts information from her that astonishes him.

He bargains with Deputy to find out where she lives in London. In the Cathedral next day he sees her threatening gestures at Jasper, and later hears from her own lips that she recognizes him. Datchery goes home.

> Mrs. Tope's care has spread a very neat, clean breakfast ready for her lodger. Before sitting down to it, he opens his corner-cupboard door; takes his bit of chalk from its shelf; adds one thick line to the score, extending from the top of the cupboard door to the bottom; and then falls to with an appetite.

These words were written by Dickens in his little Swiss chalet on 8 June 1870, only hours before he died. They are the conclusion of chapter 23. (It is clear that this is the end of a chapter because below the last line in the manuscript there is a flourish.) What was to follow? No one knows. Forster says in his *Life* of Dickens:

> Nothing had been written, however, of the main parts of the design excepting what is found in the published chapters; there was no hint or preparation of the sequel in any notes of chapters in advance . . . The evidence of matured designs never to be accomplished, intentions planned never to be executed, roads of thought marked out never to be traversed, goals shining in the distance never to be reached, was wanting here. It was all a blank.

A would-be solver of the mystery must confront the testimony of Forster about Dickens's plans for his last novel. Forster says the story

> was to be that of the murder of a nephew by his uncle; the ori-ginality of which was to consist in the review of the murderer's career by himself at the close, when its temptations were to be dwelt on as if not he the culprit, but some other man, were the tempted. The last chapters were to be written in the condemned cell, to which his wickedness, all elaborately elicited from him as if told of another, had brought him. Discovery by the murderer of the utter needlessness of the murder for its object, were to follow hard upon the commission of the deed; when by the means of a gold ring which had resisted the corrosive effects of the lime into which he had thrown the body, not only the person murdered was to be identified but the locality of the crime and the man who committed it. So much was told me

before any of the book was written; and it will be recollected that the ring, taken by Drood to be given to his betrothed only if their engagement went on, was brought away by him from their last interview. Rosa was to marry Tartar, and Crisparkle the sister of Landless, who was himself, I think, to have perished in assisting Tartar finally to unmask the murderer.

Two comments from a couple of other people close to Dickens may be mentioned as confirming Forster's account. Charles Dickens junior, the novelist's eldest son, said his father told him Jasper murdered Edwin. And Luke Fildes, the novelist's illustrator, said Dickens told him: 'Can you keep a secret? I must have the double necktie. It is necessary, for Jasper strangles Edwin Drood with it.' (In the novel it is a black scarf.)

But Forster's account did not go unchallenged. The general reliability of the *Life* was soon questioned. This takes us into the thick of the controversy about Dickens's private life, which is still a matter of dispute among scholars. And apart from this background of uncertainty specific doubts have been expressed about Forster's account of *Edwin Drood*. There is one worrying problem for those who believe Forster. He says that in July 1869 Dickens wrote to him:

> What should you think of a story beginning in this way? – Two people, boy or girl or very young, going apart from one another, pledged to be married after many years – at the end of the book. The interest to arise out of the tracing of their separate ways, and the impossibility of telling what will be done with that impending fate.

Forster says this idea was discarded, and that in a letter dated Friday 6 August 1869 Dickens wrote:

> I laid aside the fancy I told you of, and have a very curious and new idea for my new story. Not a communicable idea (or the interest would be gone) but a very strong one, though difficult to work.

Forster then says: 'I learnt immediately afterward' that 'the story . . . was to be that of the murder of a nephew,' etc.

The problem here is that the first idea for *Edwin Drood* which

Forster says Dickens wrote to him about has been shown to appear in Dickens's Memoranda Book, kept by him between 1855 and 1865, in an entry which cannot be dated later than 1862. What are we to make of this? It is agreed that Forster is not such a good witness for Dickens's last years as he is for 1840–60. Things had happened in the lives of both men to diminish their intimacy, and Forster disapproved of Dickens's public readings. So it has been suggested that when Forster wrote his biography he was anxious to show that he had been on intimate terms with Dickens to the end, and so he copied out a plot from the old Memoranda Book and said Dickens had sent it to him. As Angus Wilson has said, this is not a charge of faulty memory but of bad faith. It throws doubt on the whole of the *Life*. If Forster had been capable of it surely he would have been capable of what is also alleged, that he based his account of *Edwin Drood* not on what Dickens told him but merely on inferences from his reading of what was published.

If Forster's account is rejected the recollections of Fildes (recorded long afterwards and partly discrepant) and Charles Dickens junior (which appeared many years after his own death) cannot carry great weight. The essential truth of Forster's account is clearly the crucial question. Can it be defended?

Not all the considerations that can be urged against it are equally strong. There is no evidence of estrangement between Forster and Dickens at this time, and some evidence against it. As for the fact that Forster's account of the continuation of *Edwin Drood* could have been deduced from what was published of the novel, this makes no difference one way or the other. *Any* account would have to be consistent with what was published.

The real difficulty is the business of the Memoranda Book. Of course it could be that Dickens, considering a new story, himself consulted it. And there is no doubt that many modern scholars are convinced of Forster's general reliability and good faith, even if there are minor distortions of fact in the *Life*. All the same, this business seems fishy, and Forster's account of *Edwin Drood* must for the present remain problematic. If his word is doubted, this account becomes only one more attempt to describe the 'trajectory' of the story (such as the one I have already attempted in outlining the plot on the assumption of Jasper's guilt).

One puzzling aspect of what Forster says is the apparent

inconsistency between Dickens's statement that his new idea was 'not . . . communicable' with Forster's statement that Dickens 'immediately' communicated it to him. A little joke? or a contradiction? Charles Forsyte (1980) has argued that there need be no contradiction. It is surely probable that Dickens told Forster *something* about *Edwin Drood*; not all the details, as that would have spoilt the plot for him, but a vague outline of the story, which did not give away the real secret of the mystery; and it was *this* that Forster 'learnt immediately afterward'. It is not certain that Forster even meant to imply that Dickens revealed the incommunicable secret to him. Even if he did mean to imply that, we do not have to believe that Dickens actually did so.

Can we find out what it was? Sylvère Monod is sceptical. He thinks the 'new idea' was destined never to be communicated. And he points out that in any case, whatever the novelist may have told Forster, it is by no means certain that Dickens would not have introduced significant modifications at the last moment and departed from any intentions he may have had before June 1870. These are wise words. All the same it is hard to believe that Dickens had no idea what was to be the solution to his mystery when he embarked on *Edwin Drood*, even if he may not have decided on all the details. There is in fact reason to think he did know. The first sketch for the cover was made by Dickens's son-in-law and was approved by Dickens on 5 December 1869. It includes a dramatic scene with a man holding a lantern which does not correspond to anything in the text as we have it. Surely Dickens already had in mind, while still writing the early part of the novel, a scene that was to occur in the later part?

There have been many guesses about the new idea. A popular theory is that Edwin Drood was not really murdered but was to reappear in the denouement. And it is true that Dickens's list of possible titles for the novel, which has survived, does include some which leave open the question of what happened to Edwin. But, as Margaret Cardwell points out in her admirable edition of the novel for the World's Classics, Dickens was prepared in 1869, while still planning his own story, to print in *All the Year Round* a serial by Robert Lytton, for which Dickens suggested the title *The Disappearance of John Acland*, as it would 'leave the reader in doubt whether he was really murdered, till the end.' If Dickens was

prepared to print such a story the 'curious *and new* idea . . . strong
. . . though difficult to work', cannot be the question of whether
or not Drood was murdered.

Nor is it likely that the new idea was the innocence of
John Jasper, maintained by Felix Aylmer (1964) in his Agatha
Christie-type solution. This kind of solution, elaborately ingenious,
is open to the serious objection that Sherlock Holmes did not make
his first bow till 1887, 17 years after the publication of *Edwin Drood*.
If it is hard to believe that Dickens anticipated him, it is even
harder to believe that he could have anticipated the sophistication
of detective and mystery stories since the days of Conan Doyle.
The Victorian Agatha Christie was not Dickens but Wilkie Collins,
and in a letter to Collins of 6 October 1859 Dickens seems to deny
any interest in that kind of plotting.

> I think the business of art is to lay all that ground carefully, not
> with the care that conceals itself – to show, by a backward light,
> what everything has been working to – but only to suggest,
> until the fulfilment comes. These are the ways of Providence,
> of which ways art is but a little imitation.

There *is* a mystery in *Edwin Drood*, but not that kind of
mystery.

The truth is that for the modern connoisseur of mystery stories
Edwin Drood must be very disappointing. There is almost nothing
to find out. Every clue indicates that Jasper is the murderer. As
a detective story it is a primitive, like Mark Twain's *Pudd'nhead
Wilson* (1894). Yet the effect of the novel is anything but feeble.
We feel all the time that it is full of meaning. Dickens had never
written in this pregnant and intense way before. The sense of deep
mystery that pervades it does not derive from the whodunit but
from undisclosed personal secrets and from the haunting figure of
Jasper – a man not only leading a double life, but deeply divided
within himself. He is a brother under the skin of some other
Dickens figures, among them Sydney Carton, Arthur Clennam,
Pip, and Bradley Headstone. He can also be readily related to
other examples in nineteenth-century literature of the divided
self or *âme damnée*, in books such as Hogg's *Justified Sinner*
(1824), Balzac's *Illusions Perdues* (1837), Poe's *William Wilson*
(1839), Dostoyevsky's *Crime and Punishment* (1866), and – after

Dickens's time – Stevenson's *Dr. Jekyll and Mr. Hyde* (1886) and Wilde's *Picture of Dorian Gray* (1891). Jasper is placed in Cloisterham, and on the old cathedral city there falls both light and shadow, alternating suggestions of what is life-giving and holy, and what is sinister and corrupt and makes for death. The appropriate culmination of the novel would have been a dramatic confrontation of good and evil. It has been suggested that this might have come about through a revelation of the 'Jekyll' and 'Hyde' aspects of Jasper. (Forster's account of the projected scene in the condemned cell may support this.) Or there might have been a final confrontation between Jasper, the symbol of evil, and an opponent from among the 'good' characters.

Supposing that this were in fact to have been the story, it seems plausible that the opponent might have been Datchery, that mysterious personage whom we leave (for ever) eating his breakfast at the end of chapter 23. Many critics agree with S.C. Roberts that what we are told of him is 'the beginning of a new element in the narrative'. There are one or two straws in the wind here.

In a letter to James T. Fields of 14 January 1870 Dickens wrote:

There is a curious interest working up to No. 5, which requires a great deal of art and self-denial . . . So I hope at Nos. 5 and 6 the story will turn upon an interest suspended until the end.

Datchery first appears in no. 5 (chapter 18) and again in no. 6 (chapter 23). Was he the 'curious interest', 'suspended until the end?'? Modern scholarship lends support to the view that he was to be a key figure. The manuscript, says M. Cardwell (1982), 'confirms the importance to Dickens of Datchery or of a character playing Datchery's role.' And in her Clarendon Press edition (1972) she points out an interesting difference between Charles Collins's sketch for the wrapper of the monthly parts and the drawing by Fildes, who replaced him. Collins's sketch showed 'the second and third of three figures rushing up the staircase, with a glimpse of the fourth in the background', to be police officers, but this is not the case in Fildes's drawing. It looks as if Dickens had decided that the mystery and detection were to have remained completely private. Several literary critics, including V.S. Pritchett (1946) and Humphry House (1947), lay stress on the 'private' character of the whole of *Edwin Drood*. At any rate the police are absent from the story, as Philip Collins (1965) notes, though the fictional action seems to take place at a time when policemen were on their beats. We hear at one point that the search for the missing Edwin was 'pressed on every hand', yet the only collector of clues we see is Datchery.

Could Datchery be a policeman? Dickens had introduced the professional police detective into English fiction in *Bleak House* (1852) – Inspector Bucket. But Datchery, unlike Inspector Bucket, is a gentleman. It seems more probable that he is an amateur. Philip Collins remarks on the frequency of the motif of shadowing and pursuing in Dickens's novels. Monks follows Oliver Twist, Quilp follows Nell, Dombey chases Carker. In *Bleak House* itself Bucket the professional is reinforced by the amateurs Tulkinghorn and Guppy, all in search of secrets. Dickens is fond of amateur investigators – no doubt because they enjoy the fictional advantage of being emotionally involved with the victim or the villain. There may be a hint of this at the end of chapter 22 of *Edwin Drood*.

> John Jasper's lamp is kindled, and his Lighthouse is shining when Mr. Datchery returns alone towards it. As mariners on a dangerous voyage, approaching an iron-bound coast, may look along the beams of the warning light to the haven lying beyond it that may never be reached, so Mr. Datchery's *wistful* gaze is directed to this beacon and beyond. (emphasis added)

That Datchery was to be a *deus ex machina* may be suggested by a conversation in chapter 17, which Dickens deleted, between Neville Landless, who is suspected of the murder of Edwin, and Crisparkle. Neville says: 'It seems a little hard to be so tied to a stake and innocent; but I don't complain.' 'And you must expect no miracle to help you,' says Mr Crisparkle compassionately. 'No, sir, I know that. The ordinary fulness of time and circumstance is all I have to trust to.' At the end of the chapter lawyer Grewgious is looking up at the stars 'as if he would have read in them something that was hidden from him.' The next chapter (18) begins: 'At about this time a stranger appeared in Cloisterham' – Datchery. Is he the 'miracle'?

Who is Datchery, of the white (or grey) hair and black eyebrows? He may be a new character. But there seem to be hints that he is in disguise, and it has been usually thought that he is a character who has already appeared. Two of the proposed identifications are sensational. The first is that he is Edwin Drood himself in disguise. This was cleverly argued for in an early study, *Watched by the Dead* (by Richard A. Proctor, 1887).

But it contradicts Forster, Fildes, and a son of Dickens, three men who in different ways were close to him, and who all affirm that Dickens told them Edwin was murdered. The *John Acland* business also makes against it. The other exciting suggestion is Helena Landless, supported by Edmund Wilson in his influential essay in *The Wound and the Bow* (1941). 'The plausibles', as Alfred Hitchcock called them, will not like this idea. Helena is a lady known in Cloisterham, yet she walks about disguised as a retired buffer in broad daylight. Would a young girl be likely to know about 'the old tavern way of keeping scores'? – as likely as the Dean, one would think, or less. The Helena idea does not appear to be in Dickens's style. We learn from his letter to W.H. Wills (30 June 1867) that he was relieved to find in *The Moonstone* 'nothing belonging to disguised women or the like' (a reference to Collins's *No Name*).

Other identifications are less interesting. On Grewgious as Datchery G.K. Chesterton has surely said the last word: 'There is something pointless about one grotesque character dressing up as another grotesque character actually less amusing than himself.' Recent books on *Edwin Drood* have favoured Bazzard, amateur dramatist and author of the Thorn of Anxiety. His character seems to be quite different from Datchery's, but of course it might also be a pose: as Aylmer says, his theatrical manner may conceal deep motives. But in that case we have to invent a 'real' Bazzard about whom we know absolutely nothing. Equally uninteresting is the suggestion that Datchery is Neville Landless, or Lieutenant Tartar. Tartar knows nothing of Jasper.

One more suggestion may be mentioned, as 'getting warmer', This is the young man named Poker, who does not actually appear in *Edwin Drood*, but who teases 'the old Tory jackass' in the enigmatic 'Sapsea fragment', discovered by Forster. Forster thought Dickens had used up his material too quickly and was trying to invent some more, but it is not credible that the business of Poker could have been introduced as it stands into the novel; it is too similar to the business of Datchery. Charles Forsyte suggests that the Sapsea fragment may have been an earlier unpublished sketch which Dickens kept by him as something that might be worked into *Edwin Drood*. Or (an attractive suggestion) it may be a tentative first sketch of the Datchery idea. Once again we do not know.

Philip Hobsbaum (1972), after listing the various hypotheses about Datchery, concludes: 'Clearly, this is stalemate. The critics should confess themselves baffled.'

But I believe there is an explanation. I think Dickens was planning to wind up the story with a spectacular final coup not to be equalled in detective fiction until Agatha Christie's *Murder of Roger Ackroyd*, and I base this belief on three considerations.

1. *The period of Dickens's life during which 'Edwin Drood' was concocted.* Dickens had achieved a direct contact with his public in his readings which meant a great deal to them and to him. In April 1869 his health broke down and his doctors insisted that he should stop. But he was allowed to give twelve farewell performances in 1870. He took his last leave of his audience at St James's Hall with a little joke:

> In but two short weeks from this time I hope that you may enter, in your homes, on a new series of readings at which my assistance will be indispensable; but from these garish lights I vanish now for evermore with a heartfelt, grateful, respectful, affectionate farewell.

Dickens could not know that *Edwin Drood* was to be a farewell performance in fiction, but he may well have guessed it. If so it would be surprising if he had not considered some way of making his last bow in the novel itself. At any rate there is little doubt of the influence of the readings on *Edwin Drood*: it is full of 'stage directions.'

2. *The personal significance of 'Edwin Drood'.* While we need not accept the whole of Edmund Wilson's theory about the novel, it is easy to agree with him that John Jasper and Charles Dickens have affinities. Whether or not Dickens had a divided personality like Jasper, Jasper like Dickens is an artist, a gifted musician with a beautiful voice. His use of opium can be regarded as a symbol for the life of imagination which he leads apart from other men. He is apparently a skilful mesmerist (compare Dickens and Mrs

De La Rue) with a potentially dangerous power over his fellow men and women. He seems an alien from another world, yet he is accepted in the conventional English community, where he passes for a man of kindly feelings and good spirits. But his hymns to the God of Christianity in the decaying cathedral are false – whether or not, as Wilson thinks, his real object of worship is Kali, goddess of destruction.

We must be wary of identifying Dickens (or any other great novelist) with any one character. As Taylor Stoehr says, 'Dickens seems to be in all his characters'. This seems to prevent him taking any one role and identifying himself with it. We never have the impression, Stoehr feels, that the author himself is the hero, as we do in *Middlemarch* or *Evelina* or *The Sun Also Rises*. Critics have remarked on the thin, 'distant' quality of Dickens's first-person narrators – David, Esther, Pip. 'Dickens's people are nearly all flat,' says E.M. Forster, adding that 'Pip and David Copperfield attempt roundness, but so diffidently that they seem more like bubbles than solids.' Yet it is hard not to feel a strong personal engagement in one character - Jasper. 'His own temptations and imaginings, says Humphry House of the 'macabre Dickens', 'isolated and heightened by the peculiar, narrowing intense quality of his imagination, fed daily by the immense power he felt himself to possess over others' personalities - these were the authentic sources of his great criminal characters.' We must be wary of the kind of interpretations Monod calls '*effroyablement serieux*', but there does seem to be a serious centre of interest in this book, and it is Jasper.

But if Jasper represents an aspect of Dickens, he cannot be the puppet in whose costume Dickens would have made his 'positively last appearance'. He is a bad man in disguise; is it not likely that he will be defeated by a good man in disguise, and that is the part that Dickens himself would play? In both life and art Dickens loved the incognito and was fascinated by role-playing. 'There had always been something vaguely theatrical about his style of dress,' says Ellen Moers, who gives him a place in the line of dandies from Beau Brummell to Max Beerbohm. He could dress up to attract attention, as a Heavy Swell. But he could also, says John Reed, derive a deep satisfaction from moving secretly about the low districts of London, 'like Haroun al-Raschid in disguise'.

3. *Dickens's lifelong fascination with The Arabian Nights.* Angus Wilson has written convincingly about the profound significance of Jasper's 'oriental dream' under the influence of opium. 'Dickens is identifying the world of *The Arabian Nights* with the erotic and the violent, those parts of it which we may suppose he was conscious of when as a child he so loved it.' There are many references to *The Arabian Nights* in Dickens's work – for example in *Martin Chuzzlewit*, chapter 5, *David Copperfield*, chapters 3 and 59, *American Notes*, chapter 9. They are frequent in the *Christmas Stories*. There is the detailed account in 'A Christmas Tree' of the hold these stories had over his childish imagination. In another story he speaks of the 'sweet memories' with which the name of 'the good Caliph Haroun Al-Raschid' is 'scented'. Of yet another passage Michael Slater in his recent *Dickens and Women* says: 'As always with Dickens, *The Arabian Nights* allusions are a sure sign that his emotions are deeply stirred.' 'Under the lightest of fictional disguises he enjoys . . . that pleasure so dear to him, of exposing his deepest feelings to his beloved public without that public at all suspecting what it is that he is doing.'

If Philip Collins is right Dickens had composed a mystery plot in the real world at this time – the house at Slough, the assumed name, the double life. But psychological explanations are quite speculative. The solution I suggest does not depend on them. It is a simple one. *Edwin Drood* turns out to be an 'Arabian Nights expedition' (Dickens once invited Wilkie Collins to one in real life). Datchery is Charles Dickens himself, moving like Haroun al-Raschid in disguise among the subjects of his fictional kingdom.

This would explain why Dickens was so secretive in the notes for *The Mystery of Edwin Drood*, intended for his private use. 'They are curiously cryptic', says Arthur J. Cox, 'as if the author wished to conceal, even at the privacy of his desk, the solution to his Mystery.' All the other suggested solutions are either 'difficult' in an un-Dickensian, Agatha Christie way, or they are not credibly 'difficult' for a genius like Dickens. This solution gives a reason why Dickens played his cards close to his chest. The secret would have been uniquely exciting while it was kept, but anti-climactic if it had got out prematurely. It would also explain his reference to the 'self-denial' required in writing the Datchery numbers, and the curious phrase 'the Datchery assumption' quoted by Forster as used by Dickens. It would explain the deleted reference to 'a miracle'. A miracle is a direct intervention of God, and in a novel the novelist himself is God. There are anticipations of the idea in Dickens's earlier work. The teller of the tale of the Baron of Grogzwig in *Nicholas Nickleby* is clearly a persona of the author. There is the revelation of Master Humphrey as himself 'the single gentleman' at the end of *The Old Curiosity Shop*. There is the peculiar character 'The Shadow' which intrigued Dickens at one time. In his later years we have the sketches collected as *The Uncommercial Traveller*, in which Dickens goes about as 'Mr Uncommercial'. If Hitchcock could appear in his own films, why not Dickens in his own novel?

Of course it is impossible to say how the Dickens/Datchery figure would have been finally explained. I suspect that he would have turned out to be the person referred to by Grewgious in chapter 20: '. . . a Firm down stairs with which I have business relations, lend me a substitute' – i.e. for Bazzard, who is 'off duty at present'. This would give a reason for the mention of this 'substitute', otherwise unexplained. It would also give some relevance to the mystery about Grewgious's career and the unknown help he received in it. Would he have been the 'Agent' and the 'Receiver' of the author?

Whoever Datchery is, it seems probable that he would have played a leading part in the unmasking of Jasper. Jack Lindsay suggested that his name may have come from an unconscious reminiscence of 'Datchet' in *Cheveley* (1839), Lady Lytton's *roman à clef*, in which Datchet is the instrument for the exposure of a wicked novelist who had treated his wife cruelly. (This is a novel Dickens is sure to have read with interest, as besides Lytton it contains portraits of other figures from his own milieu, including Forster.) Who knows? A more reliable inference is that there is no reason to believe that the process of detection would have been very ingenious or elaborate. Those who know Dickens's work well will not hesitate to agree with Kate Perugini, his daughter, when she said of *Edwin Drood*: 'It was not, I imagine, for the intricate working out of his plot alone that my father cared to write this story; but it was through his wonderful observation of character, and his strange insight into the tragic secrets of the human heart, that he desired his greatest triumph to be achieved.'

Chapter 10
On *The Portrait of a Lady*

The Portrait of a Lady is one of the most accessible of Henry James's novels. It has none of the obscurity of *The Golden Bowl* (1904), or other works in James's later manner. There is no difficulty in making out what it is all about, though there may be disagreement over just what it says. Especially in its early chapters it is a sunny work, sparkling with light comedy. (A good example in chapter 1 is Mrs Touchett's strange telegram, and the discussion about what it means.) Throughout the novel James's sense of place and environment, one of his strong points, is active, and in the Italian scenes he shows himself, as so often, a painter *manqué*. But there is shadow as well as sunshine in the *Portrait*, pathos as well as comedy. And at the heart of it there is a mystery. This is not inappropriate: there is often something mysterious in portraits of women by Old Masters.

On the surface the *Portrait* is unproblematic. It appears to be a solid late-nineteenth-century novel of manners and society, rather slow-paced in comparison with Stevenson or Conan Doyle. Readers new to Henry James may find themselves restive at the comparative lack of action down to chapter 19; and James himself, while the novel was being serialized, took this objection seriously. Obsessed as he was with construction, he was apt to misjudge the tempo of his narratives. Other novels of his – *Roderick Hudson*, for example – begin too slowly and end too rapidly. This is a common fault in writers influenced by painting. However that may be, from chapter 20 onwards, when Isabel becomes involved with Osmond through the machinations of Madame Merle, a deeper interest sets in, which holds us to the end. It has been said, disapprovingly, that the story verges on melodrama, and the Victorian reader would doubtless have recognized some familiar archetypes, such as the Striking Girl, the Fairy Godmother, the Rich Uncle, and the

Sinister Conspirators. But is it a disadvantage for a novel to draw deeply on fairytale types and patterns?

The great fairytales have a meaning beyond their plain sense. What was James's meaning in this novel? His preface does not disclose a great deal. Written for the New York edition many years later, in his oblique later style, it is a pleasant biographical document rather than a retrospective critique, chiefly important for its tribute to Turgenev and its dicta on the art of fiction in general. As for this particular novel, he dwells on its 'architectural' competence. The later James was heavily preoccupied with formal considerations, and he took pride in *The Portrait of a Lady* as the most 'proportioned' of his productions after *The Ambassadors* (1903). What pleased him most was the scale of the work: he had 'built large'. But as for the characters, apart from Isabel, he merely tells us that 'I seem to myself to have waked up one morning in possession of them.'

Does a study of sources help? Various literary influences have been seen in this novel, among them Balzac, whom he always revered as a master, and later French novelists such as Flaubert, whom he had known personally during his residence in Paris; and the expatriate Russian novelist Turgenev, for whom he felt a warm personal affection. Today it is thought that James owes more to the English tradition represented by Dickens, Thackeray and George Eliot. But his deepest affinities are with none of these writers, but with the New England writer Nathaniel Hawthorne (1804–64), of whose work he published a penetrating study in 1879. He shared with Hawthorne an intense interest in American puritan psychology. Yet James felt some dissatisfaction with his predecessor. After reading Hawthorne he was left 'with a sense of having handled a splendid piece of silversmith's work'. He looked for a more robust humanity and a greater realism of presentation than he could find in Hawthorne. He wanted to express in his own work the interest in manners and the social surface that the New England fabulist had lacked.

The other limitation James saw in Hawthorne's work was what he called its 'provinciality'. James's friend and fellow-novelist William Dean Howells objected, very reasonably, that if it is not provincial for an Englishman to be English, or a Frenchman French, then it is not provincial for an American to be American.

But what James had in mind was a sort of inferiority complex which the English or French were without. He saw this as a weakness in Hawthorne's essays on England, *Our Old Home* (1863), and his ambition was to banish from his own work that 'exaggerated, painful, morbid national consciousness'. He longed to be accepted as a major writer on both sides of the Atlantic. And he was to win his fame as the poised master of an intercultural subject: Americans' relationships with Europeans. This subject is prominent in his fiction of the 1870s, in *Roderick Hudson* (1875), *The American* (1877), *The Europeans* (1878), and, most famously, in his tale of 'Daisy Miller' (1878), who was for long to typify the American girl abroad. Looking back over James's achievement not long after the novelist's death Ezra Pound, in the *Little Review* (August 1918), saw it as 'the whole great assaying and weighing, the research for the significance of nationality, French, English, American.'

Today this seems a misplacement of emphasis. Certainly James's treatment of the international theme is of historical interest. But the abiding power of his work derives less from this than from its rendering of the spiritual qualities which 'European' or 'American' came to symbolize in James's vision of the world. His early work is sometimes described as a study of the relations between crude but decent Americans and polite but corrupt Europeans. But if this was ever a fair description it had ceased to apply by the time he wrote *The Portrait of a Lady*. Madame Merle and Osmond may be associated with corrupt 'Europe', and Madame Merle speaks of herself as belonging to 'the old world', but the novel (like *The Europeans*, despite its title) is really about provincial Americans and cosmopolitan Americans. All the main characters, except Lord Warburton, are American.

Old Mr Touchett and his son, settled in England, do not seem rootless, like the Americans in Paris whom Isabel so dislikes. But their world is still an American world. And they are eccentric. 'The Touchetts aren't English at all, you know,' says the Englishman Bantling. 'They have their own habits, their own language, their own food – some odd religion, even, I believe, of their own.' Here James seems to be drawing on memories of his own family; his father, a lovable oddity, had in fact worked out his own religion (a sort of Swedenborgianism). This background of family affection may account for the attractiveness of Gardencourt, its genial warmth.

Mrs Touchett, who leads a wandering life more or less permanently away from her husband, is far from genial. To establish her in the novel James uses a technique of imagery which he may have learned from Dickens (for an example of it see Dickens's presentation of Wemmick in *Great Expectations*, 1861). We are told that she 'had a great merit; she was as honest as a pair of compasses. There was a comfort in her stiffness and firmness; you knew exactly where to find her.' James uses this kind of imagery to bring out the special quality of characters who are shown to us in only one aspect, the 'furniture' of the novel. Mrs Touchett's style of talk is in keeping. 'You use too many figures of speech,' she tells Ralph. 'I could never understand allegories. The two words in the language I most respect are Yes and No.' She is rather like the acrid Mrs Witt in D.H. Lawrence's *St. Mawr*. But as the story unfolds Mrs Touchett, like Mrs Witt, reveals unexpected facets. She had habitually denied herself tender emotion, on moral grounds. After Ralph's death she feels herself stranded; her morality has ceased to be adequate. 'It had come over her dimly that she had failed of something, that she saw herself in the future as an old woman without memories. Her little sharp face looked tragical.'

Her son Ralph is shown to us more fully. The ugly, good-natured, clever cousin, the sanctioned idler, aesthete, and sociable recluse, Isabel's true lover but condemned by sickness to an onlooker's role, he is, of the men characters, the one obviously closest to the novelist's own point of view. James's intention, as far as Ralph is concerned, is suggested by some remarks of his in *Hawthorne* about the new kind of 'good American' who, he thought, was emerging after the Civil War. 'He will not, I think be a sceptic, and still less, of course, a cynic; but he will be without discredit to his well-known capacity for action an observer.' This could be an account of James himself and it explains his fondness for characters like Ralph, or Strether in *The Ambassadors*.

There is humour and pathos in Ralph's self-description:

'I keep a band of music in my ante-room. It has orders to play
without stopping; it renders me two excellent services. It keeps
the sounds of the world from reaching the private apartments,
and it makes the world think that dancing's going on within.'

Ralph is mainly a commentator and mentor to the heroine, like
George Eliot's Daniel Deronda (though unlike Deronda he has
a sense of humour and is never pompous). He has, however, an
essential function in the plot. It is he who persuades his dying father
to leave Isabel half his own inheritance. 'I should like to put a little
wind in her sails . . . She wishes to be free, and your bequest will
make her free.' His fate is to live to witness the ironic result: the
fortune she inherits through his generosity is, precisely, the reason
for the loss of the freedom she so prizes.

Isabel's two unsuccessful suitors, while less interesting characters,
are necessary to the design. Lord Warburton is a convincing English
aristocrat, 'with his pleasant steady eyes, his bronzed complexion,
fresh beneath its seasoning, his manly figure, his minimizing
manner.' We have no difficulty in imagining what Isabel has
given up in rejecting him, 'the peace, the kindness, the honour, the
possessions, a deep security and a great exclusion.' James ensures,
through Ralph's witty comments, that we do not miss the irony of
a great landowner with radical views; but Warburton never seems
a humbug to the reader.

His rival the American businessman is also a fine manly fellow,
but he is otherwise very different. Isabel associates him with
'armoured weapons', 'plates of steel handsomely inlaid with gold.'
'He might have ridden, on a plunging steed, the whirlwind of a
great war.' He is a study in masculine strength, with attendant
limitations: 'his jaw was too square and set and his figure too
straight and stiff.' Caspar Goodwood is forcibly presented. Yet
he is a dead spot in the novel, one of those fictional characters
who obstinately refuse to come to life. James may have been
handicapped here by his convention of sexual inexplicitness, since
Goodwood represents something crucial for our understanding of
the psychological crisis of Isabel. 'There was a disagreeably strong
push, a kind of hardness of presence, in his way of rising before
her.' But as a character he always looks like a mere contrivance,
embarrassingly wheeled on and off as the action requires.

Caspar's successful rival, Gilbert Osmond, and Osmond's co-conspirator Madame Merle, belong to the mysterious side of the novel. They are not at first fully revealed to us, as Warburton and Goodwood are. We see them, down to chapter 36, in contrasting lights, through Isabel's admiration, or through Ralph's dislike and mistrust. Ralph says of Osmond: 'He's a vague, unexplained American who has been living these thirty years, or less, in Italy.' His adverse judgment is harsh: Osmond 'had always an eye to effect, and his effects were deeply calculated. They were produced by no vulgar means, but the motive was as vulgar as the art was great.' But Isabel is captivated. She first sees him as 'a quiet, clever, sensitive, distinguished man . . . holding by the hand a little girl whose bell-like clearness gave a new grace to childhood.' The image she carries away from her visit to his hill-top is of the vistas and ranges of steps and terraces and fountains of a formal Italian garden. The irony is poignant when we glance forward to the Isabel of later years, seeing a 'rigid system' close about her, 'shut up with an odour of mould and decay.'

Osmond is a subtle study. He married Isabel 'for the money', but not only for the money. (We feel that he would not have married Henrietta Stackpole for any money.) He was 'greatly in love with her'. He tells Isabel he would have enjoyed being Pope, and the suggestion of a corrupt Catholicism is often present, with his 'curtains and crucifixes'. He approves of convents, and sends his daughter Pansy to one, though not for religious reasons. His ex-mistress Madame Merle calls him '*very* bad', and says he has destroyed her soul. After her marriage Isabel discovers that, where Serena Merle is concerned, her husband 'seldom consented to finger, in talk, this roundest and smoothest bead of their social rosary' – a revealing and unpleasant image.

There is a poetic suggestiveness in the description of his house in Florence. 'It had heavy lids, but no eyes: the house in reality looked another way.' The function of the windows on the ground floor 'seemed less to offer communication with the world than to defy the world to look in.' His cold exultation over his capture of Isabel is creepy, and we shudder over his words to his bride-to-be: 'You're remarkably fresh, and I'm remarkably well-seasoned.' He fancies that 'he could tap her imagination with his knuckle and make it ring.' She first appeals to him as being 'as smooth to his general need of her as handled ivory to the palm.' Again we may look forward to Isabel's realization that she has been 'an applied handled hung-up tool'.

This manipulative acquisitiveness is more vivid today than Osmond's aestheticism, which has become 'period'. Correggio is no longer a name to drop, and the description of the contents of Osmond's villa does not make them sound very attractive. We are left uncertain about Osmond's taste (and about Henry James's?). As authorities on it we have to choose between Madame Merle, arbitress of elegances, who admired it, and Ned Rosier, Pansy's art-loving suitor, who did not. More important in the scheme of the novel is the spiritual significance of this 'avid and ambitious desire to take possession of the object for the benefit of the owner or even of the spectator' which Claude Levi-Strauss thinks one of the original features of the art of Western civilization.

The obscure psychology of the predator may lurk in the mystery that surrounds the main motif in the later chapters, Osmond's hatred of Isabel (and her fear of him). As she sees it, he hates her for having a mind of her own, while she fears him because his 'beautiful mind' seems to 'peep and mock' at her from 'a small high window'. (This suggests a childhood memory, or fantasy.) The deeper psychology of this failed marriage is not clear. We are shown it only from Isabel's point of view, and she sees it in an *ex parte* way and in exclusively moral terms. 'Under all his [Osmond's] culture, his cleverness, his amenity, his egotism lay hidden like a serpent in a bank of flowers.' As often in Isabel's meditations, the author's voice is mixed with hers, and we do not know quite how he has imagined the total situation.

It may be noted that Isabel seems to fall in love with Madame Merle at least as much as with Osmond. Madame Merle, with her thick fair hair, 'arranged "classically" as if she were a Juno or a Niobe', is a less original type of character. She has reminded some readers of splendid unprincipled ladies in Balzac and Thackeray. But she too is a fine Jamesian study. We understand something, if perhaps not all, of the spell she casts on Isabel. Isabel sees her as 'a woman of strong impulses kept in admirable order.' She is very taken with her competence, writing letters all the morning, painting water-colours in the afternoon, 'touching' the piano (she never 'plays' the piano, always 'touches' it) or doing embroidery in the evening. Madame Merle is a character physically. 'She declared that in England the pleasures of smell were great . . . and she used to lift the sleeve of her British overcoat and bury her nose in it, inhaling the clear, fine scent of the wool.'

The novelist's view of Madame Merle has some likeness to D.H. Lawrence's account of what he called 'social' beings. 'She's too complete,' says Ralph. He thinks she is 'almost as universally "liked" as some new volume of smooth twaddle.' Yet with her too there is a hint of mystery. When Isabel says to Ralph 'You don't like her,' Ralph replies: 'On the contrary, I was once in love with her.' This is never explained. Her general role is that of the manipulator. 'I don't pretend to know what people are meant for. I only know what I can do with them.' But, unlike Osmond, she has some of the reader's sympathy: she too has been Osmond's victim.

One of the best things in the *Portrait* is her meeting with Isabel at Pansy's convent, when Madame Merle, smoothly holding forth, suddenly realizes that her secret is known to Isabel.

> She had not proceeded far before Isabel noticed a sudden break in her voice, a lapse in her continuity, which was in itself a complete drama . . . What remained was the cleverest woman in the world standing there within a few feet of her and knowing as little what to think as the meanest. Isabel's only revenge was to be silent still – to leave Madame Merle in this unprecedented situation.

This is a wonderful scene. Nothing is said, yet both Isabel and Madame Merle understand the situation completely. James's art of reticence here foreshadows his later novels, with their understatement, indirectness, and their requirement (too demanding for some of us) that we read between the lines.

Pansy is the most significant, structurally speaking, of the minor characters. She remains to the end something of an enigma, though it is clear that she loves Isabel and dislikes her actual mother, Madame Merle. Her suitor Ned Rosier's attitude to 'the small serious damsel' resembles her father's: they both seem to be connoisseur-predators competing for the possession of a 'Dresden-china shepherdess'. But just how we are to interpret this is not clear – especially as there is a suggestion of homosexuality about Rosier.

There is no difficulty in interpreting Osmond's sister, the Countess Gemini, arriving from Florence 'with her trunks, her dresses, her chatter, her falsehoods, her frivolity, the strange, the unholy legend of the number of her lovers.' She is one of the most vividly evoked characters in the novel. It has been objected that she has too obvious a plot-function (to disclose the Merle/Osmond intrigue to Isabel). But she has a motive in her dislike of Osmond, and her eagerness to encourage her sister-in-law to defy him by travelling to England to be at Ralph's death-bed.

Henrietta Stackpole is one of James's most memorable comic characters. At first her vulgarity, and her eyes 'like large polished buttons', grate on us as they do on Ralph. He complains that 'she walks in without knocking at the door'. But she is also said, pleasantly, to be 'as crisp and comprehensive as a first issue before the folding'. She aspires to be 'the Queen of American Journalism': she is a portent of the age of 'the media' that lies ahead. But she amuses the reader. And she is kindly and warm-hearted, as both Isabel and Ralph readily recognize. James accuses himself in his preface of 'overtreatment' here. Henrietta was meant to be only a *ficelle*, a term he introduced into literary criticism to describe a character who can be used for as many sorts of purpose as the action may demand. Henrietta can be obtuse, or shrewdly intelligent, or charitable and generous, according to what scene she is in. Actually she is more interesting than that. At times she seems not only more sensible but more likeable than the heroine. And she contributes a welcome lightness to the story.

But of course the effect of *The Portrait of a Lady* depends on what we make of Isabel. How attractive and admirable is she if at all? About James's main aim there can be no doubt. The novel was to be the story of how a particular young woman 'affronts her destiny'. He could have told another story, for example about one of Isabel's sisters, who are described: the novel is the genre that pays homage to contingency. But he has chosen instead to 'organize an ado' about Isabel Archer. Her qualification to be the heroine is her 'fine awareness'. She can understand what happens to her.

What sort of character is Isabel meant to be? Some critics, remembering James's interest in the inveterately symbolic Hawthorne, have seen a hint of allegory in her 'fixed determination to regard the world as a place of brightness, of free expansion, of irresistible action.' There has been speculation about her historical ancestry, which may go back to Crèvecoeur's 'new man', or James's own Christopher Newman in *The American*; and parallels have been found with Huckleberry Finn or Jay Gatsby, or the antinomian heroes of J.D. Salinger or Saul Bellow. Isabel's keynote is her insistence on her independence: 'I'm very fond of my liberty.' Osmond tells her: 'You can do exactly what you choose; you can roam through space.' Space, we know, is 'the final frontier'. Does Isabel have an American obsession with boundless space? She is very taken with Saint Peter's, Rome, because it fits her 'conception of greatness', which afterwards 'never lacked space to soar'. Some readers think of Emerson and his Transcendentalism; 'Yet what is my faith? What am I? What but a thought of serenity and independence, an abode in the deep blue sky?' And the very pointedly presented discussion of clothes between Isabel and Madame Merle, in chapter 14, while not easy to interpret, does at any rate convey that free self-expression, in whatever form it takes, is a positive virtue.

But the girl we are introduced to at the beginning is very much an individual – and a limited and erring one. She is ignorant and inexperienced. Mrs Touchett says Isabel thinks she knows a great deal about the world, like most American girls, 'but like most American girls she's ridiculously mistaken.' James himself in his narrator's voice speaks of her 'meagre knowledge', 'her inflated ideals', 'her confidence at once innocent and dogmatic'. These of course can be taken to be characteristic American limitations, but they need not be. It is not only Americans who have an imagination 'by habit ridiculously active'. The special circumstances of her upbringing are part of the case. Her dead father, 'handsome and much loved', had told her nothing of the unpleasant side of life, and she and her sisters had had 'no regular education and no permanent home – they had been at once spoiled and neglected.'

She is certainly not perfect. It is hard not to see self-satisfaction in her belief that her nature had 'a garden-like quality'. We are told that 'she was always planning out her development, desiring her perfection, observing her progress'. She can seem patronizing, even a little callous. When Caspar tells her: 'You'll get very sick of your independence' she replies: 'Perhaps I

shall; it's even very probable. When that day comes I shall
be very glad to see you.' There is something curious, and
unattractive, about her ideal of happiness, 'to be in a better position for appreciating people than they are for appreciating you.'

It is not hard to accumulate evidence proving her to be a
self-centred egotist. But in the later part of the novel our
sympathy is undoubtedly enlisted for her as a tragic heroine.
And it is difficult to believe that we are ever invited to pass
a totally adverse judgment on her. Critics unfriendly to Isabel
have usually preferred to take the view that James himself does
not realize how great her shortcomings are.

This was the position taken by F.R. Leavis in his very influential
essay in *The Great Tradition* (1948). Leavis suggested an interesting
explanation for James's attitude to Isabel. He argued that it came
about because James had closely studied George Eliot's last novel
Daniel Deronda (1876), and had been deeply impressed by the
situation of the heroine, Gwendolen Harleth. According to Leavis
the story of Isabel is really a variation on the story of Gwendolen.
'Isabel Archer is Gwendolen Harleth seen by a man' – a man who,
unlike the woman writer George Eliot, is a little complaisant, a
little blind to his heroine's faults, and who does not provide
a sufficient justifying situation, as George Eliot does, for her
tragedy.

Is this view correct? There can be no doubt, as Bernard Shaw
pointed out in the 1890s, that James learned from George
Eliot. His manner is lighter and crisper, and he does not stop
for explanations and moralizing as she does, but the literary
relationship is undeniable. James had known George Eliot personally, and in a letter of May 1869 had even professed himself
'in love with this great horse-faced bluestocking'. She is mentioned in the *Portrait* as one of the modern authors Isabel reads.
Nor is there any doubt that he had carefully studied *Daniel
Deronda*. He composed a very searching 'Conversation' about it
in 1876.

But the parallel between Isabel and Gwendolen does not
seem close. Here is the opening of *Daniel Deronda*, in which
Gwendolen is seen, through Deronda's eyes, at the gaming
table.

Was she beautiful or not beautiful? and what was the secret of form or expression which gave the dynamic quality to her glance? Was the good or the evil genius dominant in those beams? Probably the evil; else why was the effect that of unrest rather than that of undisturbed charm? Why was the wish to look again felt as coercion and not as a longing to which the whole being consents?

None of that sounds like Isabel. That is not the timbre in which she is spoken of. There is no 'Lamia beauty' about her. She is never shown at the gaming table. Her character is different. Isabel is 'outgoing', forms friendly and affectionate relationships with several men and women. There is no reason to think that Gwendolen cares for anyone (except perhaps her mother) till she falls in love with Deronda. Their stories are quite different. Gwendolen's problems are due to the financial ruin of her family. For Isabel the situation is exactly opposite: old Mr Touchett's legacy makes her rich and independent. Gwendolen is tempted into a bad marriage at the expense of another's claim; she yields to temptation after a moral conflict. From then on she is full of guilt. Isabel has no moral conflict and no guilt. She is the victim of a conspiracy, like Maggie in *The Golden Bowl*, or Milly in *The Wings of the Dove*; or a case of betrayed innocence, like the child heroine of *What Maisie Knew*. Isabel is an example of *hamartia*, as Aristotle called it: not a moralistic idea of tragic disaster as the punishment for sin, but the destruction of a hero or heroine because of a false step taken in blindness. Moreover it was 'a generous mistake', as Ralph says. Gwendolen is a case of poetic justice, one egotist trapped by another. Surely we do not feel that this is true of Isabel by the time we reach the scene at Ralph's death-bed?

Leavis tends to discuss Isabel as if she were a person in real life whom James is misrepresenting. When George Eliot says 'Gwendolen was not a general favourite with her own sex' Leavis, with suggestive italics, says 'James *tells* us nothing like this about Isabel'. He admits that Isabel *is* a favourite with her own sex, but he hints that James has concealed something: in such a girl 'there must have been expressions of her "preoccupation with self" and her "sense of her own absoluteness".' This seems either to equate fiction with biography, or to require James to have written a quite different book. Leavis thinks Isabel wilful and perverse, and he points out that Isabel's good friends, her aunt and Ralph, urge her not to marry Osmond, while Gwendolen's good friends urge her to marry Grandcourt. But her aunt wants Isabel to make a socially advantageous match, such as Warburton. As for Ralph, he is in love with her, and so is a hardly disinterested adviser. Neither of them has anything definite against Osmond, though they see that he is a poseur.

Nor is it easy to agree with Leavis's assertion that 'Osmond . . . plainly *is* Grandcourt, hardly disguised'. True, both men are egotists and cold fish, and both pretend to despise public opinion while secretly much concerned with it. But few characters in fiction seem more different than the sporting Grandcourt only happy on horseback, and the scholar-aesthete Osmond brooding over his coins; the Englishman a probable baronet and peer, and the 'obscure American dilettante', as Mrs Touchett calls him, with no social position. And what about Osmond's 'beautiful mind?'? There is no suggestion that Grandcourt *had* a mind, let alone that it was beautiful. If we are to have a parallel with George Eliot Isabel's mistake is more like Dorothea's in *Middlemarch*. But Osmond and Casaubon are quite different also.

Was Isabel someone in real life? Henry James's nephew, editing his father's letters, said that two of James's most appealing heroines, Isabel Archer and Milly Theale in *The Wings of the Dove*, were 'drawn from the image' of James's beloved cousin, Mary ('Minny') Temple, who died in 1870 at the age of 24. Leon Edel in his life of James accepted this identification. Theories involving long-dead people are hard to prove or disprove. Isabel seems quite different from Milly. They do not sound as if they were based on the same person. Isabel is called beautiful, and she is a willowy brunette with grey eyes. Milly is 'agreeably angular' and her hair is exceptionally red. She is 'slim, constantly pale, delicately haggard'. She is presented quite differently from Isabel, in James's words 'circuitously . . . as an unspotted princess is ever dealt with . . . the pressure all round her kept easy for her, the sounds, the movements regulated, the forms and ambiguities.' Isabel is vibrant, self-assured, 'affronting her destiny'. Milly is a Dove. The Dove does not 'affront' anything.

A better real-life model is surely James himself. The autobiographical 'feel' of the account of Isabel's early life in chapter 3, when we see her in the old house at Albany, can be amply confirmed from Edel's biography. *The Portrait of a Lady* is in many ways a *Portrait of the Artist*. But James 'is' other characters as well – notably Ralph Touchett. And it can be plausibly argued, as indeed Edel does, that he 'is' Osmond too. Where do these identifications stop?

Biographical questions apart, the chief problem in *The Portrait of a Lady* is the ending: Isabel's final decision. Just what happens? Few will agree with H.R. Hays (*Hound and Horn*, VIII, 1934) who thought that the story is 'resolved into a conventional happy ending with a divorce and rescue by the American business man.' Surely it is made clear in Isabel's long meditation in chapter 42 that she is condemned 'for the rest of her life' to 'the house of darkness, the house of dumbness, the house of desolation.' (Apart from that, she is not in love with Goodwood.) She makes no attempt to leave Osmond, even at the direct urging of Henrietta. Warburton and Goodwood discover her unhappiness, but she sends them away. Though she disobeyed Osmond to be with the dying Ralph, she goes back to him.

Granted that this is what happens, is it artistically satisfying? James in his Notebooks says that the obvious criticism will be that he had not 'seen the heroine to the end of her situation, that I had left her *en l'air*.' If James did not see Isabel to the end of her situation, should he have given more definite hints what that would be? There may be advantages in this open-ended conclusion. It is hard to imagine any other that would have been right.

What was Isabel's motive for returning? There is some mystery here, but a few things are clear. First of all, Isabel took marriage very seriously, as Osmond says *he* does. She does not take a 'modern' view of it. 'Certain obligations were involved in the very fact of marriage, and were quite independent of the quantity of enjoyment extracted from it.' And she has a further motive for staying with Osmond in her promise to Pansy.

But several critics (Dupee, Matthiessen for instance) have felt that these motives are not dramatically adequate. Some think that Isabel in flight from Goodwood's kiss is showing herself to be puritanical, like Hawthorne – only more so. Others have seen her as essentially virginal (though she had borne Osmond a child). Her resistance and flight from Goodwood are partly on account of her aversion to sexual possession. It is the very attraction she feels towards Goodwood that makes her do what she thinks her duty and go back to her husband.

Certainly the motif of fear seems important. Isabel is afraid of Goodwood, afraid of Warburton, and (as she admits) afraid of herself. For all her passion for freedom, and her inquisitiveness about life, there is something cautious and theoretical about her. When she thinks Warburton is about to propose she wishes 'both to elude the intention and satisfy her curiosity'. Ralph tells her: 'You want to see, but not to feel.' She has been compared to an earlier James heroine, the convent-trained Madame de Mauves, as a study of the ascetic temperament. But her cry to Osmond 'We don't live decently together!' suggests that they ought to have sexual relations, which have now ceased.

The source of her fear must remain undefined, a matter of suggestion. The plot has already disclosed Isabel's illusions about her freedom; she thought she was free, but she was manipulated, not only by the conspirators, but by the fairy godmother and the saintly invalid. And the final irony may be that when some real freedom does seem to open up for her she is afraid of it. After Goodwood's assault the world around her seems 'to take the form of a mighty sea, where she floated in fathomless waters.' It is from this that she flees as her story ends. And the well-meaning Henrietta, seeking briskly to console Goodwood, is given the suitably ambiguous closing note.

Chapter 11
On The Golden Bowl

'. . . really quite unique – so that, though the whole thing is a little *baroque*, its value as a specimen is, I believe, almost inestimable'.

(Charlotte Verver in chapter 38)

The Golden Bowl (1904) is often regarded as Henry James's masterpiece, but it is a profoundly mysterious and baffling work. There are two reasons for this. One of them stares the reader in the face: the peculiarity of James's later style, a peculiarity which it shares with the other major novels from that phase of his career, *The Wings of the Dove* (1902) and *The Ambassadors* (1903). A preliminary intimidating sample of this style may be tasted in the Preface which James wrote for the New York edition of the novel (1909). Seasoned *aficionados* may be able to interpret what James says there about 'representational values' and other features of the novelist's art, such as the superiority of indirect to direct presentation; they may even grasp what he says against the kind of illustrations to novels that display recognizable characters or episodes. But few will be able to say with any confidence whether James pronounces for or against the frontispieces which adorn the New York edition!

A thorough discussion of James's late style would require an investigation of the whole problem, human and artistic, presented by the old man of Lamb House, Rye. James found some other great Victorians, such as Tennyson and Browning, both of whom he knew personally, bewilderingly unlike their work. But everyone acquainted with James agreed that he *was* like his work. The style is part of the human 'case' so amusingly documented in the Letters in Leon Edel's biography, or in the anecdotes collected in *The Legend of the Master* (Nowell-Smith, 1947). Its peculiarity has sometimes been explained by James's habit, in later life, of dictating to a secretary, who took down all his qualifications and hesitations. Whether or not that is the correct explanation, there is no doubt that many readers, including some who enjoy James's earlier work, have been as exasperated by it as his elder brother was. William James told Henry that his own stylistic ideal was 'to say a thing in one sentence as straight and explicit as it can be made, and then drop it forever', whereas Henry's was 'to avoid naming it straight, but by dint of breathing and sighing all round and around it, to arouse in the reader who may have had a similar perception already (Heaven help him if he hasn't!) the illusion of a solid object, made (like the ghost in the Polytechnic) wholly out of impalpable materials, air and the prismatic interferences of light, ingeniously focused by mirrors upon empty space.' He implored Henry to 'say it *out*, for God's sake, and have done with it.' He accused him of having become 'a curiosity of literature'. 'For gleams and innuendos and felicitous verbal insinuations you are unapproachable, but the *core* of literature is solid. Give it to us once again!' But this plea, from the greatest American philosopher and psychologist to the greatest American novelist, was not granted. These brothers had some things in common (including a sense of humour) but literary style was not one of them.

So distinctive a manner as the later James's has inevitably been much parodied, either in a friendly way, as by W.H. Auden in *The Sea and the Mirror*, or James Thurber ('The Beast in the Dingle') or maliciously, as by H.G. Wells in *Boon* or Kingsley Amis in *I Like It Here*. (The finest of all the parodies is Max Beerbohm's 'The Guerdon', revealing Beerbohm's uncanny ability to get inside the skin of Jamesian syntax and vocabulary. While we read it, it is impossible not to believe that James is the writer.) A few of its stylistic features may be noted.

1. *Distaste for adjectives*, reported by Theodora Bosanquet, James's amanuensis. Here are some examples from *The Golden Bowl*: instead of 'flat statement', he writes 'flatness of statement'; for 'bright high harmony' he writes 'brightness of high harmony'; for 'this humble welcome' he writes 'the humility of this welcome'. (On the other hand, he has a passion for adverbs.)

2. *Heightened cliché*. See the discussion of this in Lodge (1966). 'Just these things in themselves, however, with all the rest, his

fixed purpose now, his committed deed, the fine pink glow, projected forward, of his ships, behind him, definitely blazing and crackling . . .' (from chapter 12). A Jamesian development from 'he had burnt his boats'.

3. What linguists call the *cleft sentence*. Examples abound: 'Under this particular impression it was that everything in Maggie most melted and went to pieces.' Detailed discussion of this and many other of James's stylistic traits can be found in Short (1946), Watt (1960), and more fully in Chatman (1972).

4. *Ellipsis.* This is a common source of obscurity in James's later novels. Much of the dialogue is made cryptic by a speaker breaking off short, 'Your husband has never, never, never —' (chapter 33). Often the conversation in *The Golden Bowl* consists of obliquities, euphemisms, equivocations, and lies; the participants are at cross-purposes, or draw false inferences. Ellipsis serves an important purpose here.

5. *Colloquialism and slang.* A hallmark of late James is the inter-mittent appearance of colloquialism, often nestling inside quotation marks, in a context that is florid and circumlocutory. (This is a trick James has in common with Mr Micawber.) Sometimes the meaning is momentarily obscure because the slang has dated. 'It had been for all the world as if Charlotte had been "had in".' James, of course, was more than a 'society novelist', but he *was* a society novelist, and his style has the flavour of society small-talk, the variety of social nuance, expected in that kind of book. But nothing is more ephemeral than upper-class slang; as soon as it becomes current it becomes unfashionable. See Girling (1973).

6. *Deixis.* This technical term from linguistics refers to the fact that some words have a deictic or pointing function, referring backward or forward to other words. Ian Watt's discussion of James's use of 'it' in *The Ambassadors* is well known, Other examples are 'something', 'item', 'matter', 'one', 'another'. The use of these colourless words to replace abstractions – intangible nouns, or whole clauses or sentences, or even vaguer referents – is the chief cause of the difficulty in reading James's later novels. The mystified reader must be prepared to cope with a flood of *its, whats, thats, theses, whiches*, most of them of the murkiest antecedents.

7. *Personified abstractions.* James's grammar converts these into entities as substantial as – some might say more substantial than

– the persons in the story. There is a suggestive discussion by Chatman (1972) of a passage in chapter 26.

> that consciousness, lately born in [Maggie], had been taught the evening before to accept a temporary lapse, but had quickly enough again, with her getting out of her own house and her walking half across the town. . . . found breath still in its lungs. . . . It exhaled this breath in a sigh, faint and unheard.

Chatman asks 'Unheard by whom?' By Maggie, of course. 'Later, the two – she and this consciousness-with-lungs – are rejoined, like fellow-conspirators in a secret cell.' A little further on we read:

> Meanwhile . . . the prior, the prime impression had remained, in the manner of a spying servant, on the other side of a barred threshold, a witness availing himself, in time, of the lightest pretext to re-enter. It was as if he had found this pretext in her observed necessity of comparing – comparing obvious common elements in her husband's and her stepmother's ways of now 'taking' her. With or without her witness, at any rate, she was led by comparison.

This 'impression', this 'witness', has taken on flesh and blood as 'a spying servant'. 'Her observed necessity of comparing' – *who* has observed that Maggie has felt this necessity? An 'impression' – or rather, 'an impression as spying servant'.

This abundance of metaphor is the most striking feature of the style of the novel. All that the reader of *The Golden Bowl* is asked to do, said H.G. Wells, is to clamber over metaphors. When I first tried to read it I was under the impression that Maggie kept her husband in a pagoda (see the opening of chapter 25). An unwary reader might read the following sentence as saying that Charlotte had suddenly and startlingly committed a violent assault on Maggie.

> Oh, the 'advantage', it was perfectly enough, in truth with Mrs. Verver; for what was Maggie's own sense but that of having been thrown over on her back, with her neck, from the first, half broken and her helpless face staring up? (chapter 36).

It might even be said that the interpretative problems of the novel turn on the question of what is metaphorical and what is literal.

But James's metaphors are not there to mystify, but to illustrate, to exemplify, to explain, to elaborate. He has been criticized for their frequent triteness, but I think Chatman is right when he says that James's purpose in using metaphor was not poetic. He was concerned with the tissue of society and the psychology of those who live in it, with speech, current speech; and it is the dead and dying metaphors that are on everyone's lips, not the unusual, freshly minted metaphors of the poet. There has been much speculation on why James wrote like this. It is sometimes said that in his later novels, and in his revision of earlier ones such as *Roderick Hudson* (1875), his concern was to make his language more particular, specific and concrete. But what really happens is that his later style increases in *intangibility* – though at the same time, as we have seen, becoming (as if in compensation) more metaphorical. Many readers have been baffled. Vernon Lee (1923) wondered whether James was practising a kind of natural selection among readers, by making his style into an obstacle-course.

Yet it would be a mistake to suppose that the difficulties of the novel could be removed by translating the novel into a more straightforward linguistic idiom. There are, no doubt, stories by the later James in which his absurd verbal affectations merely confuse the reader and muffle whatever it was that the author had to communicate; but in *The Golden Bowl* the obliqueness belongs to the essence of the work.

And this brings me to the second reason for the obscurity of *The Golden Bowl*. The problem is not just to make out what the characters in it are up to, but what our attitude towards what they are up to is meant to be. In James's own words in the Preface, the problem is to find out what the author's 'active sense of life' is: 'to keep one's hand on it,' he says, 'is to hold the silver clue to the whole labyrinth of his consciousness.' A felicitous expression: *The Golden Bowl* is a labyrinth. Writers of short introductions to the novel (like this one) must recognize that it would be a perverse enterprise to get the reader out of the state of mind that James so clearly wants to get him into. A critic hunting for the 'silver clue' to the novel must not sound too peremptory if he is to help others to savour its special quality. 'It shook between them, this transparency, with their very breath; it was an exquisite tissue, but stretched on a frame, and would give way the next instant if either breathed too hard.' (chapter 37.) In the words of the poet Donne, it is 'gold to airy thinness beat'.

The Golden Bowl, like many of James's stories, had its origin in a situation of real life. He records in the Notebooks that he had been told

> about a simultaneous marriage in Paris . . . of a father and daughter – an only daughter. The daughter – American of course – is engaged to a young Englishman, and the father, a widower and still youngish, has sought in marriage at exactly the same time an American girl of very much the same age as is his daughter.

'I see a little tale, *n'est-ce pas?*' James wrote,

> in the idea that they all shall have married, with this characteristic consequence – that the daughter fails to hold the affection of the young English husband, whose approximate mother-in-law the pretty young second wife of the father will have now become. The father *doesn't* lose the daughter nearly as much as he feared, or expected, for her marriage which has but half gratified her leaves her *des loisirs*, and she devotes them to him. They spend large parts of their time together, they cling together, and weep and wonder together, and are ever *more* thrown together.
>
> *Mettons* that this second wife is nearly as young as her daughter-in-law – and prettier and cleverer – she knows more what she is about. *Mettons* even that the younger husband has known her before, has liked her, etc. – been attracted to her, and would have married her if she had had any money. She was poor – the father was very rich, and that was her inducement to marry the father. The latter has settled a handsome *dot* on his daughter (leaving himself also plenty to live on) and the young husband is therefore thoroughly at his ease.
>
> They feel abandoned, yet they feel consoled, with *each other*, and they don't see in the business in the least what every one else sees in it . . . A necessary basis for all this must have been an intense and exceptional degree of attachment between the father and daughter – he peculiarly paternal, she passionately filial.

James at first thought of this situation as the basis for a short story or *nouvelle*, but (as often happened) it grew in scale as he

worked on it. In the course of developing it into *The Golden Bowl*
he was excited to come upon what he called in the Notebooks an
'exquisite truth'.

> I almost hold my breath with suspense as I try to formulate it;
> so much, so *much*, hangs radiantly there as depending on it . . .
> the divine principle is a key that, working in the same *general*
> way, fits the complicated chambers of *both* the dramatic and the
> narrative lock.

As usual it is not easy to make out quite what James is saying here,
but the gist of it seems to be that he felt he had discovered a way
of actualizing the kind of highly formal and artificial plot which
had fascinated him in the Parisian theatre with the resources
of the modern novel, its breadth and inwardness, its apparent
incalculability.

So this ambitious novel-drama was to become another of James's
studies of the international theme. The 'father' becomes Adam
Verver, the plutocrat, from somewhere west of the Mississippi. He
is in Europe on a special mission, to ransack it for *objets d'art* to fill
a museum in his home town, American City, to which he plans to
retire as a sort of Citizen Kane, though in his general amiability
he more resembles Daniel Touchett in *The Portrait of a Lady*. But
Touchett has something of the New England patriarch about
him, whereas Verver is a Westerner who has made his millions
in the 'Gilded Age' that followed the American Civil War. As a
younger man he discovered a gift for business which made him
fabulously wealthy; in later life he discovered an equally great gift
for collecting works of art. He is said to be famous for his fine taste,
like one of the great European royal or noble patrons; he thinks
of himself as a 'Patron of Art', and he 'was ashamed' of Pope
Julius II's maltreatment of Michelangelo. But Julius II did at least
employ Michelangelo, while Verver does not (apparently) take up
any living artist, or commission a single work. He is only interested
in what is already established and guaranteed as old, distinguished
and admirable. One further feature of his aestheticism should be
noted: like the literary critic Northrop Frye he cuts art off from
emotion. He puts his daughter Maggie's gifts to him in a glass case,
apart from other things in his collection, because they are associated
with personality and feeling.

It is in this spirit of aesthetic connoisseurship that he and his daughter acquire a member of an ancient family, the Italian Prince Amerigo, who has charm and wit and taste, but no fortune. Amerigo is a sort of Jamesian version of Prince Stepan Arkadyovich Oblonsky, Anna Karenina's brother-in-law; good-natured, pleasant, charming – and very virile – he tells his fairy godmother Fanny Assingham that he has no moral sense. He is a Roman aristocrat: one of his favourite terms of praise is *galantuomo*. He fully appreciates the luxurious life, the bath of gold, which the Ververs generously provide for him; but he is increasingly baffled by the 'great white curtain' that seems to hang between him and his wife and father-in-law.

Later Adam marries a beautiful Europeanized American girl, Charlotte Stant – perhaps not such a resplendent piece for his collection, but at any rate a distinguished bargain. In a scene very typical of *The Golden Bowl* the tycoon makes his curious, passionless, veiled proposal to her against the background of their hunt for some Damascene tiles owned by Mr Guterman-Seuss – the same background of Jewish antiquarianism as the shop in which the Prince and Charlotte, and much later Maggie, come upon the gilded bowl (with a secret flaw in it) which supplies the title for the novel.

What the Ververs do not know is that the Prince and Charlotte had had a love affair – at any rate, a close relationship – which had been brought to an end because the pair were not rich enough to marry. Readers of *The Wings of the Dove* will remember the Kate Croy/Merton Densher situation, and Charlotte has something of the resourcefulness, vigour and ruthlessness of Kate – something, too, of that carnality (surprising in a novelist like James, so often thought of as sexless) which adds a strange touch of poignancy. But later on Charlotte seems more like the Princess Casamassima, or Madame Merle in *The Portrait of a Lady*. She is repeatedly called 'grand' and 'great', and the Verver plan for her is that she should be a gracious hostess and museum curator and a sort of super-social-secretary who will supply the American millionaires with the European polish and worldly knowledge which they lack. She will blaze splendidly with Verver diamonds.

Her other assigned function is to console Adam lest he should feel unhappy on account of the 'loss' of his daughter. But actually the father and daughter seem to spend as much time together as before, and when Maggie in due time produces a Principino (another fine 'piece' for the collection) Adam and Maggie busy themselves exclusively with the child. Not only do they leave the Prince and Charlotte to their own devices, they seem positively to encourage their public appearances together.

The 'inevitable' happens and the Prince and his stepmother resume their earlier intimate relationship, in a clandestine fashion. Maggie comes to know of it, and, without anyone ever saying anything explicit to anyone else, she conducts a fierce secret struggle to recover her husband's affection and send Charlotte off with Adam to American City.

This kind of summary would distort any novel and is particularly damaging to *The Golden Bowl*, since James's method, which he descants on in the Preface, is not to tell the story omnisciently, in the Victorian manner he banished from the modern novel, but to present it indirectly, often through 'reflectors'. The reader is expected to pick up hints, make guesses, as the characters do. In Book I we see the (very slowly moving) 'action' almost entirely from the point of view of the Prince; in Book II mainly from the point of view of Maggie. From time to time we have also a sort of choric (though not specially privileged) commentary from a bizarre couple called Colonel and Mrs Assingham, whose sole occupation in life appears to consist in gossiping about the Ververs. But we rarely are allowed to know Adam's or Charlotte's thoughts, and as the thematic material of *The Golden Bowl* again and again is concerned with 'knowledge', the question of what this or that person does or does not know about the situation as it develops constitutes a crucial part of the mystery.

The main problem of the novel is the balance of sympathy. In the Notebooks sketch of the story this seems clear. 'The subject,' James said, 'is really the pathetic simplicity and good faith of the father and daughter in their abandonment.' And in *The Golden Bowl* itself it is natural to suppose that we are meant to be on Maggie's side. She is the chief character, and half the book is devoted to her struggle to save her marriage. Some commentators on the novel side with her so extremely that they see in her an allegorical figure, a type of Christ, or a symbol of the Holy Spirit. (On this view Adam Verver, remote and enigmatic and prayed to, is

God the Father.) Other critics do not go so far in their exaltation of Maggie. They admit that though sympathetic and attractive she does commit errors. But they emphasize the deceitfulness and unscrupulousness of Charlotte – see for example Owen (1963).

There is in fact no agreement about what the novel says. A glance at the representative selection of commentaries I have included in the Bibliography will show that the critics are divided. The difficulty with the 'natural' pro-Verver reading is that we have to swallow the buying of the Prince, and this sticks in some readers' throats. They hate *The Golden Bowl* because they find in it the expression of a kind of American idealistic materialism, or materialistic idealism, serene in its conviction that money can buy anything. Also the guilty pair, whatever their sins, seem more like normal people than the quasi-incestuous father and daughter, huddled in their private world. But did James realize that he had made the Ververs repulsive? William Empson thought that he did not: James, he believed, was 'morally a very confused man'. F.R. Leavis says that 'if our sympathies are anywhere they are with Charlotte and (a little) the Prince, who represent what, against the general moral background of the book, can only strike us as decent passion; in a stale, sickly and oppressive atmosphere they represent life.' Leavis can only account for what he sees as James's strange unawareness that the Ververs might appear distasteful by supposing that he was so concerned with 'technical elaboration' that he 'lost his full sense of life and let his moral taste slip into abeyance.'

Another reading, worked out in detail by Firebaugh (1955) agrees with the critics who think the Ververs repugnant but argues that James *meant* them to be so. In that case the novel is a deliberate and scathing exposure of American acquisitiveness, aesthetic in the case of Adam, psychological and spiritual in the case of Maggie – and the moral corruption that goes with it.

A more popular reading, developed by critics such as Crews (1957), Anderson (1958), and Krook (1962), regards the novel as fundamentally a religious allegory. Anderson in particular argues that Henry James wrote the novel (together with *The Ambassadors* and *The Wings of the Dove*) as one constituent of a vast three-part symbolic 'morality' about Man, based on the ideas of his father, who was himself deeply influenced by the mysticism of Swedenborg. (George Santayana describes Henry James Senior as 'one of those somewhat obscure sages whom early America produced: mystics of independent mind, hermits in the desert of business, heretics in the churches.')

This is a specialist contribution and needs careful sifting, but it must be pointed out that even if it is accepted it does not by itself solve the problem I have mentioned. If the Ververs are to represent God the Father and God the Holy Spirit, &c., they cannot at the same time be seen as vultures of American acquisitiveness. Perhaps a more balanced view is possible, in which Maggie is seen as neither a saint nor a witch? – see Wright (1957). Of course how we read a novel depends on the assumptions we bring to it, and the subject of American cultural relations with Europe is one which can still easily stir up passions. The obscurity of the style and the proliferating, wide-ranging implications of the imagery make it certain that so long as *The Golden Bowl* has readers they will differ about it: it is Henry James's *Hamlet*. There seem to be four possibilities.

1. James meant us to sympathize with the Ververs (Adam and Maggie) and they are sympathetic.
2. James meant us to sympathize with the Ververs but they are unsympathetic.
3. James did not mean us to sympathize with the Ververs and they are unsympathetic.
4. James did not mean us to sympathize with the Ververs but they are sympathetic. (I have never come across anyone, in print or in person, who took this view.)

For the sake of completeness, a fifth possibility must be contemplated; that the novel is, as Frank Kermode puts it, one of those works by James that 'create gaps that cannot be closed, only gloried in; they solicit mutually contradictory types of attention and close only on a problem of closure.' In other words, *The Golden Bowl* may be radically ambiguous, and, whether inadvertently or not, James may not have given us enough data to reconcile the contradictions.

It is not the business of a short introduction to adjudicate among these possibilities. 'Find out for yourself!' as Maggie tells the Prince (chapter 34). But I will offer, briefly, a personal opinion. I think the allegorical interpretation of *The Golden Bowl* is difficult. If America is the New Eden, as it is in Henry James Senior's system, why is it conveyed to us that Charlotte is punished by being sent there, led by a silken halter, as Maggie imagines it? America is where the 'bad' people go in Henry James – like Madame Merle in the *Portrait*. Or was James himself in two minds about it? He loved and admired his father, the American idealist, yet he himself hated being in America and preferred to live in France or England. Other elements in the allegory do not convince me. I cannot accept Adam Verver, in his white waistcoat, as a convincing embodiment of God the Father. Do we have to believe that there is an allegory at all? There is no hint of it in the sketch in the Notebooks. (Nor, by the way, is there anything there about the Golden Bowl itself, so important for symbolic explications – see Anderson's discussion – so clumsy, obtrusive and Ibsen-like for non-symbolist readers.)

As for the balance of sympathies, I suggest that there is more of a problem about Adam than about Maggie. However unfairly, a wronged woman gets our sympathy, a cuckold our contempt. I find it impossible not to see Maggie as belonging among those radically innocent American heroines who are always treated tenderly by the novelist; Daisy Miller, Verena Tarrant of *The Bostonians*, Isabel and Henrietta in *The Portrait of a Lady*, Milly in *The Wings of the Dove*. But of course – James was well aware – none more so of the possible ambiguities of innocence.

Considered as a realistic or historical novel, *The Golden Bowl* may be thought to contain some improbabilities. One occurs at an important point in the plot, when the second-hand dealer sells Maggie the Bowl and then, stricken with remorse, comes next day to point out the defect in it and admit that he has overcharged her. This man, besides having a remarkably fine conscience for one of his profession, appears to enjoy total recall, for he not only recognizes in Maggie's room photographs of Charlotte and Amerigo, the lady and gentleman who had inspected the Bowl years earlier, but the exact date of their visit to his shop. A more serious defect is the often tedious and unlifelike conversation of the Assinghams. Edith Wharton observes that 'this insufferable and incredible couple spend their days in espionage and delation, and their evenings in exchanging the reports of their eavesdropping with a minuteness and precision worthy of Scotland Yard.'

These may be minor points, of 'treatment' rather than 'essence'. But the character of Adam Verver is central to the story, and there must be grave doubts about his credibility. James admitted in the preface to *The Reverberator* that 'before the American businessman' he was 'absolutely and irredeemably helpless, with no fibre of my intelligence responding to his mystery.' It seems pointless to compare Adam with contemporary depictions of robber barons, such as those of Theodore Dreiser in *The Financier* (1912) and *The Titan* (1914). These men – if they may be called that – belong to something imaginable as real life; Adam in comparison is a fairytale figure. If criteria of realism are relevant, it might be pointed out that the kind of art-connoisseur that he is would be more likely to be one of the second or third generation descendants of a robber baron, rather than a robber baron himself. James himself created a much more plausible first-generation millionaire in the repulsive Abel Gaw (in his unfinished novel *The Ivory Tower*).

Is the whole 'world' of the novel imaginable? One day Edith Wharton suddenly asked James: 'What was your idea in suspending the four principal characters in *The Golden Bowl* in the void? What sort of life did they lead when they were not watching each other, and fencing with each other? Why have you stripped them of all the *human fringes* we necessarily trail after us through life?' James's surprised reply was 'My dear – I didn't know I had!' But had he?

If *The Golden Bowl* is implausible, difficult to read and morally problematic, why bother with it? Many readers do not. The only 'problem' it deals with is that of people who have too much money. The impatient cannot enter into this drama of mind-readers in which nothing happens; they do not care whether there was or was not a pea under the eight mattresses. And if William James is right that 'the *core* of literature is solid', it is hard to refute them. But other readers have been fascinated by the extraordinary way in which Henry James invented a language to dramatize the inner life of human beings, and so created the twentieth-century novel of Proust, of Dorothy Richardson, of Joyce, of Faulkner. Few even of his hostile critics have denied that he had a fine comic gift, a deep and cunning insight into feelings, a subtle sense of place and atmosphere, of London seasons and weather and time of day. And to many of us he seems, with all his rarifications, to have the essential gift of the novelist, the gift of Scheherezade; in this novel which some fling aside because nothing happens, others are kept eagerly turning pages to find out what happens next.

Any interpretation of the novel must take into account the fact that James was a very unusual kind of writer dealing with an unusual kind of subject. He is making art out of people who have themselves turned life into an art; he writes about, and out of, a world of self-exiled cultivated Americans wandering about Europe – London, Paris, Rome – untroubled by any passion except curiosity, since no other great interests, such as commerce or politics, any longer compete for their attention. His is a world of fine shades, artificial, finicking even; going there we may seem to be turning our backs on reality, yet at moments, strangely enough, we find ourselves at the heart of it. To the sympathetic reader of *The Golden Bowl* the perusal of the novel can be almost as exciting an adventure as the conception and the writing of it were for James himself. For it is the artistic impression that must receive the final stress. To the reader who enjoys it the novel will appear as Bach's Chaconne for unaccompanied Violin appeared to Brahms. 'Using the technique adapted to a small instrument the man writes a whole world of the deepest thoughts and the most powerful feelings.'

Chapter 12
On The Jungle Books

The Jungle Books, the most popular of Kipling's prose works, were written in the 1890s, the second phase of his literary career. Rudyard Kipling (1865–1936) was a young English journalist who had enjoyed a spectacular success as a fiction-writer and poet, first in India and then in London, in the previous decade. Now began what literary historians have called his American period. It was a happy time in his life, when, fresh from his Indian and British triumphs, he seemed to be on the verge of making a settled home in the United States with his American wife. Ahead still lay the much publicized vendetta with his eccentric brother-in-law Beatty Balestier, the flight from the United States in dismay and anger, the near-fatal illness, the death of his young daughter Josephine (the much-loved 'Taffimai'), the embitterment over the South African War which embroiled Kipling in a mutually hostile relationship with the English liberal intelligentsia that to this day has never quite been resolved. All this was to make the last years of the century the worst period of his literary life. But none of it is foreshadowed in *The Jungle Books*, which still retain traces of that idyllic atmosphere of the early 1890s that was never to return to Kipling's work.

The Jungle Books (1894–5), like two other great English books, Lewis Carroll's *Alice in Wonderland* (1865) and Kenneth Grahame's *The Wind in the Willows* (1908), can be regarded as stories told by an adult to children. Kipling's younger daughter Elsie (Mrs George Bambridge) described to Dr A.W. Yeats in 1955 how Kipling recited the tales to the children with the lights out in a semi-dark room, and 'the cold narratives of *The Jungle Books* and *Just So Stories* in book form left so much to be desired that she could not bear to read them or hear them read.' (See an article by D.H. Stewart in *The Journal of Narrative Technique*, vol. XV, no. 1, winter 1985). But a father's rigmarole for children is only part of the composition of *The Jungle Books*. They constitute a complex work of literary art in which the whole of Kipling's philosophy of life is expressed in miniature. Many influences, some reasonably certain, others at most probable, have been at work on the narrative, and it would require a substantial book to take the road to Xanadu. Kipling discusses the book in his autobiography, *Something of Myself* (1937), but, as usual in that work, makes no attempt to analyse or explain. It must be remembered that he believed his writing to proceed from a source which was not under conscious control, which he called his Daemon (i.e. his genius or inspiration), and so he was as suspicious of talk about his or any other writer's intentions as any disciple of Wimsatt and Beardsley. However, he did leave on record two interesting pieces of inside information. The first reveals what C.S. Lewis has called Kipling's preoccupation with the Inner Ring: 'somehow or other I came across a tale about a lion-hunter in South Africa who fell among lions who were all Freemasons, and with them entered into a confederacy against some wicked baboons. I think that . . . lay dormant until the *Jungle Books* began to be born.' (*Something of Myself*, p. 8.) The second takes us to Kipling's home in Vermont where many of the stories were written.

> My workroom in the Bliss Cottage was seven feet by eight, and from December to April the snow lay level with its window-sill. It chanced that I had written a tale about Indian Forestry which included a boy who had been brought up by wolves. In the stillness, and suspense, of the winter of '92 some memory of the Masonic Lions of my childhood's magazine, and a phrase in Haggard's *Nada the Lily*, combined with the echo of this tale. After blocking out the main idea in my head, the pen took charge, and I watched it begin to write stories about Mowgli and animals, which later grew into the *Jungle Books* . . . Two tales, I remember, I threw away and was better pleased with the remainder. (pp. 113–14)

It is possible to gloss and expand Kipling's own account a little, but only a little. One point to bear in mind is that, like most people, he thinks of *The Jungle Books* as stories about Mowgli. But in fact, like many of his other books, they are collections of miscellaneous short stories. The Mowgli stories form a coherent sequence, telling the story of Mowgli's childhood and youth, from his adoption by the wolves in 'Mowgli's Brothers' to his departure from the Jungle in 'The Spring Running'. But in the first *Jungle Book* only the first three stories are about Mowgli; the other four centre on different characters and settings, and they do not form a sequence, while in the second the first four stories about Mowgli are alternated with non-Mowgli stories, the volume closing with the last Mowgli story, 'The Spring Running'. Nor is it the case that only the Mowgli stories are good, the rest being inferior. One or two of the Mowgli stories would be agreed by most readers not to be as good as the best of the other stories. Nevertheless, the *Jungle Books* are rightly remembered for the Mowgli motif, which is the most original thing in them.

The next matter requiring comment is the question about which was the first Mowgli story (i.e. the first to be written, not the first in the fictional life of the wolf boy). As we have seen, Kipling says that he had written a tale about 'Indian Forestry work', including Mowgli, before 'the pen took charge' and wrote *The Jungle Books*. Kipling is here referring to the story called 'In the Rukh', which appeared in *Many Inventions* (1893) – in this edition it is reprinted at the end of the second *Jungle Book*. All this seems clear enough though many readers, without necessarily being able to articulate their reasons, must find it difficult to believe that 'In the Rukh' and 'Mowgli's Brothers' and its successors really belong to the same imaginative or daemonic impulse. The Mowgli of 'In the Rukh' is not only fully grown-up and (rather unromantically) a forest ranger in government service, he seems somehow different in conception from the character in *The Jungle Books*. C.E. Carrington put it well when he called 'In the Rukh' 'realistic and pseudo-rational . . . not quite successful, not vintage Kipling. You don't really believe it, in spite of its verisimilitude, while "Mowgli's Brothers" is a masterpiece. It shows genius and forces a complete suspension of disbelief, so that mere verisimilitude is irrelevant.' Carrington was allowed access to Kipling's diaries of the period, and they convinced him that 'the first motion towards "Mowgli's Brothers" was a landmark, something new in his career.'

I suspect that 'In the Rukh' and 'Mowgli's Brothers' were two alternative experiments in a new mode, very likely taken up and dropped. 'Mowgli's Brothers' proved to be by far the better to follow, but 'In the Rukh' was too good for the waste-paper basket . . . Publication dates mean very little. Either or both of the stories might have lain by him in typescript for years. (C.E. Carrington in *Reader's Guide to Rudyard Kipling*, vol. VII, 1972.)

Study of the sources of the Mowgli stories must always be accompanied by the recognition that they are works of imagination, fancy, fantasy, fiction, not credible anecdotes of jungle life. It is symbolically of some significance that Kipling transferred the setting of the stories from the forests of Northern India which he knew well, and which are depicted in 'In the Rukh', to the Seoni district of Central India where he may never have set foot. The stories were written in the study, not in the jungle. Their chief literary sources are undoubtedly the anecdotes of Rudyard's father, Lockwood Kipling, in his *Beast and Man in India* (1891), full of Indian village- and jungle-lore (and these surely will have been coloured and enriched by Lockwood's table-talk), together with *Mammalia of India* (1884) and other books by Robert Armitage Sterndale. Here, for instance, we learn of the 'red dogs of the Deccan' with hair between their toes. Sterndale also alludes to wolf-child stories, e.g. Romulus, and thinks them not impossible. (On this matter Carrington's opinion, based on expert advice, seems plausible; there could in real life be an individual, X, who was suckled as a baby by a wolf, and there could be an individual, Y, who was a wild man of the woods, but X and Y could not be the same person.) Another source that may be mentioned, perhaps as much of value to Kipling as their conversation, was probably the photographs of the Seoni district (now in the Carpenter Collection in Washington) which his friends Professor and Mrs Hill took during their vacations there in the late 1880s.

A few other possible minor sources or allusions in the Mowgli stories will be touched on in the Notes. But one requires special mention here, since it is the only stimulus Kipling himself acknowledged. This is *Nada the Lily* (1892), a novel by his friend Sir Henry Rider Haggard (1856–1925). Kipling wrote to Haggard that it was a 'chance sentence' in that book – well worth reading for its own sake, a powerful study of Chaka, a sort of Zulu Napoleon – that

started me off on a track that ended in my writing a lot of wolf stories. You remember in your tale where the wolves leaped up at the feet of a dead man sitting on a rock. Somewhere on that page I got the notion. (From H. Rider Haggard, *The Days of My Life*, 1926.)

For fuller discussion of this, and many other elements in the concoction of *The Jungle Books*, the reader is referred to chapter 6 of that excellent book *Kipling and the Children* (1965) by Roger Lancelyn Green.

But no study of sources, known or hypothetical, can be of more than peripheral importance when we are dealing with so distinguished an artist as Kipling at his best, and discussion of *The Jungle Books* should be made to centre, not on their origins, of which we can know little, but on their meaning. This is something, of course, that readers will find out for themselves. It will be one thing if and when the reader is a child discovering the stories for the first time; another thing if the reader is an adult in that situation; yet another thing if the adult re-reads them, remembering the child reading. And of course one child, or one adult, or one adult remembering a child, is very different from another. All the same, those readers who have reported on their readings – the critics – do seem very often to converge in their interpretations and judgments, and (whether this was their purpose or not) concur in one observation at least: *The Jungle Books* are very *odd* works, not really quite like anything else by Kipling, or any other writer. A little conjecture why this is so may perhaps be permitted.

Even when they are read only as fairytales, it is clear that the Mowgli stories are the expression of a powerful myth. They tell the story of how the baby abandoned in the jungle by his parents when the tiger attacks is brought up by animals (he is adopted by the wolves, a mighty people, and secures strong protectors, the head wolf Akela, the bear Baloo and the black panther Bagheera), and through a combination of what they have to teach him about the Jungle with his own innate capacities as a human being he becomes Master of the Jungle. The boy reader identifies with Mowgli and enjoys the transformation into joyful fantasy of the impulse to dominate. But at the same time the stories are carrying a message to him, which is only partly explicit. The explicit message is educational. Elliot L. Gilbert in *The Good Kipling* (1972) points out that the Mowgli stories are what he calls a *Bildungsroman*. In realistic fiction this genre is concerned with the struggle of a young man or woman to discover his or her 'identity', to discover as far as may be possible the truth about themselves. Gilbert shows how this kind of story is told in *The Jungle Books* in a fairytale, fabulous form. Mowgli spends his whole life among animals. But as he approaches manhood he begins to find that he is not like the animals. A central symbol for this is Mowgli's eyes. They are the source of his power over the beasts, who cannot meet his gaze. From the beginning they have been the sign that he is not one of the beasts: 'the look in Mowgli's eyes was always gentle. Even when he fought, his eyes never blazed as Bagheera's did. They only grew more and more interested and excited.' Mowgli has passed through a preliminary training which in many ways is like that suitable to animals. But a time comes when he must move beyond his animal 'brothers', and realize the truth about himself, and accept the responsibility of being a man, and the recognition that it sets him apart.

This theme of growing up, of becoming a new self, runs through much of *The Jungle Books*. Rikki-tikki-tavi, the mongoose, washed away from his parents by a summer flood, the White Seal discovering how to release his people from the threat of death, and finding himself at the end occupying on the new beach the position his father had held on the old, Purun Bhagat leaving the life of a Westernized statesman to take up the totally different existence of an ascetic hermit – all these stories, so different in setting and circumstances, are all exploring the theme of self-discovery and the realization that a new life has begun.

Much of Kipling's fiction for children and young people can be described as educational. The didacticism of *Just So Stories* (1902), meant for little ones, is only playful, a parody of Victorian 'instructional' pabulum, but the pedagogic element in *Captains Courageous* (1896–7) and the *Puck* books (*Puck of Pook's Hill*, 1906, and *Rewards and Fairies*, 1910) is meant seriously and is part of the meaning of those books. Obviously Baloo, Bagheera etc. are schoolmasters in animal costume, and a good deal of the subject is the acculturation of a late-Victorian child, put into symbolic form. But in other ways the Mowgli stories are not really like the educational books, but belong with another area of Kipling's fiction that came from deeper down in him, something more personal, and with more potent 'unconscious' or latent content; belong, in short, with 'Baa Baa, Black Sheep' (in *Wee Willie Winkie*, 1888), known to be based on the terrible experiences of Rudyard's own childhood, and, above all, with *Kim* (1900–1), the novel-poem which was the supreme imaginative correlate of all that India had meant to him. In other words, Mowgli belongs with Punch of 'Baa Baa, Black Sheep' and with Kim, as a study of the Waif. He belongs with Kim, and not with Punch, in so far as he is a waif who finds helpers and an environment which is co-operative with him and which he can eventually control. In this respect – the achievement of domination – Mowgli differs from another famous waif of late nineteenth-century literature, Mark Twain's Huck Finn. Both boys feel the lure of the uncivilized, the freedom from the restraints of the man-made world, but while Huck 'lights out for the Territory' Mowgli ends in the government service, like Kim.

It cannot be denied, then, that the message of the Mowgli stories is political. In much of his fiction of the 1880s Kipling had studied various casualties of the imperial system in India. He had projected an unfavourable view of the activities at the top of the Indian government, in the summer capital of Simla. He had written stories showing the weakness of the imported 'sahibs', some of whom became too remote, in their clubs and other British-dominated institutions, from the life of the people they were trying to govern. He had also seen the opposite weakness, the ruler who identifies too much with the subject people and 'goes native', like McIntosh Jellaludin. In the 1890s Kipling was putting forward a positive project for the salvation of the Indian Empire by the improvement of its administration. The key figures would be people with a similar background to Kipling's own, the English born in India, who knew both worlds, and could pass from one to another, and back again, without being compromised.

We can see something of these ideas at the back of the Mowgli stories. As John A. McClure points out (in *Kipling and Conrad*, 1981), they can be read as an allegory of imperialism. Mowgli is learning the art of a colonial ruler, and the animals represent the natives, the subject people. He enforces his domination by what in the political jargon of the time was called Orientalism. He moves freely among the people, they are his 'brothers' yet at the same time he is not of them. Similarly Kim is the 'Little Friend of all the World', but in the last resort he uses the inside knowledge he has gained from living with the Indians to serve the imperial government. The problem for the reader about this consciously dual role played by the hero, slipping back and forwards across the border, is partly one of political (and moral) judgment. 'Fraternalism' (as it may be called) can be, and is, made very attractive by Kipling's literary art, the mutual happiness of Mowgli and the animals, Kim and the Indians. But it clearly begs the question of why the country-born figure has to dominate at all, or why, if he has to, he should not be in truth fully one of his own people, 'Jungle-dwellers' or 'Indians', according to which symbolism is being used. And we wonder whether 'fraternity' in the end can really mean very much apart from the 'liberty' and 'equality' with which the slogan of French republicanism associates it. There is also the imaginative difficulty that in practice fraternalism seems to amount to the hero's behaving like a spy (which is what Kim, in the Great Game, actually becomes). McClure, writing as an American very consciously in the post-Vietnam War perspective, is very severe on this aspect of the Mowgli stories, and it is not necessary to take such a harsh view of Kipling's politics to feel rather uncomfortable in those scenes between Mowgli and Bagheera in which the human hero asserts his superiority over the panther who is the 'natural' king of the Jungle. The appeal to fraternalism ('We be of one blood, ye and I') which is the key to Mowgli's success looks a bit strained when it is juxtaposed with the naked assertion of power, as in this passage from 'Letting in the Jungle':

> Once more Mowgli stared, as he had stared at the rebellious cubs, full into the beryl-green eyes [of Bagheera] till the red glare behind their green went out like the lighthouse shut off twenty miles across the sea; till the eyes dropped, and the big head with them – dropped lower and lower, and the red rasp of a tongue grated on Mowgli's instep.
>   'Brother-Brother-Brother!' the boy whispered, stroking steadily and lightly from the neck along the heaving back.

This tableau of the mighty panther licking the feet of the boy who calls him 'Brother' is psychologically convincing, but the ethical and political implications – if we take it as of symbolic significance – are problematic. That at least must be conceded to McClure's view.

Those who would prefer a more inclusive, less tendentious reading of the stories, one that does more justice to the magical atmosphere, the moralized fantasy, characteristic of *The Jungle Books*, should concentrate less on their function as sweetening the pill for the indoctrination of a Victorian imperialist, and more on the manifest theme of the stories, one central to Kipling's philosophy. This word does not seem entirely inappropriate, though it must be kept in mind that his philosophy was largely intuitive and not worked out on a systematic logical basis.

We have come here, of course, to 'The Law', and what it meant to Kipling. McClure sees it merely as a formulation of Social Darwinism. But a more sympathetic and profounder and perhaps truer view of this concept is taken by Shamsul Islam in his book *Kipling's 'Law'* (1975). He shows the reiterated emphasis, and the religious seriousness and solemnity, with which Kipling invests it.

> 'Listen, Man-cub,' said the Bear, and his voice rumbled like thunder on a hot night. 'I have taught thee all the Law of the Jungle for all the peoples of the Jungle – except the Monkey-Folk who live in the trees. They have no Law. They are outcasts.'

In the words of Kipling's most notorious line of verse (from 'Recessional', 1897) they are 'lesser breeds without the Law.' But what does this *mean*? Whatever it means exactly, it permeates *The Jungle Books*, and not only the Mowgli stories. Purun Bhagat, going about with his begging bowl, passes through a busy Simla street and is stopped by a Muslim policeman for obstructing the traffic, and 'Purun Bhagat salaamed reverently to the Law, because he knew the value of it, and was seeking for a Law of his own.' We think of *Kim* (for which the story of Purun Bhagat is in some ways a 'trailer') in which the Lama says 'I follow the Law – the Most Excellent Law.' In the animal stories we constantly 'hear the call / – Good hunting all/That keep the Jungle Law!' ('Night-song in the Jungle'). It is said to be 'the oldest law in the world', 'arranged for almost every kind of accident that may befall the Jungle People, till now its code is as perfect as time and custom can make it.' Baloo told Mowgli that the Law was like the Giant Creeper, because it dropped across everyone's back and no one could escape. On the day of the Water Truce, Hathi the elephant tells the story of 'How Fear Came', a Jungle parallel to the story of the Fall of Man in the Garden in *Genesis*. 'The first of your masters has brought Death into the Jungle, and the second Shame. Now it is time there was a Law, and a Law that ye must not break.'

All this makes it sound as if the Law were a matter of the arbitrary commands of a god. But it is not. Nor is it either, simply a collection of prudential or 'utility' principles. It has something in it of both the prescriptive and the descriptive, but it is not fully reducible to either. In an extended discussion Dr Islam identifies the essential elements of the Law. The most important of these is that it is rational, the antithesis of *dewanee* (Urdu for 'madness', 'irrationality'.) All the Jungle People fear that, 'the most disgraceful thing that can overtake a wild creature.' The rational basis of the Law is shown, for instance, in the reason why the Law of the Jungle forbids the killing of Man:

> The Law of the Jungle, which never orders anything without a reason, forbids every beast to eat Man . . . The real reason for this is that man-killing means, sooner or later, the arrival of white men on elephants with guns, and hundreds of brown men with gongs and rockets and torches. Then everybody in the Jungle suffers.

The Law of the Jungle is geared to the attainment of the common good. 'The strength of the Pack is the Wolf, and the strength of the Wolf is the Pack.' ('But every wolf has full right under the Law to fight', as cross Mowgli once forgot when he tried to stop two young ones fighting.) In case of danger to the community the Law prescribes immediate offensive action to protect the society from disintegration. In 'Kaa's Hunting' the lawless monkeys intrude into the Jungle, and the followers of the Law take immediate action against them. In 'Red Dog' the Pack decides, on the advice of Mowgli and Akela, to fight rather than surrender to the enemy. Similarly Rikki undertakes grave dangers in fighting against the cobras, symbols of lawlessness, to restore the peace and harmony of the whole community of the bungalow and its garden. The Law enjoins ethical values: moderation, respect for elders; kindness to both young and old; fortitude; the value of keeping one's word; the danger of pride and the need for humility. 'Hold thy peace above the kill', Bagheera advises Mowgli. Finally, devotion to duty and work are advocated.

In personal relationships, Mowgli and his friends go beyond the explicit code of the Seeonee Wolf Pack. Much is made of the love between Mowgli and the animals; the risks Baloo and Bagheera and Kaa take to rescue him from the Bandar-log; the willingness of the wolf brothers to sacrifice their lives for his sake; Mowgli's decision to stay with the pack when the red dogs attack. Love is shown in the emotion of grief at loss, as when the animals lament at Mowgli's departure from the Jungle. The scene is charged with emotion. 'It is hard to cast the skin,' says Kaa, as Mowgli sobbed and sobbed, with his head on the blind bear's side and his arms round his neck, while Balloo tried feebly to lick his feet.

Mowgli also goes beyond the code in his idea of justice. He hears the word from Messua's husband and he says 'I do not know what justice is, but – come thou back next rains and see what is left.' Mowgli's concept of justice is close to revenge: in 'Letting in the Jungle' McClure comments on the savagery of this story, and suggests that it arises from Kipling's own hysterical vindictiveness, deriving from his days of impotent suffering in the House of Desolation. But we must also remember that this is a primitive society.

The thoughtful reader of the stories is reminded from time to time that not all the Law is natural law, the eternal law ordained by God. Some of it is positive law, and therefore requires law-making, authority and promulgation. This aspect of the Law is shown by the proviso that the leader of the pack can make new rules for a situation not already dealt with. 'The word of the Head Wolf is Law.' Finally, there is a good deal in the stories about the importance of custom and tradition. As Noel Annan has said, Kipling in much of his work is preoccupied with what holds society together. In *The Jungle Books* it is clear that religion and custom, convention and morality, and laws, are forces of social control. The individual breaks these rules at his peril.

All this is communicated to the youthful reader in language which he can understand, and in terms of a morality which is second nature to him, a morality of 'just deserts' and 'just reward'. Yet it is conveyed by way of a masterpiece of storytelling, which can be enjoyed without a thought of the didactic content. Imaginative, aesthetic and sensuous, the Jungle is 'there' as a complex evocative symbol, of which the full significance cannot be paraphrased.

The Jungle Books were once very popular, but may not be much read now. This may be due to reasons for some of which Kipling was responsible, and for some of which he was not responsible. One of the latter was the appropriation of the Mowgli theme by the American writer Edgar Rice Burroughs (1875–1950), with his series of stories, beginning with *Tarzan of the Apes* (1914), about the son of an English aristocrat abandoned in the jungle as a baby and reared by apes. (Kipling read *Tarzan* and remarks that the author had 'jazzed' the motif of the *Jungle Books* 'and, I imagine, had thoroughly enjoyed himself.') A later misfortune, also not Kipling's fault, was the Disney cartoon of *The Jungle Book*, harmless entertainment and nothing to do with Kipling, but marred even as that by Disney's awful cuteness. More responsibility on Kipling's part may be assigned to the use made of Mowgli and his friends by Baden-Powell and he had no objection to this, but the activities of those dear little boys called Wolf Cubs make it more difficult to see *The Jungle Books* as the profound works of literature which they really are. But above all it is Kipling's 'views' (which W.H. Auden said time would pardon) that probably do most to turn readers away in the late twentieth century. Nor is it easy to separate the views from the art, nor what is distasteful from what is permanently valid in the views. All that need be said of this here is that it would surely be a pity if any consideration of 'views' should prevent any reader, old or young, from flying through the air with Mowgli and the Bandar-log, or joining Mowgli in the 'armchair' of the aged python's coils, or savouring the tremendous scene in 'Red Dog' when the Bee People swarm among the ancient rocks.

Of the Mowgli stories in the first *Jungle Book*, 'Mowgli's Brothers' is in a class by itself. It creates the whole world of the Jungle, and by implication suggests essentially everything that is to follow in the other stories about him. From the moment when Father Wolf carries the 'naked brown baby' in his mouth to Mother Wolf in the cave we know that we are in the company of a great storyteller, like Aesop. The stories seem always to have existed. We do not think of anyone as making them up. Yet the Kipling ideology is slyly present. The baby already reveals his membership of the Master Race as he looks up into Father Wolf's face and laughs when the wolf was checked in midspring, and when he is 'pushing his way between the cubs' to get to Mother Wolf's teats. Later,

> Father Wolf taught him his business, and the meaning of things in the Jungle, till every rustle in the grass, every breath of the warm night air, every note of the owls above his head, every scratch of a bat's claws as it roosted for a while in a tree, and every splash of every little fish jumping in a pool, meant just as much to him as the work of his office does to a business man.

He is a citizen of two worlds by now, called 'Mowgli the Frog' (it has been suggested) because the frog is an amphibian. The simplicity of the writing, appropriate to the child reader, can take on a Swift-like mordancy when for a moment an adult reader is envisaged:

> The Lame Wolf had led them for a year now. He had fallen twice into a wolf-trap in his youth, and once had been beaten and left for dead; so he knew the manners and customs of men.

'Mowgli's Brothers' has many fine things. But it has the inevitable defects of a pioneer work; the construction is a little jerky, compared with such masterpieces of flowing narration as 'Kaa's Hunting' or 'Red Dog'.

'Kaa's Hunting' is the rival of 'Red Dog' for the title of the best Mowgli story. The humour of Mowgli and his bear and panther schoolmasters, the humour of their relations with Kaa, will not be lost on the child reader, while the adult can relish how cleverly it is done. The imaginative symbols of the story are two, the Bandar-log and Kaa. It is fairly plain what the monkeys represent, though this is not a simple allegory: the Bandar-log may be a glance at the bad side of American democracy (we remember that the Seeonee Pack are pointedly called 'the Free People'); they may also remind us of London (or any other) literary circles. But essentially they are a standing metaphor, available for application according to the relevant experience of the reader. The symbolism of Kaa goes deeper. What do Kaa and his coils represent? Snakiness, coldness, the physical and moral strength of a power emancipated from passion; age, memory . . . Soon it becomes clear that the symbol is polyvalent, cannot be exhausted in a formula. The young reader, gripped by the story and the humour, is insensibly learning about new possibilities in *human* life (not really about pythons). With the Cold Lairs we have an imaginative extension that goes beyond the simple moral tale of the naughty boy who played with the monkeys. And in the powerful scene when Kaa hypnotizes the Bandar-log, while Baloo and Bagheera too fall under the spell, and uncomprehending little Mowgli looks on untouched, the theme of *The Jungle Book*, in so far as it turns on Mowgli, is neatly dramatized.

'Tiger! Tiger!' is a disappointment. The showdown between Mowgli and Shere Khan has been long awaited; it is crucial to the saga. But the adult reader may be almost as puzzled as the child reader as to just how Shere Khan was killed. And it is a minor mystery why Kipling, having conceived Shere Khan as the second-rate, nasty character he is, should have reminded us in the title of Blake's Tyger, 'burning bright'. Perhaps there is an intentionally ironic effect here. Perhaps, also, the fact that (as in 'Red Dog') Mowgli gets others to do his killing for him, has something to do with the hidden unromantic theme: that getting things done in the real world is less a matter of personal heroics than of ingenuity and the capacity for collective organization. But none of this, even if it is meant to be there, makes the story very good. It is chiefly interesting for Mowgli's relations with the Man Pack. These (apart from the mysterious English at Khanhiwara) are portrayed unfavourably. The life of the village is one of mud walls, narrowness, superstition, prejudice. The exception is Messua. Here warm human feeling comes in, indicated with great tact and delicacy. Messua is clearly in love with 'Nathoo': is he with her? 'Nathoo', as Messua sees him, is someone who might well have grown up to be the Mowgli we meet in 'In the Rukh'. But this Mowgli is a more complex figure, with his ambiguous position between the Jungle and human worlds, that is to be beautifully worked out in 'The Spring Running'.

'The White Seal' has probably been much less read than the

Mowgli stories. In a book by Edith Nesbit, a disciple of Kipling, it is remarked as an oddity that one of the characters knows it. 'The White Seal' has been under-rated: it is superior to its counterpart, 'Quiquern', in the second *Jungle Book*, for although in both stories Kipling has mugged up a lot of information it is worn more lightly in the earlier story. Kotick, the White Seal, is an anomaly, like Mowgli, and like Mowgli he saves his people. There is some delightful descriptive writing, and the humour of Sea Cow as an old gentleman is lively, though gentle; there is a flavour of Lewis Carroll's Mock Turtle about him. There is also a flavour in the whole story of Charles Kingsley's *The Water Babies* (1863), a work which Kipling knew well: a blend of sensuous realism with fantasy similar to Kingsley's water world. 'The White Seal' may also be called, on its smaller scale, a *Bildungsroman*. It is a charming story (the accompanying poetry has more charm than the verse in the *Jungle Books* usually has) and the work of a master writer, but we do not feel the Daemon as conspicuously present.

In contrast, 'Rikki-tikki-tavi' seems to be a story that was born not made. The adults and children who enjoy it together are enjoying the same things. Also the story may be more obviously attractive than the Mowgli stories, though they are deeper and more powerful. Rikki has the moral virtues Kipling wants us to admire, but he is less part of the official machinery than Mowgli. There are no bears etc. lecturing on civics; and the Law is only present by implication. The mongoose has his own law, he is an empiricist. The story beautifully creates the world of the Indian bungalow and the garden. The sinister Nag and his wife Nagaina render the Kipling aphorism: 'the female of the species is more deadly than the male.' There is humour in Darzee and his wife. The balance of sympathies is well held: the fallacies of Darzee, the realism of his wife, the timidity of Chuchundra versus the bravery of Rikki, the evil Nag, and Nagaina even more savage but more sympathetic, trying to save her children.

'Toomai of the Elephants' may have been the first *Jungle Book* story to be written. It is more in the tradition of the Ernest Thompson Seton animal stories: none of the elephants speak, and even Little Toomai cannot converse with Kala Nag. Toomai himself is pleasantly sketched, but he is a slight character. The story was made into a British film, *Elephant Boy* (London Films,

1937). Apart from the co-director, Zoltan Korda, and the Indian actor Sabu, there were intelligent people connected with it, the director Robert Flaherty and the actor Walter Huston, but it deserved Graham Greene's scathing review (reprinted in *The Pleasure Dome*, 1972). Greene says that 'Kala Nag's attack on the camp should have been the first great climax of the picture.' But the 'scene is thrown away'. The elephants do not dance as Kipling described them. Greene notes something crude and cruel in Kipling's mind. 'We are expected to feel satisfaction at the thought of the wild dancers driven into the stockade to be tamed.' Yet it is only when Kipling speaks, in his own dialogue, when Machua Appa apostrophizes Toomai, that 'the ear is caught and the attention held.'

'Her Majesty's Servants' is even more minor. It is enjoyable, but slight. The world of the pack-animals, with the human narrator hearing everything, lacks the secrecy and magic of the Jungle. The story is memorable only for the finale, which in its context amounts to a mighty peroration on Kipling's great theme of obedience – without which you cannot run an empire, conduct an orchestra, control the traffic, perform a surgical operation, etc. etc. Politics apart, this is the verbal music to which the reader, coming to it as the epilogue of the first *Jungle Book*, cannot but thrill.

> . . . Mule, horse, elephant, or bullock, he obeys his driver, and the driver his sergeant, and the sergeant his lieutenant, and the lieutenant his captain, and the captain his major, and the major his colonel, and the colonel his brigadier commanding three regiments, and the brigadier his general, who obeys the Viceroy who is the servant of the Empress. Thus it is done.'
>
> 'Would it were so in Afghanistan!' said the chief; 'for there we obey only our own wills.'
>
> 'And for that reason,' said the native officer, twirling his moustache, 'your Amir whom you do not obey must come here and take orders from our Viceroy.'

The Second Jungle Book is superior to the first. Three at least of the Mowgli stories are first-rate, and there is at least one other story ('The Miracle of Purun Bhagat') which is unsurpassed in Kipling's work generally. 'How Fear Came' is chiefly valuable for deepening the myth of the Jungle, giving it the suggestion of a scripture and a theology. The horrors of drought are hinted at, without disturbing the atmosphere of a bedtime story – suitable for a bath night: 'Mowgli, lying on his elbows in the warm water, laughed aloud, and beat up the scum with his feet.' But Mowgli himself plays only a subordinate part in the story. And the suggestion that the Jungle is 'fallen' is not altogether in harmony with other stories, in which it is innocent and Eden-like in contrast with the greater corruptions – and greater opportunities – of human civilization.

In 'Letting in the Jungle' Mowgli plays the main part, but it is not one of the best of the stories. The dialogue between Mowgli and Hathi is impressive. But the process of arranging Mowgli's revenge seems to take a long time, and perhaps it drags a little. Again, as in 'Tiger! Tiger!', the human world comes off poorly; apart from the hostility of the villagers, the grown-ups lack magic, as in one of Edith Nesbit's stories; the fairytale fades into the light of common day. Once again Mowgli is not permitted to shed human blood: he gets others to wreak his revenge for him. There is no doubt that his conduct is savage and cruel, and this is an aspect of Kipling that admirers have to face. He wrote a number of revenge stories. But they come to an end with 'Dayspring Mishandled' (1928), one of Kipling's best stories, in which the avenger gives up his revenge. For the young Kipling, however, revenge was still sweet.

'The King's Ankus' needs no apologia, and no explanation. At least one critic has called it the best of the Mowgli stories. Two considerations could be urged against that view. First, it is less rich in atmosphere than 'Kaa's Hunting', or 'Red Dog'. The easy way in which the Jungle 'properties' are handled in the early pages suggests that if Kipling had decided to turn these stories into a series 'The King's Ankus' might have been the prototype. Secondly, Mowgli's role is somewhat marginal. He learns something – something very terrible – about human greed and wickedness, but we learn nothing new about him. The story, which is very well told, is a traditional one, and the analogy with 'The Pardoner's Tale' of Chaucer, about the men who went in search of Death, is apt. But, although Kipling greatly admired Chaucer, the two stories seem quite independent. The moral is equally forceful in both of them.

'Red Dog' is surely the masterpiece of the Mowgli stories in this book. Kaa is again impressive. He is *seen* wonderfully here:

For a long time Mowgli lay back among the coils, while Kaa, his head motionless on the ground, thought of all that he had seen and known since the day he came from the egg. The light seemed to go out of his eyes and leave them like stale opals, and now and again he made little stiff passes with his head, right and left, as though he were hunting in his sleep.

Kipling's poetic genius is kindled, as in 'The Mother Hive' (1908), by the opportunity to evoke the world of bees.

For centuries the Little People had hived and swarmed from cleft to cleft, and swarmed again, staining the white marble with stale honey, and made their combs tall and deep in the dark of the inner caves, where neither man nor beast nor fire nor water had ever touched them. The length of the gorge on both sides was hung as it were with black shimmery velvet curtains, and Mowgli sank as he looked, for those were the clotted millions of the sleeping bees. . . . As he listened he heard more than once the rustle and slide of a honey-loaded comb turning over or falling away somewhere in the dark galleries, then a booming of angry wings, and the sullen drip, drip, drip, of the waste honey, guttering along till it lipped over some ledge in the open air and sluggishly trickled down on the twigs.

The story is the most 'epic' in quality in the Mowgli series. J.M.S. Tompkins compares it to scenes in Tolkien's *Lord of the Rings*. A precedent may be found in Macaulay's 'Horatius': the *Lays of Ancient Rome* are an earlier example of the use of legendary, mythic material in the education of the young Victorian imperialist. But the use of the beast-fable perhaps limits the power and scope of the story, whereas Macaulay's use of Livy and 'the brave days of old' enhances them. Roger Sale has complained that the destruction of the *dhole* by the wild bees is anti-climactic, and perhaps Mowgli's craft and cunning a little eclipse his warriorhood. Otherwise the story is replete with the traditional motifs of heroic fable: the Lone Wolf, the death of Akela. Finally, it represents the climax of the Mowgli *Bildungsroman*: his victory over the red dogs makes him Master of the Jungle.

'The Spring Running' makes a better epilogue than the too 'arty' 'In the Rukh'. It may have too little 'story', perhaps, to attract the young reader. Yet it may be that he will sense dimly what it is about and respond to it without knowing why. The cold word 'puberty' is here replaced by this marvellous and delicate evocation of the upsurge of a new kind of life. As often in Kipling, it is through the use of *sound* that much of the effect is created.

There is one day when all things are tired, and the very smells, as they drift on the heavy air, are old and used. One cannot explain this, but it feels so. Then there is another day – to the eye nothing whatever has changed – when all the smells are new and delightful, and the whiskers of the Jungle People quiver to their roots, and the winter hair comes away from their sides in long, draggled locks. Then, perhaps, a little rain falls, and all the trees and the bushes and the bamboos and the mosses and the juicy-leaved plants wake with a noise of growing that you can almost hear, and under this noise runs, day and night, a deep hum. *That* is the noise of the spring – a vibrating boom which is neither bees, nor falling water, nor the wind in tree-tops, but the purring of the warm, happy world.

Of the non-Mowgli stories in this book the best is 'The Miracle of Purun Bhagat'. Possibly it is not really in place in the *Jungle Books*. It has the Indian setting of the Mowgli stories, and the animals, but they are part of the furniture, not protagonists. This may have led to the tendency of critics to forget about it when they are considering Kipling's claim to be the greatest short-story writer in English. At any rate, it is a very fine story. The theme resembles the Lama motif in *Kim*. The life-history of the Bhagat is the three 'Lives' of *Piers Plowman* in miniature: Do-Well, Do-Better, Do-Best. The Bhagat turns from the Active life of an Indian statesman to the Contemplative life of a hermit, and at the crisis of the story illustrates the Unitive life, when he emerges from his mystic solitude to save his people. Kipling's distinction comes out in his ability to grasp why men have turned to contemplation, though he himself is committed to the life of action. Yet, fine story though it is, 'The Miracle' does not rank with the greatest things in short fiction, such as Tolstoy's 'The Death of Ivan Ilyitch', or Melville's 'Billy Budd'. Though it is not a fairytale, there is something of the distanced, frozen quality of a fairytale about it.

The art with which nature is depicted suggests the art of Kipling's uncle-in-law, Burne-Jones. It is lovely, but somehow lacking the quality of major creation. Perhaps Kipling could only resolve the East/West opposition by giving it this distanced, 'framed' kind of setting? But the essential point of the story is its insight into the heart of Purun Dass:

> Even when he was being lionised in London he had held before him his dream of peace and quiet – the long, white, dusty Indian road, printed all over with bare feet, the incessant, slow-moving traffic, and the sharp-smelling wood-smoke curling up under the fig-trees in the twilight, where the wayfarers sit at their evening meal.

'The Undertakers' has perhaps been too much ignored. The critics who have mentioned it, such as R.L. Green, do not much like it, and it is not orientated towards the young reader. It is a rather slight story, told in an unusual way, largely through flashbacks, in the conversation of the three predators, the Mugger, the Jackal and the Adjutant. They are all unpleasant characters, but there are some telling ironies, and the whole story can be relished for its sardonic, Ben Jonson-like comedy. There is also a possible complexity of feeling about 'progress', when the Mugger says: 'Since the railway bridge was built my people at my village have ceased to love me; and that is breaking my heart.' But in its context this has no pathos, because we cannot sympathize with the evil crocodile.

'Quiquern' is no one's favourite. The amassing of detail is both laborious and obvious, and the story must be a candidate for the weakest story in both the *Jungle Books* (it is inferior to its charming opposite number in the first book, 'The White Seal'.) That said, the anecdote on which the story turns is unusual and attractive. But it may be too slight for so much treatment. Indeed 'Quiquern' is almost all 'treatment'. One way to enjoy it is to see it as a story about story-telling. There were no limits to the sophistication and artifice with which Kipling could practise, and reflect on, the ancient art which he had mastered. At the end of 'Quiquern' he plays with the whole notion of 'fiction', and gently and humorously touches on the strangeness, and the chanciness, of it all.

Kotuko . . . scratched pictures of all these adventures on a long, flat piece of ivory with a hole at one end. When he and the girl went north . . . he left the picture-story with Kadlu, who lost it in the shingle when his dog-sleigh broke down one summer on the beach of Lake Netilling at Nikosiring . . . a Lake Inuit found it next spring . . . sold it to a man at Imigen . . . he sold it to Hans Olsen, who was afterward a quartermaster on a big steamer . . . [which stopped] at Ceylon, and there Olsen sold the ivory to a Cingalese jeweller . . . I found it under some rubbish in a house at Colombo, and have translated it from one end to the other.

Chapter 13
E. Nesbit and The Book of Dragons

E. Nesbit [Edith Nesbit, 1858–1924] was a prolific author of the late nineteenth and early twentieth centuries. Like 'Mother' in *The Railway Children* she wrote to support her family. By 1898 she had come to enjoy a modest reputation as a readable purveyor of light fiction, some of it written in collaboration with her husband Hubert Bland. Her output included children's stories in the Mrs Molesworth tradition, but without the distinctive quality she was to develop later. She wrote much verse, and longed to be a poet. Philip Larkin includes her in *The Oxford Book of Twentieth Century English Verse* (1973). But her narrative poems in the manner of Tennyson (*Lays and Legends*, 1886) are now forgotten. Some of her best work is in her short stories, especially the striking tales about the return of the dead, 'Mansize in Marble' and 'John Charrington's Wedding'. But it is for her books about children that she is remembered. These began with the stories of the Treasure Seekers which were published in magazines during 1898 and collected in book form in 1899. From now on she was recognized as one of the leading British writers for children. The immediate stimulus to write *The Story of the Treasure Seekers* came from an invitation by *The Girls' Own Paper* to reminisce about her own childhood, but she may also have been influenced by Kenneth Grahame's *The Golden Age* (1895) and its continuation *Dream Days* (1898), which describe the doings of a family of five orphans relatively free of adult supervision.

Nesbit's books about children fall into three categories.

1. Pure fantasy, as in *The Book of Dragons* (1900).
2. Non-fantastic (if often improbable) books about children seen from the children's point of view. This category includes the trilogy about the Bastables: *The Story of the Treasure Seekers* (1899),

The Wouldbegoods (1901), and *The New Treasure Seekers* (1904). It also includes *The Railway Children* (1906). The Bastables appear, seen from an adult point of view, in *The Red House* (1902).
3. Books containing a fantastic element or marvel, but otherwise realistic, a genre used by Nesbit's contemporary F. Anstey [Thomas
. Anstey Guthrie, 1856–1934] in *Vice Versa* (1882), *The Brass Bottle* (1900), and other books. In *The Brass Bottle* an Arabian Jinnee is let loose in Victorian London. At the end of *Five Children and It* the children turn to Anstey's novel to find a way out of their difficulties. This category includes the trilogy about the Five Children: *Five Children and It* (1902), *The Phoenix and the Carpet* (1904), and *The Story of the Amulet* (1906). To the same category (magic in the modern world) also belong *The Enchanted Castle* (1907), and *The House of Arden* (1908).

E. Nesbit's gift is agreed to be for the depiction of children. Some of her admirers like to claim that she was the first writer to see them as real human beings, unsentimentally (but this claim, as we shall see, has been contested.) She usually takes a family of children of various ages up to 10 or 11 and involves them in adventures, sometimes brought about by magic, sometimes not. Many of the stories are about the predicaments children get into when searching for treasure in everyday surroundings. There is always some domestic trouble in the background, a parent missing, a lack of money: many of the children's adventures come about through attempts to restore the family's prosperity. In its more fantastic aspects Nesbit's writing belongs to a kind recognized as distinctively English, with its infusion of magic, its parody of logic, and its surrealistic wit and humour. Famous examples are Edward Lear and Lewis Carroll, and Nesbit has affinities with them as a writer, though as a person she was much less inhibited than they were: Noël Coward, who came to know her well, described her as the most genuine Bohemian he had ever met.

The narrator of the Bastable books is the eldest boy Oswald (not avowedly, but the reader soon discovers this.) His attempts to present objectively his own abilities and good qualities result in an unintentionally amusing self-portrait. Perhaps this is merely for the benefit of the adult reader, but with Nesbit we can never be sure how many of her subtleties are taken in by children without their being fully aware of them. As with Henry Adams and Norman Mailer, Oswald's use of the third person gives him both a commanding and an irritating quality as narrator. It would be interesting to know, but hard to find out, to what extent boys (or girls) find it easy to identify with him.

In the other trilogy, about the Five Children, character interest is less prominent: though these books too are full of comedy, it does not derive mainly from this source. It would not be inaccurate to describe them as fairy stories, but there is an essential difference between them and traditional folktales, even if we encounter these, as many of us do, in the Grimms' *Household Tales* (1824–6), in which, as J.M. Ellis shows in his recent book *One Fairy Story Too Many* (1983), they are partly rationalized and brought into line with conventional ideas. In folktales the magic suffuses everything. You cannot make sense of a story like 'Rumpel-stilt-skin' unless you are prepared to take it on its own terms. The world of folktales has its own laws, physical, metaphysical and moral. In contrast, in her Anstey-type stories, Nesbit confines the magic to one marvel: everything else belongs to the ordinary world. She excels in the consistent working out of stories based on a fantastic premiss. Though a rapid and casual writer she is careful about details: she anticipates the questions children are likely to ask, even if her answers are often cleverly evasive.

Unlike some other fantasists Nesbit makes the marvel interesting in itself. In *Five Children and It* the Psammead has a distinct character as the small irritable strange-looking creature who grumbles all the time at having to fulfil the wishes of the children, afraid it may injure itself in the process. To add to the comedy something always goes wrong with the Psammead's miracles: we are regaled with a display of human folly. The method is different from that of the Bastable trilogy. We remember 'It' rather than the Five Children. Many readers probably cannot recall their names. They are in a sense more credible than the Bastable children, less naive, more endowed with competence and common sense, but they are not highly individualized as the Bastable children are.

Like all good modern writers of fairy stories Nesbit uses traditional motifs and gives her own turn to them. Humphrey Carpenter (in *Secret Gardens*, 1985) notes that the Psammead probably derives from the bad-tempered Cuckoo and Raven in Mrs Molesworth. It is a distinctive character all the same. In *The*

Phoenix and the Carpet the magic carpet is a traditional device, but an original slant is given to it: the carpet has been repaired and parts of it are not magic (a neat emblem of the genre of the whole book). The Phoenix not only has its legendary attributes but its personal ruling passion (vanity). This book apparently suggested Rudyard Kipling's stories in *Puck of Pook's Hill* (1906) and *Rewards and Fairies* (1910). (There had already been influence in the other direction: the Bastable children play games based on Kipling's *Jungle Books* (1894–5).) It has been said that the Puck books are more didactic than *The Phoenix and the Carpet*; and certainly they contain, in a form devised to please young readers, Kipling's pondered insights into English history. Nesbit merely writes to entertain. But there are lessons in *The Phoenix and the Carpet* also. A contrast has been seen between conservative Kipling and socialist Nesbit. The children in the Puck books are always being asked to admire unusual and heroic individuals, who performed their assigned tasks in an exemplary way. Nesbit is more concerned to show children the workings of a society as a whole: in what ways the people of other periods differed from, and in what ways they resembled, the present time.

But the main difference between Kipling and Nesbit is that in the Puck books Dan and Una are mere spectators; they do not take part in the 'past' or 'future' events, as the children in the Nesbit books do, and the Traveller in Wells's *Time Machine* (1895), whatever logical difficulties this may entail. In Kipling the genre is that of the Historical Pageant: in Nesbit it is the Exciting Adventure. The sense of an enjoyment shared between author and reader is more important than edification. Graham Greene in *A Sort of Life* (1971) recalled his youthful delight at the end of the book, when the magic bird has gone and a great box arrives full of everything the children have ever desired, 'toys and games and books, and chocolates and candied cherries, and paint-boxes and photographic cameras.'

The design on the reader in Kipling does not mean that the Puck stories had less appeal than the Nesbit books. It is doubtful whether the teaching was ever the source of interest. I suspect that both the Imperialist and the Fabian would have been forgotten if they had not been able to create that sense of the mysteriousness of the past which gives it its special thrill. C.S. Lewis (whose own writings for children owe much to Nesbit) said that *The Story of the Amulet* was his favourite among her books, because it first opened his eyes to 'the dark backward and abysm of time'. And Stephen Prickett, in *Victorian Fantasy* (1979) shows how Nesbit uses the fantastic to illuminate history and make it 'real'. *The Story of the Amulet* displays more than routine invention in the conjuring-up of the Egypt of the Pharaohs, Babylon, Caesar's Britain, and a glimpse of a future utopia which has a definitely Wellsian flavour. Not only are the particular episodes excellent: the frame story is excellent too, with the mystery of the missing half of the Amulet, lost in the past, and the surprising conclusion to the story.

But in these books the magic is merely a datum: it could be presented on television, the great enemy of the imagination. In *The Enchanted Castle* it pervades the whole atmosphere of the book. The story tells how four children encounter magic in the gardens of a great deserted house. Here the magic is not, as in Anstey, or the Five Children books, only a postulate: it suggests the co-presence of another world with our own. 'There is a curtain, thin as gossamer, clear as glass, strong as iron, that hangs forever between the world of magic and the world that seems to us real. And when once people have found one of the little weak spots in the curtain which are marked by magic rings and amulets, and the like, anything may happen' (from *The Enchanted Castle*). There is something disturbing, even nightmarish, in the scene when the statues of dinosaurs come to life in the moonlight, and in the grotesquerie Graham Greene remembered, when the Ugly Wugglies, made of masks and umbrellas, suddenly come alive and applaud the children's play from their roofless mouths, while they clap their empty gloves. *The House of Arden* belongs to the same mixed genre but does not reach so deeply into primitive fancies and terrors. The characteristic Nesbit comedy appears in the marvel, here the Mouldiwarp, a mole that appears on the family coat of arms: it can be summoned only by poetry composed in its honour, which is difficult for Edred and his sister Elfrida, since neither of them has any vestige of poetic gift.

With or without the use of magic, Nesbit wrote gripping and convincing stories of children. How she creates life on the page cannot be explained by a formula, but the secret seems to lie in her ability to use adult skills for the expression of a child's imaginings, yet without patronage or betrayal. Children are not themselves good storytellers; they 'had the experience but missed the meaning' (T.S. Eliot, *East Coker*). Nesbit seems to be able to give the 'experience' and the 'meaning' together. As she put it: 'The reason why these children are like real children is that I was a child once myself, and by some fortunate chance I remember exactly how I used to feel and think about things.' (Quoted from the introduction to *E. Nesbit: Fairy Stories*, ed. Naomi Lewis, Knight Books, 1979.) There is also an element of 'generation politics': Nesbit seems to be on the child's side in a way in which many writers for children are not. In 'The Cockatoucan, or Great-Aunt Willoughby' (in *Nine Unlikely Tales for Children*, Ernest Benn, 6th impression, 1929) a young Edwardian seems to confront an elderly Victorian:

> She had been to her Great-aunt Willoughby's before, and she knew exactly what to expect. She would be asked about her lessons, and how many marks she had, and whether she had been a good girl. I can't think why grown-up people don't see how impertinent these questions are. Suppose you were to answer, 'I'm top of my class; Auntie, thank you, and I'm very good. And now let's have a little talk about you. Aunt dear, how much money have you got, and have you been scolding the servants again, or have you tried to be good and patient as a properly brought up aunt should be, eh, dear?'

In 'Whereyouwanttogoto' (in *Nine Unlikely Tales for Children*) there is a similar authorial dissociation from authoritarianism: 'You are intelligent children, and I will not insult you with a moral. I am not Uncle Thomas. Nor will I ask you to remember what I have said. I am not Aunt Selina.'

Edith Nesbit apparently had a difficult and insecure childhood (though with periods of great happiness). She believed that her early sufferings were in many ways representative of the sufferings of children at that time, and that they should not remain for ever unarticulated but should be preserved and shown from the inside. I have suggested that her point of view represents a combination of the adult's with the child's. It might be more accurate to say that she undermines the normal contrast between adult and child: they are both alike because they are both human. Children may have more limitations, they are physically weaker, exposed to some kinds of exploitation, material and moral, that adults may be able to avoid. But they can have all the adult qualities, both admirable and unadmirable: they can be clever, witty, temperamental, greedy, naive, ingenious, as adults can. The slang and manners have of course dated: the characterizations have not.

Does this put E. Nesbit in a class by herself? Her achievement stands up well to comparison with famous things in canonical literature: *What Maisie Knew*, or *Huckleberry Finn*. The sense that what the reader reads is 'just happening' is better preserved in the Bastable books than in these. Henry James has a design on us (to keep us convinced of the incorruptible innocence of Maisie) and in *Huckleberry Finn*, though Mark Twain disclaimed any plan or intention in his preface (and I have never seen any convincing evidence that he did not mean what he said), there are places in the novel where we feel the presence of the collusive author. But in the Bastable books there seems to be no storyteller behind Oswald. Adult moralizing is now and then introduced, but Oswald accepts it, and his acceptance of it is part of his character: he is an establishment type. Similarly in the books in which E. Nesbit herself is the narrator there is no getting beyond a humorous, kindly, maternal presence,. (The relation between this and the historical Edith Nesbit is disputed by her biographers: some regard it as an extension of her actual personality, others say she did not really like children – as has been said of some other famous writers of children's books.)

There has not been until recently much critical debate about E. Nesbit. After the 1914–18 war her work became for a time unpopular, but from the interwar years onward there was a considerable and steady rise in her reputation, and nowadays Puffin editions are scattered about in many houses. She has become a comfortable literary fixture, read, but not argued about. But during the last few years a new view of her work was put forward, chiefly by the American critic Gore Vidal. According to this view she should be seen less as a Late-Victorian/Edwardian entertainer and more as a radical and subversive author, anticipating trends which surfaced in the 1960s and 1970s. Biographical considerations give this a certain plausibility: we know of the unconventionality (by the standards of her time) of Edith Nesbit's domestic ménage and private life, and her close association with Wells and Shaw and other 'advanced' figures of the day.

But much in Nesbit's work, and life, can be urged against this new reading. I think Humphrey Carpenter has put cogently the objections to seeing Nesbit as a pioneer of Children's Liberation. The friendly adult (sometimes the narrator herself) who takes the children's side in the stories can sometimes be suspected of Fifth Columnism. Carpenter thinks Nesbit's leftism only skin deep, more a matter of short hair and smoking in public than of any real understanding of socialist ideas. She may have been excited by contact with the avant-garde; but when Women's Suffrage became an issue she opposed it. It is true that the Queen of Babylon, in *The Phoenix and the Carpet*, comments adversely on the treatment of 'slaves' (i.e. the working class) in modern London; but there is no deep concern with social change or reform in her books. The children, even if afflicted by poverty, remain middle class: all the families, however reduced their circumstances, have servants; and the parlourmaids, cooks etc. are assumed to be socially inferior. Carpenter notes that in *Five Children and It* it is assumed that servants cannot see the result of the Psammead's magic. But I think he makes too much of this point. The author has to convey to us that the Psammead is a fantasy of the children, without actually saying so. She can be accused of clumsy plot-machinery here rather than unthinking snobbery. In real life children make all sorts of concessions to reality in their shared fantasies, and do so with the utmost nonchalance.

Still, it cannot be denied that Nesbit's stories are about middle-class children and imply middle-class values. And it is also true that she had a good deal of influence (regretted by Carpenter) on writers for children. Until the rather self-conscious revolt against them in the 1950s it was usual to choose middle-class children as protagonists. In Nesbit this can be excused as merely a period limitation, yet as Carpenter reminds us, her forerunners, such as Charles Kingsley and Mrs Ewing, had made poor children their heroes, and they were often the centre of interest in Mark Twain.

Carpenter's most telling point seems to me the contrast he draws between her books and Grahame's *Dream Days* and *The Golden Age*. In Grahame's books the children are not patronized but are allowed to have their own point of view, firmly critical of adults, and this is given authorial support. In his books, unlike Nesbit's, it is the adults not the children who make fools of themselves. In comparison with Grahame it can be said that Nesbit's attitude to children is patronizing. Carpenter grants that the semi-fantasy books do not make this impression, but then the issues of the real world are less challenging in them than in the Bastable books. Are these criticisms of Nesbit fair? It must be conceded at any rate that she was not a forerunner of modern feminism. E. Nesbit is above all motherly. Then (to make use of a formal distinction drawn elsewhere by C.S. Lewis) the realism of her books, where there is any, is of presentation rather than content. There is a safety net under the stories: the children are never in real danger, the misery and horror of the real world are kept out, many of the underlying assumptions and attitudes are gentle. From a modern point of view this may be seen as a limitation of her books. They are also, on the face of it, directed to boys rather than girls. Edith Nesbit herself, it seems, was boyish, and her flattery of the boy reader can be egregious: in 'The Book of Beasts', the first story in *The Book of Dragons*, when Lionel goes to be crowned 'he was a little sorry at first that he had not put on his best clothes, but he soon forgot to think about that. If he had been a girl he would very likely have bothered about it the whole time.' But we must not forget the duplicities of the humorist and ironist that were also part of E. Nesbit.

Nor can the sense that Nesbit is pro-child – pro-girl as well as pro-boy – be eliminated. No doubt her critique of the adult world is less destructive than that in *The Golden Age* and *Dream Days*. But she is not in that business. These books have not been loved as Nesbit's books are (or Grahame's own *The Wind in the Willows*). She writes books that adults and children are meant to enjoy together. But her comedy at the expense of male complacency (as in the character of Oswald) is none the less trenchant because it is affectionate.

If there really is a subversive, 'modern' E. Nesbit, she is to be found less in her realistic books than in her satiric fantasies, where she is closer to Lear and Carroll. In *The Book of Dragons* we have a sense of free play, rare in her work, which links it with the *Alice* books and *The Hunting of the Snark* and *The Book of Nonsense*. Victorian seriousness was relieved by a glimpse of

> Fantastic beauty, such as lurks
> In some wild Poet, when he works
> Without a conscience or an aim.
>
> (Tennyson, *In Memoriam*, section 34)

Nonsense literature has for long been a recognized field of academic study, but it remains difficult to discuss such things without falling into the solemn absurdities satirized in F.C. Crews's *The Pooh Perplex* (1963). The popularity and survival power of fantasy suggest that it is rooted deep in the mind, but attempts to explain it destroy the means by which its effect is achieved. To analyse E. Nesbit's charm is like cutting open a rubber ball to see what makes it bounce, a feat performed by more than one of her boy protagonists, and authorially condemned. Critics who are occupationally tempted to allegorize should remember the shrewd saying of George MacDonald that fairytales may *contain* allegories but cannot *be* allegories. The fugitive suggestion of allegory is part of the fascination of these tales, but the fugitiveness is essential.

E. Nesbit's stories in *The Book of Dragons* have something of this quality, though superficially, with their humour and sophistication, they are remote from fairytales and folktales. They were first published in the *Strand Magazine* in 1899. The *Strand* was intended primarily for adult readers, and humorists like Anstey who appeared in it did not have a child public in mind. The stories were collected in book form in 1900, with the exception of 'The Last of the Dragons', which appeared in *Five of Us –and Madeline*, first published posthumously in 1925. The nine stories are now most conveniently available in *The Complete Book of Dragons*, illustrated by Erik Blegvad (Hamish Hamilton, 1972). Erik Blegvad's illustrations show the dragons as dinosaur types, while H.R. Millar, who illustrated the dragon stories for the *Strand*, gives them a more traditional character. In any case there is no doubt that the dragons were suggested by dinosaurs, as in *The Enchanted Castle*. The source for them was Hawkins's stone statues of dinosaurs at the Crystal Palace (transferred in *The Enchanted Castle* to a castle in the West of England.) This suggestion of the Wellsian, modern world view immediately differentiates them from traditional dragon mythology, which was apparently not based on any knowledge of the gigantic prehistoric reptiles. But

Nesbit used very little popularized science about the great lizards. And she uses very little traditional dragon-lore either, though part of the attraction of *The Book of Dragons* is the variety in appearance and character of her dragons. She makes use of the European and Near Eastern connotations of the dragon as an evil power (though in those cultures there are also traditions in which it is beneficent). But she does not draw at all on the traditions of the Far East which honour dragons. Nor on the other hand, is she interested in the dragon as a warlike emblem, as in the royal ensign of England, instituted by Uther Pendragon, father of King Arthur. What the stories communicate is no deep use of dragon-lore but the presence of a writer of exuberant and carefree invention. She invents new landscapes, with an unforgettable use of light and colour, a sense of space, and lots of weather.

The dragons are all different and have different fates. In 'The Book of Beasts' the Red Dragon, culpably released from the book by little King Lionel, returns to the book's pages at the end. In 'Uncle James' the dragon eventually turns into a little, crawling, purple newt with wings. In 'The Deliverers of their Country' there is a plague of dragons, of various sizes, who at the end of the story are all washed away (with one exception, the size of an earwig) in the Universal Tap Room. In 'The Ice Dragon' there is a spectacular description of a great shining winged scaly clawy big-mouthed dragon, made of pure ice, with deep clear Prussian-blueness, and rainbow-coloured glitter. (He is melted by a bonfire.) The dragon in 'The Dragon Tamers' is made almost entirely of iron armour, a sort of tawny, red-rust colour. After years of eating nothing but bread and milk his plates and wings drop off and he grows furrier and furrier, and he is the beginning of all the cats. 'The Fiery Dragon' in the story of that name, grows small at night and is eventually put into a dragon-proof bottle. In 'Kind Little Edmund' the dragon is female: immense and yellow, like a monstrous centipede. She goes down into the centre of the earth in search of her baby, the drakling. In 'The Island of the Nine Whirlpools' the dragon is hardly more than a pantomime figure. The King takes his daughter to the Lone Tower which stands on an island in the sea, a thousand miles from anywhere. He engages a competent dragon and a respectable griffin to look after her. The dragon grows old and horrible and is drowned in the whirlpool, while the griffin is killed when the eagle part and the lion part of it fight each other. 'The Last of the Dragons' is by way of being an epilogue. We emerge in the light of common day, in the 1920s. The last of the dragons lived in Cornwall, before English History began, had no interest in Princesses, liked drinking petrol, was sentimental when called 'Dear', and eventually became the first aeroplane.

The all-pervading presence of the fireside narrator prevents the creation of an enclosed world, such as that in 'The Blue Mountain' (in *Nine Unlikely Tales*), in which we feel from the inside what it would be like to live in an ant-hill.

> the people of Antioch . . . were very black, and generally lazy. They scurried up and down in their rocky little city, and always they seemed to be driven by most urgent affairs, hurrying to keep important appointments. They ran about all day long, attending to their business, and hardly stopping even for their dinner or their tea, and no one ever saw any of them asleep.

In *The Book of Dragons*, in recompense for the lack of an enclosed world, we are given a display of the varied types of literary effect which are possible when there is a self-conscious narrator. 'The Book of Beasts,' the first story, can be seen as a manifesto of the newly emergent art of E. Nesbit. We may see a suggestion of allegory: the Book represents the power of literature, or the imagination, seductive but dangerous. But this interpretation does not work. Some of the Beasts that got out go back in again, two of them (the Butterfly and the Blue Bird of Paradise) stay out permanently, and a Beast that was not originally in the Book, the King's own Rocking-Horse, is allowed to go into it. I have failed to see any way in which this could be decoded as a discourse about the relation of art to life. The charm of 'The Book of Beasts' is that it plays with two kinds of marvel, very different. The first is an 'improbable possibility': an ordinary little boy is made King. This is not a wish-fulfilment story: Lionel as King seems to be even more ordered about and rebuked and slapped by adults than he was before. The other marvel introduces the transgression motif, as in the Garden of Eden, or *Peter Rabbit*. Lionel opens the Book and unintentionally releases the Butterfly and the Blue

Bird of Paradise, and the next day he lets the Red Dragon out. 'And then Lionel felt that he had indeed done it.' The story has no clear moral. Lionel brought trouble on himself and his people by opening the Book, but he and they are saved by the Hippogriff (perhaps from Ariosto?) whom he also releases from the Book. What the young reader really gets is not a moral but an introduction to English comic style. The conversation between Lionel and his Prime Minister is an anticipation of the dialogue of Noël Coward and Evelyn Waugh.

> 'But hadn't my great-great-however-much-it-is grandfather a crown?'
>
> 'Yes, but he sent it to be tinned over, for fear of vanity, and he had all the jewels taken out, and sold them to buy books. He was a strange man; a very good King he was, but he had his faults – he was fond of books. Almost with his latest breath he sent the crown to be tinned – and he never lived to pay the tinsmith's bill.'

'Uncle James' is wholly satirical. The mock-explanations for the extraordinary natural history of Rotundia sound like a parody of Victorian popular science. In 'The Fiery Dragon' we have the prettiest of the tales: it hovers gracefully on the brink of sentimentality. Princess Sabrinetta is rescued from having to marry the boorish Prince Tiresome (who hunts with hippopotamuses) by the swineherd Elfinn, but Elfinn's hands are burned by the dragon, and he can only be cured by having the burn kissed 77 times and have someone willing to die for him. The allusion to Christianity here is uncharacteristic of Nesbit and may be due to the influence of Hans Andersen.

'Kind Little Edmund' is different again, a weird tale of a round cave with a hole in the middle, in which a large pale person is sitting, with a man's face and a griffin's body, and a snake's tail and a cock's comb and neck-feathers. This is the cockatrice, who lived on fire: its fire has gone out. Kind Little Edmund helps, and in return the cockatrice tells him things they don't know at school. The manoeuvres of the cockatrice and the she-dragon and the drakling, crawling through holes and tunnels and caverns, invite commentary of a psychoanalytic kind. Artistically speaking all this bizarre vitality is a foil to the cruel repressive schoolmaster in the story, who treats the marvels recounted by Edmund as all lies. He canes Edmund seven times in the course of the story.

'The Dragon Tamers' has a flavour of William Morris.

> Then the dragon begged them to fasten him up at once, and they did so, with the collar and chains that were made years ago – in the days when men sang at their work and made it strong enough to bear any strain.

But as usual lesson and allegory are evaded. The gold that brings the happy ending is not earned through work, whether spiritualized or not, but just found.

'The Island of the Nine Whirlpools' is rich in traditional fairytale features: the magician King, angry because the Queen asked the witch for a *child*, not a *boy*, and got a daughter; the Queen turning to stone and coming to life again at the end (cf. *The Winter's Tale*). Yet the rescue of the Princess at the end is accomplished by 'scientific calculations'. 'My Princess,' he [the hero] said tenderly, 'two great powers are on our side: the power of Love, and the power of Arithmetic. These two are stronger than anything else in the world.' The mood of romance is quietly dispelled at the end in a glance at the adult reader, over the head of the child:

> I have no doubt that you will wish to know what the Princess lived on during the long years when the dragon did the cooking. My dear, she lived on her income; and that is a thing which a great many people would like to be able to do.

The elusive quality of these stories is typified by the tricks Nesbit plays with what Roland Barthes calls the 'cultural' code. This is the information emanating directly from the author about the 'real world'. Nesbit does not (like Flann O'Brien in *At Swim-Two-Birds*) play tricks with all the storytelling codes; she has no wish to puzzle or disturb her young readers. But she loves to tease them, and at the same time gently mock the grown-ups who are supposed to tell them what they ought to know. Many examples of her ironic duplicities can be found in 'The Ice Dragon'. This tale can be seen as a brief epitome of the whole of Nesbit's writing for children. There is the everyday setting, which for readers in the 1980s has acquired an enchantment of its own: fireworks at the Crystal Palace. But there is also the finely evoked beauty of the winter night, the Aurora Borealis, and the gradual transition to a dream world as the boy and girl go up the great slide on the way to the North Pole. The Transgression motif appears: the children were told not to go on the grass, but '"They said the *lawn*," said Jane. "We're not going on the *lawn*."' The evil sealskin dwarfs add a touch of domestic horror. The melting-away of the dragon corresponds to the return to ordinary life. The whole story is a parody of a homiletic tale for children, with its misleading information about the North Pole, etc., and its inconsequent 'moral', which is as follows: moth-eaten things are no good for anything, not even lighting fires. 'The Ice Dragon' is typical of Nesbit's unusual gift for writing satire without destroying the sense of wonder.

The best story in *The Book of Dragons* is, I think, 'The Deliverers of their Country.' As often in science fiction the story starts with a common experience: 'It all began with Effie's getting something in her eye.' Sometimes the narrative voice speaks through Effie, in 'free indirect style'; sometimes it blends with a more authoritative voice. Voices of authority in this story are strongly adult, contemptuous of children, medical and scientific.

> 'Dear me,' he said, 'dear dear *dear* me! Four well-developed limbs; a long caudal appendage; five toes, unequal in length, almost like one of the Lacertidae, yet there are traces of wings.'

But for all their long words the authorities are totally impotent in face of the dragon-plague. This is made wonderfully vivid, a prophetic anticipation of 1940, England attacked from the air. The scientists fail, and the children succeed – with the help of St George. This unexplained saint, whom the English presumably picked up in the Crusades, was often evoked in Edwardian conservative fantasy, like *Where the Rainbow Ends*. Nesbit gives him a characteristically deflationary treatment.

So the children told him [St George] all about it; he turned over
in his marble and leaned on one elbow to listen. But when he
heard that there were so many dragons he shook his head.
'It's no good,' he said, 'they would be one too many for poor
old George. You should have waked me before. I was always for
a fair fight – one man one dragon was my motto.'
Just then a flight of dragons passed overhead, and St George
half drew his sword.
But he shook his head again, and pushed the sword back as
the flight of dragons grew small in the distance.
'I can't do anything,' he said; 'things have changed,since my
time. St. Andrew told me about it. They woke him up over the
engineers' strike, and he came to talk to me. He says everything
is done by machinery now; there must be some way of settling
these dragons.'

The tone and meaning of the story are epitomized in the moment
when St George *half draws* his sword. The defeat of the dragons
is also unheroic, and appropriately English: the deliverance of the
country is in the end due to the weather.

The reader is left in uncertainty over whether the children have
played any part at all in what happened. That there *were* 'dragons'
– or something like them – is proved by the preservation of a single
specimen by the professor (the doctor, Effie's father, having thrown
away the one he got out of Effie's eye.) But the country shows no
gratitude to, or even awareness of, its 'deliverers'. Father merely
regrets not having preserved his specimen. Mother scolds. It is
another example of the paradox that runs through Nesbit's work:
the role of the children is both everything and nothing. Perhaps
this is because what children in her work ultimately symbolize is
the Imagination.

Chapter 14
Father Brown and Others

G.K. Chesterton himself did not attach great importance to the Father Brown stories. Ordered in batches by magazine editors and publishers, they were written hurriedly for the primary purpose of helping to finance his Distributist paper, *G.K.'s Weekly*. And though they have proved to be the most popular of Chesterton's writings, critical attention to them has been casual. This is partly because they are detective stories; and the detective story is commonly dismissed, without argument, as a very low form of art. That it is also a very difficult and demanding form, in which many clever writers have failed, is not regarded as relevant. Nor is there much respect for the innovators in this genre, or much comment on their remarkable rarity. If there were, Chesterton's reputation would stand very high; for his detective stories, while they may not be the best ever written, are without doubt the most ingenious. But to show ingenuity and originality in the detective story is for the superior critic merely to have a knack for a particular sort of commercial fiction. It is not the sort of thing he takes seriously. And Chesterton himself, it seems, would have agreed with him.

I shall try to give reasons why these stories should be taken seriously. But I must admit at the start that there are two (sometimes overlapping) classes of reader whom I cannot hope to convince. The first consists of those who loathe detective stories; the second, of those who are so prejudiced against the Roman Catholic Church that they cannot read stories in which a priest is presented sympathetically. All I can say to these readers is that the Father Brown stories are much more than detective stories, and if they can overcome their repugnance to the genre they will find a good deal that might interest them in another context; and secondly, that the element of strictly Roman Catholic propaganda in the stories is small. Furthermore, Father Brown is neither a realistic nor even an idealized portrait of a priest. Chesterton is not competing with *Morte d'Urban*, or with Bernanos; nor is he competing with Robert Hugh Benson. Anti-clericalism is irrelevant.

What is Chesterton saying in the Father Brown stories? Their meaning must be understood in terms of their genre. Whatever else these stories may turn out to be, they are certainly, on the face of it, light fiction, in a recognizable genre. And this genre was invented by Poe. Scholars have found remote antecedents and forebears for Poe's detective tales, but there can be no doubt that the modern detective tale derives from him. His tales of the Chevalier Auguste Dupin are magazine fiction. But they are also offered as moral fables. The virtue they ostensibly celebrate is Reason. Dupin is not concerned with the legal consequences of crime, like Inspector Maigret, nor is he concerned with its moral and religious implications, like Father Brown. For him, a crime is nothing but an intellectual problem. When that is solved, his interest lapses. Poe makes a great show of the rigorous deductions and inexorable logic of Dupin. He is inhumanly patient, penetrating and clear-headed. But this show of rationality is largely bluff, part of the game that Poe plays with his readers. It is notable that 'The Mystery of Marie Rogêt', which to all appearances is the most dully realistic and scientific-looking of the three Dupin stories, based on a real-life case, is in fact the most impudently fraudulent. Dupin's solution does not emerge from his reasoning: his reasoning, indeed, leads him in quite another direction. But Poe, surprised, no doubt, by a belated development in the real-life case, cunningly inserts the suggestion here and there that Dupin was all the time on the right track. At the end all that the bemused reader is clear about is that the rabbit has been produced from the hat. *How*, is nobody's business. And the classical detective story, created by Poe, is not a triumph of reason, but a conjuring trick. This is evident in the most famous, and the best, of the three Dupin stories, 'The Purloined Letter'. Everyone remembers the motif of this story: that some things are too obvious to be noticed. And this is the secret of successful conjuring. The simple suppose that 'it must be up his sleeve'. But it isn't: it's in front of your nose. The successful conjurer, like George Orwell, knows that the hardest things to see are the things that are in front of your nose.

Those who are prepared to enjoy a classic demonstration of this, in a detective story which is nothing but a detective story, should read John Dickson Carr's novel *The Black Spectacles*.

Chesterton, like all detective story writers, derives from Poe. Indeed, it might be said that he derives from a single story of Poe: many of the Father Brown stories can be regarded as ingenious variations on the theme of 'The Purloined Letter'. The suggestion of realistic police work, which we have in 'The Murders in the Rue Morgue' and 'The Mystery of Marie Rogêt' did not attract him. Father Brown keeps away from the secular authorities:

> 'The Coroner has arrived. The inquiry is just going to begin.'
> 'I've got to get back to the Deaf School,' said Father Brown. [He has just solved the mystery.] 'I'm sorry I can't stop for the inquiry.'

There are no chemical analyses or careful checking of alibis in these stories. Nor is there the dry intellectuality of Dupin. For between Poe and Chesterton comes Conan Doyle. It is, of course, Sherlock Holmes who humanized the figure of the Great Detective, the symbol of reason and justice. The Sherlock Holmes stories are in some ways inferior as literature to the Dupin stories. Holmes has a less distinguished mind than Dupin. But Dupin is a colourless character, and his confidant is even dimmer. It is the personalities of Holmes and Watson that we remember, the Baker Street 'atmosphere', in those rooms where it is always 1895, the inimitable blend of exotic excitement and reassuring cosiness.

As a conjurer, Doyle must rank low. The card often emerges patently from Holmes's sleeve. In that excellent tale 'The Bruce-Partington Plans', the solution turns on Holmes's realizing that the dead man's body was on the roof of an underground train. But this is a mere guess. Often Doyle does not even pretend to play fair with the reader. However, this does not matter. Doyle was the master of something rarer than conjuring: magic. It may be, indeed, that magic is not compatible with conjuring. At any rate, Doyle rose to a high rank among literary magicians when he invented Dr Watson. For it is Watson, not Holmes, that is responsible for the magic. It is only when we see the great man through his eyes that the whole conception reveals its unique triumphant blend of absurdity and sublimity. It is he who possesses the secret, more than Stevenson does in the *New Arabian Nights*, of evoking romance from the prosaic. London place names like 'Norwood' and 'Blackheath' will for some readers of Dr Watson's memoirs always retain overtones of mysterious romance.

All this was naturally congenial to the author of *The Napoleon of Notting Hill*. Chesterton was fascinated by the romance of the prosaic.

> His dubious eye roamed again to the white-lettering on the glass front of the public-house. The young woman's eyes followed his, and rested there also, but in pure puzzlement.
>
> 'No,' said Father Brown, answering her thoughts. 'It doesn't say "Sela", like the thing in the psalms; I read it like that myself when I was wool-gathering just now; it says "Ales".'

This slight example may serve to illustrate how much all these writers – Chesterton, Stevenson, Doyle – are disciples of Dickens, the great master of the unfamiliarity in the familiar. But Chesterton was perhaps the closest of them all to the detective story side of Dickens. The novel of Dickens that has most in common with Chesterton is *The Mystery of Edwin Drood*. It will be said that this is not merely a detective story, that it has imagination and moral seriousness. All the same, it is a detective story, and as such it is genuinely mysterious. And this is not only because it is unfinished. Neither *Barnaby Rudge* (*pace* Poe) nor *Bleak House*, which are both *inter alia* detective stories, would have been hard to solve if they had been left unfinished at a point comparable to the point where *Edwin Drood* breaks off. The quality of Chesterton's work at its best, in the Father Brown stories, is comparable to that of *Edwin Drood*. It is true to its genre: it is full of suspense, sensation, genuine clues, red herrings, 'atmosphere', real mystery and spurious mystery. But Chesterton, though he might talk light-heartedly about batches of corpses despatched to the publisher, is serious, as Dickens is serious in *Edwin Drood*. In these stories murder is murder, sin is sin, damnation is damnation. Every imaginative writer must choose his genre, and every genre has limitations. Those of the detective tale are obvious, and the most serious is this: no character can have depth, no character can be done from the inside, because any must be a potential suspect. It is Chesterton's triumph that he turned this limitation of the genre into an illumination of the universal human potentiality of guilt and sin. No character in the stories matters except Father Brown. But this is not a fault, because Father Brown, being a man, epitomizes all their potentialities within himself. 'Are you a devil?' the exposed criminal wildly asks. 'I am a man,' replies Father Brown, 'and therefore have all devils in my heart.'

This ability to identify himself with the murderer is the 'secret' of Father Brown's method. Some readers have misunderstood Chesterton's intention here. They suppose that Father Brown is credited with special spiritual powers, pertaining to his role as a priest. They see him as a thaumaturgic Sherlock Holmes. One adverse critic saw, in Father Brown's ability to divine the truth where plodding mundane detectives fail, a typical dishonest trick of the Catholic apologist. But it is made quite clear that Father Brown owes his success not to supernatural insight but to the usual five senses. He is simply more observant, less clouded by conventional anticipations and prejudices, than the average man. The kind of clue he notices is not cigar ash or footprints, but something like this:

> 'I am sorry to say we are the bearers of bad news. Admiral Craven was drowned before reaching home . . .'
> 'When did this happen?' asked the priest.
> 'Where was he found?' asked the lawyer.

A moment later the priest realizes that the lawyer has murdered Admiral Craven. If you are told that a seaman, returning from the sea, has been drowned, you do not ask where his body was 'found'. Admiral Craven was found in a landlocked pool; Father Brown realized that Mr Dyke could only know that because he had put him there. Most of the clues in the stories are of this kind. It is true that at the end of this story ('The Green Man') Father Brown does show some knowledge which, in the terms of the story, he could not have acquired by natural means; he knows that Mr Dyke committed the murder because his client, the Admiral, discovered that he had been robbing him. This is a fault in the story. But the same sort of fault can be found in greater writers when they are winding up the plot. Shakespeare makes Iago confess that he dropped Desdemona's handkerchief in Cassio's chamber. Surely a man like Iago would never have confessed anything. The essential discovery that Father Brown makes in this story is the identity of the murderer, not his motive.

Chesterton takes pains to emphasize that Father Brown has no supernatural powers, by frequently contrasting him with false mages who claim them. (Examples are to be found in stories like 'The Song of the Flying Fish' or 'The Red Moon of Meru'.) Their characteristic sin is spiritual pride. They are quite happy to be accused of crimes which they have not committed, if the crimes are thought miraculous. For contrast, we have a story like 'The Resurrection of Father Brown', in which Father Brown is subjected to the overwhelming temptation to claim credit for a false miracle: that he has risen from the dead. Without hesitation, dazed as he is, he discredits the story.

Father Brown is, then, not a thaumaturge. But it must be granted that, apart from his powers of observation, he has exceptional moral insight. It is well known that Chesterton conceived the idea for this character after meeting a priest whose 'unworldliness' proved to be compatible with an inside knowledge of crime and wickedness. His 'innocence' was of a kind that would have shocked the would-be sophisticated young men whom Chesterton soon afterwards heard patronizing the clergy for their ignorance of the world. Chesterton makes a good deal of play with the contrast between Father Brown's appearance, moonfaced, blinking, dropping his umbrella, and the reality of his insights into men's minds and hearts. But Chesterton's aim is not really a psychological study of such a man. Almost at once Father Brown becomes largely a mouthpiece for Chesterton's own wit and wisdom. Here are a few examples:

'There is a limit to human charity,' said Lady Outram, trembling all over.

'There is,' said Father Brown dryly, 'and that is the real difference between human charity and Christian charity.'

'He's a pretty rotten fool and failure, on his own confession.

'Yes,' said Father Brown. 'I'm rather fond of people who are fools and failures on their own confession.'

'I don't know what you mean,' snapped the other.

'Perhaps,' said Father Brown wistfully, 'it's because so many people are fools and failures without any confession.'

'There is one mark of all genuine religions: materialism.'

'The quality of a miracle is mysterious, but its manner is simple.'

'And can you tell us why,' he asked, 'you should know your own figure in a looking-glass, when two such distinguished men don't?'

Father Brown blinked even more painfully than before; then he stammered: 'Really, my lord, I don't know . . . unless it's because I don't look at it so often.'

'Now, in my opinion that machine can't lie.'

'No machine can lie,' said Father Brown, 'nor can it tell the truth.'

'If you convey to a woman that something ought to be done, there is always a dreadful danger that she will suddenly do it.'

'I agree that the woman wants to kill the co-respondent much more than the petitioner does.'

'Yes,' said Father Brown, 'I always like a dog, so long as he isn't spelt backwards.'

These could all have been starting-points for Chestertonian essays. The artistic reason for Father Brown's powers of repartee, and his wittiness in general, is that we look straight at him as we do not look at Sherlock Holmes, who is reflected in the – sometimes exasperated – admiration of Dr Watson. Chesterton has dispensed with a Dr Watson; and so Father Brown has to seem brilliant to *us*. And the only way this can be done is by making him brilliant. The remarks I have quoted are only a small selection. Father Brown by himself has no solidity. He is not a credible priest; he seems to be away from his parish as often as Dr Watson was away from his practice. He comes and goes from nowhere. The temptation to make him a semi-symbolic figure must have been great. Agatha Christie succumbed to a similar temptation in her stories about *The Mysterious Mr Quin*.

But this is false to the genre. Chesterton's stories, though often fantastic, are not fantasies. Again and again it is emphasized that Father Brown in himself is an ordinary man: an extraordinarily ordinary man.

But Father Brown's ordinariness is ordinariness *à la* Chesterton. He shares his creator's aesthetic sense. Indeed his detective powers are closely connected with his aesthetic sense. He knows what is the 'right' crime for the 'right' criminal. The whole of the story called 'The Wrong Shape' is built around this aesthetic criminology. The reformed criminal Flambeau, hunted and converted by Father Brown in the early stories, has similarly an aesthetic sense about his crimes. He chooses the right sort of crime for the right setting, as in 'The Flying Stars'. (Some memories of the fabled exploits of Vidocq, who fascinated Balzac, must have gone into Flambeau's creation.) It is an aesthetic sense that sometimes provides Father Brown with an essential clue; as in 'The Worst Crime in the World', where his perception of the balanced arrangement of a hall enables him to spot that one suit of armour, out of what must have been a pair, is missing. And Chesterton, as often, notes the curious and sometimes topsy-turvy relationship between aesthetic fitness and moral fitness:

> 'It's a wonder his throat isn't cut,' said Mr Smart's valet Harris, not without a hypothetical relish, almost as if he had said, in a purely artistic sense, 'It's a pity.'

The 'hypothetical relish' explains a good deal of our pleasure in the fantasies and atrocities of the stories.

Finally, Father Brown's detective skill owes much to that linguistic sensitivity which he shares with his creator. He finds himself thinking of foreign voyages in a house in Cornwall.

> 'Besides the butler, the Admiral's only servants were two negroes, somewhat quaintly clad in tight uniforms of yellow. The priest's instinctive trick of analysing his own impressions told him that the colour and the little neat coat-tails of these bipeds had suggested the word 'Canary', and so by a mere pun connected them with Southward travel.

Other characters share it at times.

He was a man with more literary than direct natural associations; the word 'Ravenswood' came into his head repeatedly. It was partly the raven colour of the pine-woods; but partly also an indescribable atmosphere almost described in Scott's great tragedy; the smell of something that died in the eighteenth century; the smell of dank gardens and broken urns; of wrongs that will never now be righted; of something that is none the less incurably sad because it is strangely unreal.

Such things show the literary critic in Chesterton, the power of verbal analysis which we associate with a critic of our own day like William Empson, and which Empson himself has praised in Chesterton. But sometimes this linguistic sensitiveness is employed in the interests of logical clarity. Chesterton has a feeling for the niceties of idiom, and their conceptual implications, which recalls a philosopher like the late Professor Austin. Here are a few examples:

> 'I said it was his hat. Or, if you insist on a shade of difference, a hat that is his.'
>
> 'And where is the shade of difference?' asked the criminologist, with a slight sneer.
>
> 'My good sir,' cried the mild little man, with his first movement akin to impatience, 'if you will walk down the street to the nearest hatter's shop, you will see that there is, in common speech, a difference between a man's hat and the hats that are his.'

> 'Hang it all,' cried Simon, 'a man gets into a garden, or he doesn't.'
>
> 'Not necessarily,' said the priest, with a faint smile . . .
>
> 'A man gets out of a garden, or he doesn't,' he cried.
>
> 'Not always,' said Father Brown.

[The whole story – 'The Secret Garden' – must be read for the explanation.]

'Have you ever noticed this – that people never answer what you say? They answer what you mean – or what they think you mean. Suppose one lady says to another in a country house "Is anybody staying with you?" the lady doesn't answer "Yes; the butler, the three footmen, the parlourmaid and so on," though the parlourmaid may be in the room, or the butler behind her chair. She says "There is *nobody* staying with us".' [A nice glimpse here of the Edwardian scene, which is indeed the point of the well-known story from which this comes, 'The Invisible Man'.]

Father Brown, then, is represented as at the same time an ordinary man, of simple tastes, who enjoys simple pleasures, and a clever, shrewd person, with observation and sensitiveness beyond the ordinary. But he is not a mystic. He remains true both to traditional theology, and to the genre of the detective story, in never decrying reason. It is when Flambeau, disguised as a priest, does this that Father Brown is certain he is a fraud. Of course, Father Brown is represented as a religious man. It is not by accident, and not merely to find a new twist to the Sherlock Holmes formula, that Chesterton makes him a priest. But once again Chesterton is at pains to dissociate him from anything exotic, any suggestion of the allegedly subtle lures of Rome. What he means us to feel about Father Brown is what he makes an American Protestant feel, in one of the stories which is set in South America:

> He could hardly be expected to sympathize with the religious externals of Catholic countries; and in a dislike of mitres and croziers he sympathized with Mr Snaith, though not in so cocksure a fashion. He had no liking for the public bowings and scrapings of [the clericalist] Mendoza . . . The truth was this: that the only thing he had ever met in his travels that in the least reminded him of the old wood-pile and the provincial properties and the Bible on his mother's knee was (for some inscrutable reason) the round face and black clumsy umbrella of Father Brown.

Again and again in these stories Chesterton shows how much the common dislike of Catholicism is (or was) due to dislike of 'religious externals'. But the deeper religious meaning of these stories is to do with something more important than cultural considerations. The abundance of quacks, mystagogues, sorcerers in them is not only due to the desire to point a contrast with Father

Brown. It is to illustrate, in terms proper to the genre in which Chesterton is writing, his belief that what Christianity has shown is that the age-old effort of man to grasp the Divine is bankrupt. Man cannot come to God. Christianity says that God came to man. This was what Chesterton was saying over and over again, in different tones and with varying degrees of humour or earnestness. Orwell claimed that writers like Chesterton seem to have only one subject: that they are Catholics. One might as well retort that Orwell's only subject seems to be that he was not one. Either the Catholic faith is relevant to the whole of life, or it is relevant to none of it. That, at any rate, was Chesterton's position.

In the end, then, the priest's 'steady humble gaze' owes its power to more than observation. When he realized that the doctor did the murder, he 'looked him gravely and steadily in the face'; and the doctor went away and wrote his confession. He is an atheist, and he begins his confession: '*Vicisti Galilaee!*' But he goes on at once 'In other words, damn your eyes, which are very remarkable and penetrating ones.'

The religious meaning is central in the best of these stories. But some of them contain a good deal of effective social satire also. I have already mentioned 'The Invisible Man', that ingenious fable of the people who 'don't count'. Wells, we know, had another idea of the 'invisible man'; and Ralph Ellison has another. Seeing the invisible in Chesterton's story means what Ellison means: discovering human brotherhood. Some of the incidental themes in this story are interesting, especially considering its date. We note that the victim Isidore Smythe is a characteristically modern man, who not only has a fast car but, more remarkably, a complete staff of robots to wait on him. Another parable, with a keen edge of social satire, is another well-known story, 'The Queer Feet'. The point of this story, as a detective story, is that a gentleman's coat looks the same as a waiter's; but the stratagem of Flambeau, the owner of the 'queer feet' which now saunter like a gentleman and now scurry like a waiter, is possible only because of the great gulf fixed between gentlemen and waiters. It is the 'outsiders', first of all Death (the dead waiter at the beginning of the story), then the crook Flambeau, and finally the shabby Father Brown, who point the satire on the Twelve True Fishermen. Chesterton, like Kipling, vividly describes the ritualism of English upper-class life; but he sees it more ironically than Kipling. The members of the select club The Twelve True Fishermen parody the twelve apostles, who were fishermen, and fishers of men like Father Brown, who can bring the reformed criminal back from the ends of the earth with 'a twitch upon the thread'. Light and amusing as the story is, it is an exposure not only of social class, but of plutocracy employing the traditions of social class, to eliminate brotherhood. Yet all the Fishermen are very likeable, and the story ends with an amusing touch. After their silver has been recovered, thanks to Father Brown, their first thought is to invent a new addition to their ritual by way of commemorating its recovery. The members will in future wear green coats, to distinguish them from waiters.

But the most memorable of the stories are not witty parables like these, but imaginative fairytales. What some readers remember most in the Father Brown stories is Chesterton's powers of description. His liking for a twilight setting – dawn or dusk – has been noted; and so has the constant sense we have that the action is taking place in a toy theatre, where the weird and wonderful backcloth dominates everything, and the tiny puppets that gesticulate in fight or dance in front of it seem faceless and featureless. And these backcloths have a decor which links Chesterton to Swinburne and the Decadents. His moral and religious outlook could not be more different from theirs; but his imagination has been formed on their work. Lurid, or fanciful, or grotesque decoration dominates stories like 'The Wrong Shape' or 'The Dagger with Wings'. Of course this decoration is there in part to distract us. A classical detective story exists to fool the reader; and Chesterton likes to avert our attention from the 'simple centre' to the 'rococo excrescences'. These are Chesterton's own expressions, which come from an incidental brief discussion of *Hamlet* in 'The Queer Feet'. Every successful crime, he says, like every successful work of art, has at its centre something simple. It is Chesterton's task as conjurer to arrange this scene, with bizarre figures in a bizarre setting, so that we shall miss the explanation of the mystery, which always turns on some straightforward, mundane motive. (In more than half the stories the motivation for the crime is nothing more metaphysical or *outré* than greed.)

However, I think the unforgettable descriptions of gardens, houses, landscapes and the effects of *light* in these stories are not mainly there for camouflage, or merely for scene painting. I think they have something to do with the meaning of the stories; and this in turn has something to do with the attraction of the detective story, as a genre, both to Chesterton himself and to his readers. But first of all let us note that, even at the level of the plot, the descriptions are highly relevant. This passage from 'The Hammer of God', read in its context, contains the explanation of the mystery. Two men look down from the top of a church.

> Immediately beneath and about them the lines of the Gothic building plunged outwards into the void with a sickening swiftness akin to suicide. There is that element of Titan energy in the architecture of the Middle Ages that, from whatever aspect it be seen, it is always running away, like the strong back of some maddened horse. This church was hewn out of ancient and silent stone, bearded with old fungoids and stained with the nests of birds. And yet, when they saw it from below, it sprang like a fountain at the stars; and when they saw it, as now, from above, it poured like a cataract into a voiceless pit. For these two men on the tower were left alone with the most terrible aspect of Gothic; the monstrous foreshortening and disproportion, the dizzy perspectives, the glimpses of great things small and small things great; a topsy-turvydom of stone in the mid-air.

This is the sort of passage that we feel is 'too good' for a detective story. Yet it is surely an artistic virtue, if only a minor one, that the height of the church and the way the landscape below it looks like 'a map of the world' should, for the attentive, explain both the crime's motive, and the method of its commission.

But my main reason for quoting the passage is to call attention to the phrases about 'monstrous foreshortening and disproportion', 'dizzy perspectives', 'glimpses of great things small and small things great'. These are clues to Chesterton's imagination. First of all, it was intensely visual. He began as a painter and we can find the painter's eye in all his descriptions. But – more important – it was child-like. Passages like this, from 'The Sins of Prince Saradine', abound in his writings:

A large lemon moon was only just setting in the forest of high grass above their heads, and the sky was of a vivid violet-blue, nocturnal but bright. Both men had simultaneously a reminiscence of childhood, of the elfin and adventurous time when tall weeds close over us like woods. Standing up thus against the large low moon, the daisies really seemed to be giant daisies, the dandelions to be giant dandelions. Somehow it reminded them of the dado of a nursery wall-paper.

This child-like quality in Chesterton attracts some readers and repels others. Those whom it repels dislike the association he makes between childish fantasies about winged daggers and flying vampires, and serious themes of good and evil. They feel that the former degrade the latter. This sort of criticism has been levelled against a later writer, Charles Williams, who also attempted to use thriller material as a means of saying something serious. I cannot answer this objection, except by saying that Chesterton himself seems to have been aware of it, and tries to answer it in his story 'The Dagger with Wings'. Here the real mystery of nature is contrasted with the spurious mystery, the 'white magic', which the criminal mystagogue exploits. Father Brown, as usual, appears as the agnostic: 'I do believe some things, of course, and therefore, of course, I don't believe other things.' The wickedness of the mystagogue and murderer Strake is explained as the perversion of a good thing: his power as a storyteller. He enjoys his masquerade as the man he has murdered. 'He enjoyed it as a fantasy as well as a conspiracy.' The monistic mumbo-jumbo with which he tries to deceive Father Brown is recognized by Father Brown as 'the religion of rascals'. In contrast, the cold of the air, as Father Brown walks home after the exposure and arrest of Strake, 'divides truth from error with a blade like ice'. Crime and insanity in this story are associated with changing colours, pantheistic unities, mixed-upness; goodness and innocence with the whiteness of snow, the dualism of black and white, truth and error, artifice and nature. The villain Strake has the wilfulness, the perversity, the distortions, of a naughty child. It is the normal imagination of the child that shows him up.

We might say, then, that Father Brown is imagined by Chesterton as a child whose vision is undistorted. The psychological critic will no doubt see in the contrasting distortions of perspective, the 'wrong shapes', the murderous yet strangely unheated fantasies of the stories, some relationship to the child's bizarre notions of the behaviour of adults. For reasons of temperament, period and literary mode, Chesterton avoids overtly sexual themes in the Father Brown stories. Yet it was presumably the real Father Brown's knowledge of sexual depravities that shocked Chesterton. And in 'The Secret of Father Brown' the priest confides to his interlocutor that he 'acted out' in his imagination all the crimes that he had investigated. What renders Father Brown invulnerable is precisely this anterior playacting.

The main critical problem posed by these stories, as by Chesterton's work as a whole, is how to distinguish between the child-like and the childish. Some of his books of stories, in a vein similar to the Father Brown series – *Four Faultless Felons*, *The Paradoxes of Mr Pond*, *The Poet and the Lunatics* – seem often childish in a bad sense. (The best of them is perhaps an early one, *The Man Who Knew Too Much*, in which Horne Fisher is a kind of 'political' counterpart to Father Brown.) These inferior stories offer the illustrated working-out of a verbal conundrum, rather than a mode of exploring the world. But Chesterton's passion for paradox cannot be wholly reduced to that. It lies at the heart of his genius, as well as of his tiresomeness. Hugh Kenner's able work on *Paradox in Chesterton* needs supplementing with a study which will discriminate between the profound and the shallow in Chesterton's wit. At least it can be said of Chesterton that his paradoxes, if sometimes they lack profundity, are never merely silly and flashy, as Oscar Wilde's can be, because they reflect a consistent view of life. And when Dean Inge describes him, with a note of animosity Chesterton rarely provoked in his opponents, as 'that obese mountebank who crucifies truth head downwards', an admirer of Chesterton might be moved to retort with the words of the painter in 'The Fantastic Friends' (*The Poet and the Lunatics*):

'The world is upside down. We're all upside down. We're all flies crawling on a ceiling, and it's an everlasting mercy that we don't drop off . . . We were talking about St. Peter. You remember that he was crucified upside down. I've often fancied his humility was rewarded by seeing in death the beautiful vision of his boyhood. He also saw the landscape as it really is: with the star-like flowers, and the clouds like hills, and all men hanging on the mercy of God.'

Chapter 15
'A Home for the Truth': Literary Criticism in the Letters of Raymond Chandler

It is quite common to find valuable literary criticism in the letters of authors. What makes Raymond Chandler's unusual is the attention he gave to questions of critical principle and literary theory. The main reason for this was no doubt his peculiar status in literature, and his acute sense of it, which enforced on him a degree of critical self-consciousness rarely found in popular writers. He was an intellectual (much as he disliked the description) and a highbrow. A highbrow writing in a lowbrow genre may be expected to adopt one of two attitudes to it. He may conceal his highbrowism and deliberately write down to his readers. Or he can introduce a note of sophisticated mockery into his treatment of the genre. Chandler chose neither course. Through his handling of the persona 'Philip Marlowe' he devised a different resolution of his problem – though he came near at times to the second alternative; there is an element of self-parody in his work which becomes more prominent in his later (and weaker) novels. He was too essentially a critical writer, too little a born romancer, ever to be among the great bestsellers.

He would probably have had interesting thoughts about literature and the theory of literature and criticism if he had never written a line of creative work: the bent of his mind was reflective, even philosophical, but he needed to rationalize his own practice and clarify, for himself as much as for others, what he was doing. He had also a temperamental combativeness which made him keen to defend the mystery novel as a serious literary form, in face of the indifference or contempt of conventional critical opinion. His awareness of this gave a drive and edge to his thought about 'theory' that dispel the suggestion of unprofitable speculation often popularly associated with the word, as well as the expectation of pretentious verbiage which has accompanied its vogue in the academic world. As a theorist, he was thoroughly businesslike.

Chandler's theory of literature was never promulgated by him in an article or essay. Professing to agree with Samuel Johnson that writers should be paid, he received no publisher's invitation to expatiate on literary matters. His only well-known critical essay to be published, 'The Simple Art of Murder' (1950), is not, like De Quincey's famous essay with a similar title, a piece of bravura, but a hard-hitting polemic against the 'English' type of detective story, reinforced on the positive side by an exaltation of Dashiell Hammett. It is an often quoted contribution to the perpetually recurring controversy over the best way to write a detective story, or 'novel of detection' as Chandler preferred to call it. Naturally this topic is often the centre of interest in his literary discussions. But it brought other topics in its wake, and his relevant letters, read as a whole, can be seen as an often intensive, if intermittent, discussion of central questions of literary theory: what is literature? or (more usually) what is 'good' literature? Is there a specifically literary good, and if so what is it? Is it one or many? In what way are politics, morals, etc. relevant in criticism? Or can criticism be purely structural? etc. He disliked the parochialism of critics of mysteries who steered clear of such questions.

To get his treatment of literary problems in focus a brief reminder of his life and work is necessary. Raymond Chandler (1888–1959) described himself as 'a half-breed.' His father was an American, originally from a Pennsylvania Quaker family; his mother, also of a Quaker family, was Anglo-Irish. He grew up in England and went to the same English school as P.G. Wodehouse (Dulwich College). Resemblances between the two writers have been noted. Both Chandler and Wodehouse lived a good deal in the United States. Both developed highly individual styles which won them popularity on both sides of the Atlantic. The influence on both of some strong and idiosyncratic teacher at Dulwich has been conjectured, in view of the presence of Edwardian slang in both, together with a special kind of elaborate irony or sarcasm suggestive of a pedantic schoolmaster. And it can be plausibly argued that under the surface both novelists accept the moral positions implied in Kipling's *Stalky and Co.* So far as I know they had no personal contact, but the published selection of Chandler's letters includes cordial letters to W. ('Bill') Townend, a writer who was a school friend from Dulwich College and a frequent correspondent of Wodehouse, whose letters to him have been collected under the title *Performing Flea* (1953).

Chandler began writing as a belle-lettrist and reviewer in a London literary atmosphere still redolent of the aesthetic 1890s. He was apt to reflect sardonically on the incongruity of his having made his first real impact as a writer for *Black Mask*. He believed that he could have been a fine essayist, and wondered whether like Max Beerbohm he had been born half a century too late and should have belonged to 'an age of grace'. That Chandler was a stylist, to the point of preciosity, seems to have been discovered earlier by his British than by his American critics, for whom he was just another writer of mysteries, despite W.H. Auden's praise of him in an essay on detective stories entitled 'The Guilty Vicarage' (1948), in which Auden says that his 'powerful' novels are not really detective stories at all but studies of evil (Chandler was doubtful about this). Even today he receives little or no mention in histories of United States literature. Yet he was a stylistically self-conscious, indeed scholarly, writer. As much as H.L. Mencken he was aware of the American vernacular, both written and spoken, as a distinct form of English, which he carefully and deliberately learned in order to use it in his fiction. The reason was of course partly commercial, but Professor Frank MacShane's detailed account of Chandler's methods of composition in his life of the writer puts it beyond doubt that there were artistic motives at work also. Writing in 1946 of his boredom with the Marlowe story he was trying to finish, Chandler speaks of his suspicion that the 'quality that finally put these stories over was a sort of half-controlled poetical emotion', which was not really centred on the manifest subject-matter of 'blood and mystery'.

His best-known novel is *The Big Sleep* (1939), because of the Warners' film (1946), produced by Howard Hawks, with Humphrey Bogart as Marlowe. Chandler himself expressed admiration for Bogart's performance, and many have taken it as definitive of the character, though his letters show that there is another aspect of Marlowe [to be mentioned later] which did not, and probably could not, get into the film. The three other indisputably successful Marlowe novels are *Farewell, my Lovely* (1940, used as the basis for the RKO film *Murder my Sweet*; *The High Window* (1943), filmed by Twentieth Century-Fox as *Brasher Doubloon* (1947), and *The Lady in the Lake* (1944), filmed by MGM in 1947. (There have been other film, television and radio adaptations since Chandler's time.) Criticisms may be made of some things in these novels, such as the construction in *The High Window*, and the unsatisfactory, though important, character of Degarmo in *The Lady in the Lake*, but they are masterpieces of the genre. The later Marlowe novels are by general consent inferior, though *The Little Sister* (1949) is very gripping, and while there are things in *The Long Goodbye* (1953) which suggest that the author was losing interest in his genre it has a curious personal flavour that makes it the most poignant of his novels. Finally, *Playback* (1958) is obviously a failure, the perfunctory work of a tired man, while the fragment 'The Poodle Springs Story' (1959) shows no sign that it could ever have recovered from its unfortunate opening situation with Marlowe married to a rich wife.

All these novels use the 'private eye' device. The most famous writer of private-eye stories before Chandler was Dashiell Hammett (1892–1961), of *Maltese Falcon* and *Thin Man* fame, whom Chandler was proud to acknowledge as his master. The device has to be clearly distinguished from other 'tough guy' fiction, for instance the work of James M. Cain (1892–1977), famous for *The Postman Always Rings Twice* (1934). Cain's typically staccato, breathless manner probably derives from the style of Ernest Hemingway (Hammett's relation to Hemingway is more problematic). Chandler admired Hemingway but did not like Cain's work, and he hated the common habit of bracketing it with his own. There was 'a hell of a lot of difference' between what he called his vernacular style and what he called an illiterate or *faux naif* style such as Cain's. It hardly needs more than a glance at Chandler's use of similes to show that his style is sophisticated in a way that is not dramatically appropriate to a tough-guy narrator. And even if these are discounted as baroque flourishes the writing is full of descriptive touches which slip (as they were intended to do) past the guard of readers who think they are only enjoying the story line. Here again this kind of subtlety would be out of place in the tough-guy mode. Chandler claimed that the classical education he had received at Dulwich gave him a sensitiveness to style which most contemporary American writers lacked, as well as a sense of proportion and sound critical standards.

The private-eye device survived Chandler and is still used in American fiction, but the Sam Spade/Philip Marlowe type has gone out of fashion. Chandler's disciple Ross Macdonald in his later novels makes his private eye (Lew Archer), who is poor and disillusioned but still a man of integrity, sadly conscious of being an anachronism. There now is a nostalgic, almost lavender quality about the 'mean streets' of Chandler's Los Angeles and New York. In his successors, such as Elmore Leonard, the places and the crimes are different, and there is a naked brutality, a fuller consciousness of politics, and a crazy, murderous madness beside which Chandler's books seem innocent. What is most dated is his seeming assumption that Marlowe's coolness about the depravity he witnesses will shock, or at least provoke, the reader. Yet in Leonard, as in John D. MacDonald (who died recently) of Travis McGee fame, the moral core of the hero remains the same. The man who must go down the mean streets is still not himself mean. For all his callousness and cynicism, he is still a righter of wrongs. The new version presumably seems less implausible to contemporary readers because he is prepared to go further than Marlowe in taking the law into his own hands, like the Clint Eastwood/Charles Bronson characters in films. But though these characters are tougher, less romantic, than Marlowe their continuity with Marlowe, and behind him with the knight errant, is still unbroken.

A clear idea of Marlowe's creator, his character as a writer and his critical and moral standards, first emerged in *Raymond Chandler Speaking*, a collection of passages taken from all over Chandler's work, edited by Dorothy Gardiner and Kathrine Sorley Walker (first British publication 1962). But the main source for his literary views is now the invaluable selection from his letters, admirably edited and annotated by Frank MacShane (first British publication 1981). Chandler himself had considered publishing such a book, saying that he sometimes seemed to have been more 'penetrating' in his letters than in any other form of writing. He was devoted to his wife, an invalid for many years, and was never far from her, and this made letter writing an essential part of his relationship with the world outside. Although he often has his actual correspondent in mind when he is writing, the letters are largely the self-communings of an insomniac who stayed writing them far into the night. They convey a sense of extraordinary isolation, both physical and spiritual, reflecting as they do the anomalies of the writer's position, as the practitioner of a form of writing designed to be marketable who none the less takes his work with intense seriousness and sees it as an art; as a half-humorous, half-scandalized observer of Hollywood and Southern California whose taste and temperament resembled those of an English aesthete of the 1890s; and a classically trained conservative who scornfully rejected the notion of rules for good writing.

In his letters he deals with many literary topics: criticism; the work of other authors, often but not always practitioners of his own genre; the genre itself and the requirements for success in it; its relation to 'good' fiction and to literature generally. (In what follows the numerals in square brackets refer to the relevant pages of MacShane's selection from the letters.) Like many authors, he complains that the critics (especially the Americans) do not understand what he is doing and praise or blame him on irrelevant grounds. He attacks the snobbish and out-of-date attitude of British reviewers to American books. 'Fancy a so-called intelligent reviewer handling Faulkner's *Intruder in the Dust* as though it were just another thriller' [201]. Chandler has a poor opinion of the little magazines. For them, intelligence consists only in 'a constant and rather laboured effort to find different meanings for things than other people have found.' He sounds even more like George Orwell when he condemns their absorption in political ideology, and adds: 'So after a while these magazines all perish; they never achieve life, but only a distaste for other people's views of it' [201]. His positive account of criticism is that it is something of high value but extremely rare, since it requires at the same time real distinction of mind together with a complete absence of egotism and self-promotion. 'Good critical writing is measured by the perception and evaluation of the subject: bad critical writing by the necessity of maintaining the professional standing of the critic' [114]. His most memorable formulation deserves to be quoted in full:

It is not enough for a critic to be right, since he will occasionally be wrong. It is not enough for him to give colorable reasons. He must create a reasonable world into which his reader may enter blindfold and feel his way to the chair by the fire without barking his shins on the unexpected dust mop. The barbed phrase, the sedulously rare word, – these are amusing, but useless. They place nothing and reveal not the temper of the times. The great critics, of whom there are pitiably few, build a home for the truth. [113]

The most famous American critic of his time, Edmund Wilson, Chandler speaks of with dislike, although Wilson had praised his work in print and exempted it from his general strictures on the detective story. It seems to me that one reason for this was Chandler's *pudeur*, never far from the surface in his writings, which caused him to recoil in contempt and distaste from Wilson's venture into pornography, *Memoirs of Hecate County*. Wilson's attack on Somerset Maugham may have been a contributory cause, for among the creative writers who practised criticism it is Maugham of whom he speaks with the greatest respect. He gives a convincing explanation for the curious, and still prevalent, highbrow hostility towards this writer. The highbrows find it hard to forgive popularity, even modest popularity such as Chandler's own. What they cannot bear is popularity plus a pretension to any kind of literary distinction. Among Maugham's books Chandler has a special admiration for *Ashenden*. 'However great a novel you may claim, or others may claim for you,' he wrote to Maugham, 'there are other great novels. There are not other great spy stories – none at all. I have been searching and I know.' There are a few good tales of adventure with a spying element, but they always overplay their hand; the difference between their bravura and *Ashenden* is like the difference between the opera *Carmen* and Mérimée's grim little story. Whether Chandler would have found anything to interest him in the great flood of spy stories in the 1960s and 1970s is doubtful. He would certainly have condemned the moral confusions of some of them.

Chandler thinks Maugham's success in general is due to his knowledge of what can and what cannot be done in art. He could have written the story of L.P. Hartley's *The Go-Between* to perfection, but he would not have written it through the eyes of a twelve-year-old boy: he would have known that this was impossible [367]. Chandler was interested in Maugham's personality as he inferred it from Maugham's writing. He suspected that Maugham's declared attitude of not caring much emotionally about people was a defence mechanism; as a wise man he must have known that, however transient and superficial most friendships are, life is a gloomy affair without them. He thought Maugham's strongest point as a writer was his perception of character and motive, as if he had been a great judge or great diplomat. He has no magic (Chandler's key term) and very little gusto. His style, often praised, seemed to Chandler no more than competent mandarin english which often only narrowly escapes dullness. He can convey the setting for emotion but rarely the emotion itself. As a technician he was far ahead of 'the good second-raters' (Galsworthy, Bennett, Marquand) but 'he can never make you lose your breath or lose your head, because he never loses his.' Entirely without folly or silliness, he would have made 'a great Roman' [205].

It is doubtful whether the later, posthumous revelations about Maugham's homosexuality would have made Chandler change his opinion of him. But he was unsympathetic to homosexuals both as people and as writers. He thought no good novel had been written about homosexuality (he does not consider the possible claims of Proust) but there could be an interesting picture of the 'peculiar mentality' of homosexuals, their sense of taste, their surface brilliance, their 'fundamental inability to finish anything'. (Again surely Proust is a counter-example, with his agonized and finally successful struggle to complete his vast novel when mortally ill.) He accepted that the prominence of homosexuality in English culture was something that had to be tolerated, but he maintained that homosexuals, however artistic and full of taste, lacked deep emotion; wonderful with surfaces, they were unconvincing as novelists, because they see life through mirrors [420].

There are other sharp and succinct accounts of contemporary writers, both British and American, in the letters. Chandler met J.B. Priestley [265] and characterized him as 'rugged, energetic and versatile, and in a way very professional, that is, everything that comes his way will be material and most of the material will be used rather quickly and superficially.' He found Priestley's social philosophy a little too rigid and a little too conditioned by the fact that he found it impossible to see much good in anyone who had made a lot of money ('except by writing, of course'), or who has a public school accent or military bearing, anyone in short who has speech or mannerisms above the level of the lower-middle class. This was a limited point of view, and Chandler thought Priestley a rather limited man. His point of view as a writer did not arise from an artistic perception; rather, his artistic perception, such as it was, was strictly limited by a point of view he already had. This is an interesting suggestion about a certain type of writer, which goes beyond the particular example.

Among the accepted classics of fiction Chandler always speaks warmly of Henry James. He admits that the webs James spins are sometimes tenuous, but this was because he was striving to say something with absolute, exquisite precision. In contrast, Elizabeth Bowen in *The Heat of the Day* was merely a parody of James, mistaking involution of style for subtlety of thought [151]. At the other extreme Chandler saw a Hornblower novel by C.S. Forester as having some interest of content (the detail of the handling of ships, the manoeuvres for battle etc.) but no interest from the formal and stylistic point of view, and hence dull; the emotions were on a level with G.A. Henty, and Forester had no conception of character; except for his seamanship he never gets above the level of 'slick magazine writing' (detested by Chandler).

Among the modern Americans Chandler praises Scott Fitzgerald for the 'charm' of his writing (a rare quality in literature) and vehemently dispraises Eugene O'Neill, a play by whom gives him the opportunity for a critical generalization. Calling him 'a second or third rate talent', he observes that one indelible sign of this was that O'Neill was only effective when dealing with something that bordered on fantasy. If it were not for the grim purpose and the appearance of solemnity of thought he would be seen to rank beside Pinero or Henry Arthur Jones; he was utterly artificial, nothing he wrote had any real content [142].

Chandler's remarks on writers outside his genre tend to be *obiter dicta* and do not usually take up theoretical issues. He is sometimes a very effective 'practical' critic, as when he quotes the following from a novel:

But the girl's expression hadn't changed. She had broken off a twig from a bush and was absently running it along the stone fence, as if though she were pondering what he had just said.

and comments 'The last clause and the "absently" throw away the effect. You either describe an action and let the reader make the deduction of the inner reaction it expresses, or else you describe the inner reaction and view what she does from within. You don't do it both ways at the same time.' [142].

In dealing with other writers in his own genre Chandler engaged with larger issues. He is mostly concerned with his contemporaries and never refers to the pioneer British detective stories, which are to be found in Samuel Warren and other nineteenth-century legal writers. About the most famous figure in the genre, Sherlock Holmes, he is not enthusiastic [110; 194]. He grants that the stories are enjoyed, but thinks this more due to nostalgia and tradition, and to qualities which did not originally make the principal interest of the Sherlock Holmes stories, than to their intrinsic merits either as literature or as fictional detection. Doyle understood 'the uses of eccentricity', but to a person with   . any knowledge of police procedure his policemen are utterly absurd. Chandler under-rates the contribution of the stories to criminology and real-life detection: Scotland Yard *did* learn from Sherlock Holmes. But he is no doubt right to say that Doyle's 'scientific' premises are unreliable. No sophisticated person can find the mysteries very mysterious. On the other hand we do not have the privilege of reading Holmes fresh from the presss. Holmes is an unforgettable character, with a few immortal lines of dialogue, but the stories as stories are pretty thin. As to the continuing fascination with Holmes, Chandler usefully generalizes: when a fictional character becomes a person people want to read about, the author has to provide more of him; unfortunately the author becomes weary of the character just about the time when the public is becoming attached to him.

Chandler quarrelled with the British development of the detective story after Holmes. He admitted that Dorothy L. Sayers was no fool and agreed that her minor characters were proof that she tried to anchor her stories in reality; but he thought her aristocratic amateur detective Lord Peter Wimsey snobbish and unreal. Her attempt to turn detective stories into novels of manners was not successful, and even if it had been successful would merely have resulted in the substitution of one trivial form of writing for another. Perhaps surprisingly he has a liking for the plodding kind of English detective story represented by R. Austin Freeman and Freeman Wills Crofts. He ranks Freeman, rightly, above Crofts; Freeman's writing is stilted, but it is not dull in the ways Crofts's is, i.e. flat; he is simply old-fashioned. Chandler likes even his Victorian love affairs.

Chandler always insists on the highly artificial, 'classical' character of the detective story as a form, but he is interested in the way in which truth and reality come into it. In Crofts and Freeman there is an ethical aspect to the writer/reader relationship: the reader has to feel that the writer has played fair, that essential clues have not been withheld from him. Freeman breaks this rule, in his scientist-detective Dr Thorndyke, who makes use of esoteric information; but this is a small lapse in comparison with the misdeeds Chandler found in Agatha Christie. He found her unreadable not merely or mainly because of her flat writing but because of the violence done to plausibility in her treatment of character and motive. He is equally severe on John Dickson Carr, who though American in origin and upbringing lived in England and practised the English type of detective story, his speciality being ingenious plots and apparently impossible murders in locked rooms etc. (the prototype is a French story, Gaston Leroux's *Mystère de la Chambre Jaune*). But Chandler does not answer the strongest point made by Carr and other British critics of 'The Simple Art of Murder', that Philip Marlowe is quite as unrealistic as Lord Peter Wimsey or Carr's Dr Fell, etc. There may be realistic elements in the stories, but then Christie, like Sayers, if not Carr, gives a still recognizable picture of quite a lot of English life; it is only the detection that is fantasy. And there is probably a large number of readers who, as far as the detection is concerned, remain merely observers and make no attempt to fathom the mystery. Chandler's strongest point against Carr was suggested to him by a profile of Carr in the *New Yorker*, in which Carr was reported as saying that 'he hated the act of writing'. Chandler could not understand how a writer could hate the act of writing. Plotting could be a bore, even if you were good at it, but to get no joy out of creation in words was for Chandler simply not to be a writer at all.

Chandler goes further into the theory of the genre in his sympathetic criticism of Eric Ambler's *Judgment on Deltchev* [269]. He saw in it the danger of falling between two stools, the common mishap of the intellectual dealing with thriller material; a danger he says he himself had to fight against all the time. Such a writer has to keep his characters and stories operating on a level which is understandable to the semi-literate public, yet at the same time give them the intellectual and artistic overtones which that public does not seek or demand or even recognize, but which 'somehow subconsciously' it accepts and likes. The criticism of Ambler is not that he became too intellectual but that he let it become apparent that he was being intellectual. 'The lucky writers are those who can outwrite their readers without outthinking them.'

The only British novelist of detection Chandler praises is Michael Innes. To read him is to have the pleasure of coming into contact with a 'whole literate mind'. Innes (J.I.M. Stewart in real life) is, to use a word not current in Chandler's time, a writer of postmodernist fiction, making no pretence of concealment of the artificiality of his genre, but parading it. Chandler admired and envied Innes, but he could not take that way. He remained fundamentally a realist. In general, Chandler thinks the British novel of detection superior to the American in the days when the Americans followed the British lead, since the British, while they may not be the world's best writers, are 'incomparably the best dull writers'. With Dashiell Hammett the American novel broke with the genteel tradition (contrast Philo Vance with Nick Charles) and introduced characteristically 'American' virtues of irreverence and indecorum. Chandler had a particular liking for the work of Erle Stanley Gardner, a personal friend. He was not, privately, uncritical of Gardner's undistinguished writing, but he liked the Perry Mason stories because of their inventiveness, preferring them to those Gardner wrote under the alias of A.A. Fair. Those stories had the same defect as Rex Stout's Nero Wolfe stories: an eccentric character outstays its welcome. The best detective is Perry Mason, 'an ordinary guy with extraordinary qualities.' Finally, discussing *The Moving Target*, by Ross Macdonald, who was to succeed Chandler as leader in the private-eye genre, Chandler excuses its

derivativeness from *The Big Sleep* and *The Thin Man*, saying he was
'Elizabethan' about such matters, but castigating its frigidities of
style (a motor car 'acned with rust') which jerk away the attention
of the reader from the thing described to the pose of the writer.

Chandler again and again regrets the lack of serious consideration
given to detective fiction. 'A column and a half of respectful attention will be given to any fourth-rate, ill-constructed mock-serious
account of a bunch of cotton pickers in the deep south' [27], while
a work of real literary skill and careful craftsmanship is relegated
simply because of its genre and the way it is marketed. He gave
careful thought to the definition of the detective novel. He saw it
as centring on clues, physical and psychological; the physical clues
were only important in so far as they pointed to the psychological
clues, and the art (and ethics) of the concealment of these is the
essence of the genre. As for the demand often made for a surprise
ending, he thought no denouement could fool the *aficionado*, unless
the writer cheats. Otherwise he has to accept that it will be
transparent to some readers. The important thing is that the
reader will accept it. A surprise ending is no good if the reader
doesn't believe it. Chandler emphasizes the element of fantasy in
the mystery story, and regrets that his readers apparently fail to
perceive the 'burlesque' aspect of his work. The means the writer
uses are realistic, in the sense that such things happen to people
like these and in places like these. But the realism is superficial.
The potential of emotion is overcharged, the time and events are
compressed in violation of probability, and 'although such things
happen, they do not happen so fast and in such a tight frame of logic
to so closely knit a group of people' [150]. Hence a Racine-like,
'classical', quality of the detective story.

Chandler defended the private-eye device, while admitting that
it was a fantasy; it was an exaggeration of something possible, unlike
Lord Peter Wimsey etc. The technical problem in presenting
Marlowe was that he was a first-person character and therefore
under the disadvantage that he must be a better man to the reader
than he is to himself. The real mystery of Marlowe is why such an
intelligent man should work for a pittance. Chandler's answer to
that is the whole of the real story, the hidden story that is never
made manifest: the struggle of a fundamentally honest man to make
a living in a corrupt society.

In the end Chandler had to confess mixed feelings about the genre he practised and defended. There was an inner contradiction in it: the better you wrote a mystery, the more clearly you demonstrated that the mystery was not worth writing. So it came about that inferior writers – Carr, Christie, Gardner – were the most successful: good writers, like Chandler, create a schism between the melodramatic exaggerations of the story and the way they tell it. At the same time he had no patience with the claims made for fashionable highbrow or middlebrow fiction. The gap between a good mystery and the best 'serious' novel of the day is scarcely measurable in comparison with the gulf between a 'serious' novel and the masterpieces of antiquity – Pindar, or Horace, or Sophocles.

But 'good of its kind' – the usual defence of his genre – came to be a formulation that did not satisfy Chandler. He was firmly of the opinion that the fact that a book is readable and popular should not be regarded as a sign that it lacked literary merit – an absurd view. But he was puzzled about such cases as Nevil Shute. He sat up all night to finish *No Highway*, yet he knew that it contained no real literary art. If (as he was inclined to think) the only relevant 'kind' is literature itself, then the criterion of excellence must be quality of performance, and more than once Chandler has to fall back on 'intensity'; which returns us to Walter Pater and the 1890s. He goes deeper into the question of style when he reflects [88] on the mystery of human personality. The personality he prizes cannot be projected if you try to do this; it comes over when you are thinking of something else. The depth that is missing from modern literature will never be restored while writers remain 'machine minders'; they have all the facts and all the answers, they are technically slick, but they are 'little men who have forgotten how to pray'.

Chandler's achievement in fiction, reinforced by his letters, is considerable. He performed the unusual feat of bringing erudition and high culture to thriller writing without making his hero improbably learned and cultivated. He brought the mystery story and the discussion of its problems into the mainstream of literature. In the area of critical theory he brought the insights of a practitioner to the enigma of literature. Despite all the efforts of philosophers and theorists over the ages, it seems clear that there are no general descriptive criteria of literary excellence. If there are any general criteria at all (a problematic assumption) these are purely evaluative. But a particular genre of literature probably does have descriptive criteria of excellence, and Chandler's letters suggest what these are for the form of it that he practised. The logical problem is how these criteria are to be related to the more general criteria usually called literary standards. Chandler did not solve that problem; but he had unusually helpful things to say about it.

Chapter 16
The Poetry of C.S. Lewis

C.S. Lewis, for a great part of his life, longed to be a distinguished poet, second only to Yeats among the poets of his time. But many of his warmest admirers now agree that verse was not a form in which he excelled. We have only to remember even a limited amount of his prose output – say, *The Allegory of Love* and *The Screwtape Letters* and *Surprised by Joy* – to realize its immense range and variety. His verse shares with his prose the unmistakable Lewisian characteristic of unfailing readability. But in comparison it seems thin and restricted, and for the most part strangely lacking in the strong personal stamp of his prose style. Lewis was a superb and learned connoisseur of English poetry. He could compose successfully – even extemporise – in the style of many English poets. But (perhaps for that very reason) a personal style eluded him. In his verse we sometimes see themes which he treated in his prose, and usually the prose treatment is more satisfying. It is tempting to think of him as essentially a prose mind, whose verse is valuable chiefly for the light it sheds on Lewis the man; attracting the kind of biographical interest which Lewis himself deprecated in *The Personal Heresy*.

I long held this view of Lewis's poetry: but I have come to think that there is a small number of the poems in which he touches greatness, poems that are not like anything else he wrote. But before coming to these I will briefly touch on his poetry as a whole. The early collection *Spirits in Bondage* (1919) shows Lewis as a young poet in the late Romantic tradition; though it is not derivative from Swinburne, Swinburne is not far in the background. Appropriately the content is an illogical but curiously attractive mood of anger with God both for His cruelty and for His non-existence: a mood which was later to recur in Lewis's work as late as *A Grief Observed* (1961). More substantial is the long narrative poem *Dymer* (1925). It is probable that *Dymer*, a fantasy-romance, deals in a mythological way with Lewis's feelings about his dead mother and, perhaps, with his father. The poem should be of intense interest to readers intrigued by Lewis's enigmatic personality. As he himself admitted, its symbolism invites psychoanalytic reconstruction. But taken by itself the poem would probably not be remembered. The verse suggests John Masefield's influence, but it has not often the clarity and purity of Masefield. There are too many passages in which the diction is undistinguished, and quite a few of the lines are unmetrical. Stylistically much of *Dymer* deserves the common use of 'Georgian' as a dismissive epithet. It gets its true significance only when related to Lewis's life and to his later poems. His other narrative poems for the most part fall into the category of poetic exercises. They sometimes anticipate what was to be the technical skill and craftsmanship of Lewis's best lyric poems, but none is in itself memorable. A possible exception is *The Queen of Drum* (1933). High claims have been made for this by Walter Hooper. But while it is better written than *Dymer* I do not think it as substantial in interest as the best of the short poems. Its attitude towards romance and Romanticism is central in Lewis's work as a whole, but Lewis was to find ways of expression for this which make *The Queen of Drum* look marginal.

I now turn to Lewis's short poems. Rarely written about, in comparison with his work in apologetic, literary history, or prose fiction, they are in my view the basis on which his reputation as a poet should rest. The first characteristic to note is that they show differences of style but no sense of a continuing and developing literary personality, like Yeats's. In this respect they are more like the poems of a poet Lewis had no use for, Ezra Pound. Occasionally they can be dated by external references, but never on internal grounds. After Lewis became a Christian in 1929 his poetry is all of a piece. Secondly, though some of the poems are explicitly Christian, there is in them little of the religious apologist; the outstanding exception is 'The Apologist's Evening Prayer', which movingly articulates Lewis's discomfort, which some of his readers have also felt, about the over-confident reliance on ratiocination in his religious writings. In his poems Lewis is much more vulnerable, self-critical, even at times self-abasing, than he is in his prose. Finally (and this is true of the less inspired poems as well as the great ones) the verse is packed with meaning. Yvor Winters once claimed that the short poem is the greatest of literary forms, because there the reader can be in touch throughout with a great mind at full stretch. This is true of Lewis's best short poems. They may have been under-rated just because, like many of Ben Jonson's poems, they say much in little.

As the author of the phrase 'the personal heresy' it is surprising how much of Lewis's charm as a writer depends upon our sense of his personality (as his friend J.R.R. Tolkien, perhaps a little ambivalently, noted.) It is possible to read many of the poems as confessional, if not in the crude sense autobiographical. But some of his best poems do not seem to be personal communications. 'Hermione in the House of Paulina' is an example. Here Lewis, speaking through the *persona* of Shakespeare's Hermione in *The Winter's Tale*, seems to be saying something with a deep personal significance, yet we cannot say what it is. The only clues I have to offer are that he once said to me that, though a reluctant playgoer, he had been deeply moved by a performance of *The Winter's Tale*; and that he once remarked in print that it might have been better if Shakespeare had made Paulina a fairy or an angel and so got rid of his 'improbable possibilities'. I also suspect that in this poem Lewis is thinking of a critical doctrine which he held in common with Tolkien, about the great beauty (in its proper place) of the *eucatastrophe*, or 'happy ending'.

All the other poems I will discuss come from *The Pilgrim's Regress* (1943), a prose allegory interspersed, in the fashion of Bunyan's *Pilgrim's Progress*, with lyrics. The *Pilgrim's Regress* is not one of Lewis's best books. Though it contains some fine things its arguments are often crude and its satire heavy-handed. Yet amid the pamphleteering wilderness there now and then springs up a well of pure inspiration. It is as if with a profound unconscious tact he had reserved for verse the expression of his finest and most sensitive perceptions. His verse *sings* in *The Pilgrim's Regress* as it rarely does elsewhere (though he can manage the drum and trumpet as well as Kipling). And he treats psychosexual problems with deep inwardness and avoidance of false notes.

One of the most revealing of his poems is 'Posturing' (p. 89).[1] Those who equate C.S. Lewis with the *persona* of the jolly pipe-smoking extrovert which he sometimes used may be surprised at the insight he shows into the element of *narcissism* that lies at the back of some of his most profound work.

> Thou givest grapes, and I,
> Though starving, turn to see
> How dark the cool globes lie
> In the white hand of me,
> And linger gazing thither
> Till the live clusters wither.

(An effective touch here is 'the white hand of me' instead of the familiar 'my white hand'.) The turns and twists of the argument, subtle as in a Metaphysical poet, suggest the movements of a snake. As the poem comes to its culmination the stanza form broadens out:

> Then and then only turning
> The stiff neck round, I grow
> A molten man all burning
> And look behind and know
> Who made the glass, whose light makes dark, whose fair
> Makes foul, my shadowy form reflected there
> That self-Love, brought to bed of Love may die and bear
> Her sweet son in despair.

Lewis, as is well known, was hostile to the 'Modernist' movement in poetry. His rejection of T.S. Eliot is manifested in 'A Confession', placed first by the editor in the 1964 collection of his poems. I can find no trace of Eliot's influence in any of them. But at times (for example when dwarves living under mountains figure in the symbolism) I am reminded of W.H. Auden, who became a friend of Lewis in his later life. And sometimes, when the relationship of men and women is concerned, there is a wry dryness that suggests Robert Graves, another ex-Georgian (Lewis as a combatant in the 1914–18 war will surely have been interested in Graves's *Goodbye to All That*). But the great difference between Lewis and all the 'Moderns' is his use of a full-blooded, un-ironic style of strong rhetorical power, with its soaring praise of God.

Thou only art the Lord,
Thou only art holy. In the shadowy vast
Of thine Osirian wings Thou dost enfold the past.
There sit in throne antediluvian, cruel kings,
There the first nightingale that sang to Eve yet sings,
There are the irrecoverable guiltless years,
There, yet unfallen, Lucifer among his peers.

    (from 'When the Curtain's Down', p. 97)

At the other extreme are the poems – groping, glamourless, bewildered – which seem to have been written after the death of his wife Joy. Colourful imagery and sonorous verse have gone: the poet has forsaken his singing robes for sackcloth and ashes. 'Joys that Sting' (p. 108) is one of the best of these poems. Lewis always writes convincingly of love bereaved: these were poems which he had to write. With other aspects of love his touch is uncertain. I do not think he is successful on the theme of the desire of one adult for another. Masterly as his poem 'Lilith' (p. 95) is, I feel the temptation it deals with is masturbation, a variant of the theme of narcissism. However that may be, no poet has found a better description of masturbation than 'the unrelished anodyne'. The part played by physical sexuality in Lewis's life, the nature of his relationship with the two 'women in his life', must remain one of the many enigmas which he presents to the biographer. To me 'Lilith' suggests not a real relationship with a woman but the paper libidinousness of the letters to Arthur Greeves. But apart from all that the poem is one of his finest. Lewis is writing verse as good as his prose.

Eager, unmasked, she lingers
Heart-sick and hunger sore;
With hot, dry, jewelled fingers
Stretched out, beside her door,
Offering with gnawing haste
Her cup, whereof who taste,
(She promises none better) thirst far more.

This poem offers an inward treatment of the Wicked Mother figure who is externalized in the excellent poems, influenced by Anglo-Saxon verse, about dragon-slaying.

Perhaps the most purely beautiful of Lewis's poems is 'Angel's Song' (p. 107). Delicate as the verse of Christina Rossetti, this poem takes us, artistically speaking, into another world from the clumsiness of *Dymer*. Comparatively young as he was when he wrote it, Lewis had already arrived at the insight that the capacity for bereavement and loss is one of the things which make us truly human. The Song is put into the mouth of an Angel who cannot know this.

> Sorrow it is they call
> This cup whence my lip
> (Woe's me!) never in all
> My endless days can sip.

A similar thought, expressed less lyrically, more meditatively, underlies 'Scazons' (p.118). (Lewis, the scholar, likes to suggest classical metres.) I first came across this poem in one of Walter de la Mare's anthologies, at a time when I had never heard of C.S. Lewis, and it made a great impression on me.

> Walking to-day by a cottage I shed tears
> When I remembered how once I had walked there . . .

'Scazons' seemed to me – to use a distinction Lewis himself accepted – a 'found' rather than a 'made' poem. The argument, difficult to paraphrase, seems to be that, in conferring His individuality on man, God has also created the possibility of a peculiarly poignant suffering: 'Gods are we, Thou hast said; and we pay dearly.'

At one time I would have said confidently that Lewis was not a poet but a maker of witty light verse (as he certainly was). But I now see a vein of true poetry in his work, something that came, not from the bullying, smothering quality of the inferior things he wrote, in both prose and verse, but from the gentle, sensitive human being which his friends knew he was.

Notes and References

CHAPTER 1: Did the King See the Dumb-Show?

Notes

Line-references are to J. Dover Wilson's edition (1934).

In addition to the sources referred to below, see also Harry Berger, 'What did the King know and when did he know it?' in 'Shakespearian Discourses of Psychoanalysis', *South Atlantic Quarterly*, 88 (1989), 811–62, which was unknown to me when I originally wrote this essay.

1   The passage may be found in *Selected Essays*, ed. Annan (1964), p. 168.
2   A.J.A. Waldock, *Hamlet: a Study in Critical Method* (1931).
3   J.W. Cunliffe, *Early English Classical Tragedies* (1912), pp. xxxix ff. Cf. also W. Creizenach, *English Drama in the Age of Shakespeare* (1916); Enid Welsford, *The Court Masque* (1927); E.K. Chambers *The Elizabethan Stage*, vol. I (1945); W.J. Lawrence, *The Elizabethan Playhouse* (1912–13). Cf. also F.L. Lucas's note on *The White Devil*, II.ii., in his edition of the play (1958).
4   B.R. Pearn, 'Dumb-show in Elizabethan drama', *Review of English Studies* (1935).
5   A.A. Jack, *Young Hamlet* (1950).
6   J. Dover Wilson, *What Happens in Hamlet* (1935).
7   S.L. Bethell, *Shakespeare and the Popular Dramatic Tradition* (1944).
8   H. Granville-Barker, *Preface to Hamlet* (1927).
9   A solution on these lines is suggested by E.L. Ferguson, 'The play scene in *Hamlet*', *Modern Language Review* (1919). Cf. also W. Babcock, *Hamlet: a Tragedy of Errors* (Indiana, 1961).
10 Babcock, *Hamlet: A Tragedy of Errors*.
11 G. Bullough, 'The murder of Gonzago', *Modern Language Review* (1935).
12 Excerpts are given in Furness's Variorum edition of *Hamlet*.
13 W.W. Greg, 'Hamlet's hallucination', *Modern Language Review* (1917).
14 E. Prosser, *Hamlet and Revenge* (1967).
15 F.C. Kolbe, *Shakespeare's Way* (1930).

16 *Tractatus*, VI. 43.
17 Preface to G. Wilson Knight's *The Wheel of Fire* (1930).
18 L. Tolstoy, *Shakespeare and the Drama* (1906), in *Recollections and Essays*, tr. A. Maude (1937).
19 P. Vellacott, *Sophocles and Oedipus* (1971).
20 J. Berger, *Success and Failure of Picasso* (1965).

CHAPTER 2: Spenser and *The Faerie Queene*

References
Alpers, P.J. (1967) *The Poetry of the Faerie Queene*.
Nelson, W. (1963) *The Poetry of Edmund Spenser*.
Sale, R. (1968) *Reading Spenser: An Introduction to The Faerie Queene*.

CHAPTER 3: *Paradise Lost*: Changing Interpretations and Controversy

Notes
1 A. Pope, *Postscript to the Odyssey* (1723).
2 See his *Rambler* articles 86, 88 and 94 on Milton's versification, and 139 and 140 on *Samson Agonistes*.
3 M. Arnold, *Mixed Essays* (1879).
4 C. Williams, introduction to *The English Poems of Milton* (World's Classics, 1940).
5 T.S. Eliot, 'Milton I' and 'Milton II', in *On Poetry and Poets* (1957).
6 Originally an article in *Scrutiny*, II (1933).

CHAPTER 4: Text and Context: Pope's 'Coronation Epistle'

References
Ault, Norman (1949) *New Light on Pope*.
Brower, R.A. (1959) *Alexander Pope the Poetry of Allusion*.
Derrida, Jacques (1977) *Limited Inc*.
Mack, Maynard (1985) *Life of Pope*.
Maud, R.N. (1958) *Review of English Studies*, IX, 146–51.
Reeves, James (1969) *Commitment to Poetry*.
Reeves, James (1976) *Reputation and Writings of Alexander Pope*.
Rogers, Pat (1974) *The Augustan Vision*.
Sherburn, George (ed.) (1956) *The Correspondence of Alexander Pope*.

CHAPTER 5: Johnson as a Poet

References
Works of Samuel Johnson, Yale Edition (from 1958).

Samuel Johnson, *The Complete English Poems*, ed. J.D. Fleeman, Penguin English Poets (1971).

James Boswell, *The Life of Samuel Johnson, LL.D.*, ed. G.B. Hill, rev. L.F. Powell (1934/1964).

CHAPTER 9: The Choir Master and the Single Buffer

References

New Oxford Illustrated Dickens 1947–8.

The Mystery of Edwin Drood, ed. Margaret Cardwell (1972) and her edition for the World's Classics (1982).

The Letters of Charles Dickens, Nonesuch edn (1938) and Pilgrim Edn (from 1965).

The Speeches of Charles Dickens, ed. K.J. Fielding (1960).

All the Year Round (1859–70).

Felix Aylmer, *Dickens Incognito* (1959) and *The Drood Case* (1964).

Richard M. Baker, *The Drood Murder Case* (1951).

R. Bulwer-Lytton, *Cheveley* (1839).

G.K. Chesterton, *Criticisms and Appreciations of Dickens* (1911).

Agatha Christie, *The Murder of Roger Ackroyd* (1926).

Philip Collins, *Dickens and Crime* (2nd edn, 1965).

Wilkie Collins, *No Name* (1862), and *The Moonstone* (1868).

Arthur J. Cox, *The Mystery of Edwin Drood* (Penguin edn, 1974).

C.G.L. Du Cann, *The Love Lives of Charles Dickens* (1961).

E.M. Forster, *Aspects of the Novel* (1927).

John Forster, *Life of Charles Dickens* (1872–4).

Charles Forsyte, *The Decoding of Edwin Drood* (1980).

Leon Garfield, *Conclusion to The Mystery of Edwin Drood* (1980).

George Gissing, *Charles Dickens* (1898).

Philip Hobsbaum, *A Reader's Guide to Charles Dickens* (1972).

Humphry House, *All in Due Time* (1955).

William R. Hughes, *A Week's Tramp in Dickensland* (1891).

Jack Lindsay, *Charles Dickens: A Biographical and Critical Study* (1950).

Karl Marx, *Selected Writings* (Penguin edn 1970).

Sylvère Monod, *Dickens the Novelist* (1967).

Ellen Moers, *The Dandy: Brummell to Beerbohm* (1960).

V.S. Pritchett, *The Living Novel* (1946).

Richard A. Proctor, *Watched by the Dead* (1887).

John R. Reed, *Victorian Conventions* (1975).

S.C. Roberts, *The Mystery of Edwin Drood* (1955).

Montague Saunders, *The Mystery in the Drood Family* (1914).

Michael Slater, *Dickens and Women* (1983).

Taylor Stoehr, *Dickens: The Dreamer's Stance* (1965).
Angus Wilson, introduction to *The Mystery of Edwin Drood* (Penguin edn, 1974).
Edmund Wilson, *The Wound and the Bow* (1941).
Robin Wood, *Hitchcock's Films* (1965).

CHAPTER 10   On *The Portrait of a Lady*

Select Bibliography

1   Writings by Henry James

The *Bibliography of Henry James*, by L. Edel and D.H. Laurence, 1957, rev. 1961, is definitive.

James wrote 22 novels (including 2 unfinished). It is widely agreed that the best are as follows:
(In James's earlier manner)
Roderick Hudson (1875)
The American (1877)
The Europeans (1878)
Washington Square (1880)
The Portrait of a Lady (1881)
The Bostonians (1886)
The Princess Casamassima (1886)
The Tragic Muse (1890)

(In James's later manner)
The Spoils of Poynton (1897)
What Maisie Knew (1897)
The Awkward Age (1899)
The Sacred Fount (1901)
The Wings of the Dove (1902)
The Ambassadors (1903)
The Golden Bowl (1904)

James wrote 112 tales, edited and introduced by L. Edel, 12 volumes, 1962–4. There is a new critical edition by M. Aziz, of which 2 volumes have appeared (1973 and 1979). *Selected Tales* in Everyman's Library, ed. by Paul Messent and Tom Paulin (1982), may be augmented by the following, which reflect various aspects of James's work:

(The international theme)
Madame de Mauves (1875)
Daisy Miller (1878)

('Society')
The Liar (1888)

(Writers and artists)
The Aspern Papers (1888)
The Lesson of the Master (1888)
The Figure in the Carpet (1896)

(Bizarre tales)
The Pupil (1891)
The Turn of the Screw (1898)
The Great Good Place (1900)

The complete plays were edited by L. Edel (1949).

Of James's extensive critical writings the following are especially notable:

Hawthorne (1879)

Partial Portraits (1888), which includes the 'Conversation' on *Daniel Deronda*.

The Art of the Novel, ed. R.P. Blackmur (1934) – James's critical prefaces.

The House of Fiction, ed. L. Edel (1957), includes essays on various novelists.

Selected Literary Criticism, ed. M. Shapira, 1963.

Among the travel-books *English Hours* (1905) and *The American Scene* (1907) are of special interest.

James's autobiography (which includes biographical studies of his family) was edited with introduction and notes by F.W. Dupee (1956).

There are said to be 15,000 of James's letters extant; they are being edited by L. Edel (vols. 1–3, 1974–80).

The *Notebooks* were edited (1947) by F.O. Matthiessen and K.B. Murdock.

2   Writing about Henry James

The life by Leon Edel (5 vols, 1953–72; Peregrine edn in 2 vols, 1977, omits all references) is the most praised – and abused – literary biography of modern times. Its 'bioliterary' approach may be questioned, but it is indispensable.

The quantity of critical writing is enormous, and continues to increase. For earlier criticism R. Gard's volume (1968) in the 'Critical Heritage' series is recommended. There is a *Bibliography of Second-ary Works* by Beatrice Ricks (1975), and a handy list of them in Tony Tanner's booklet on James in the 'Writers and their Work' series (1979).

On *The Portrait of a Lady* (henceforth referred to as PL) the following, listed in alphabetical order, are of particular interest:

Oscar Cargill, *The Novels of Henry James* (1962), instructive about possible sources of PL.

F.W. Dupee, *Henry James* (1951, rev. 1965), a 'Jacobite', 'establishment' view, but sensible and judicious.

Maxwell Geismar, *Henry James and his Cult* (1964), has valuable insights when it leaves off being an exasperated diatribe against the 'Jacobites'.

David Gervais, *Flaubert and Henry James* (1978), a thoughtful and thought-provoking comparison between the virtuous heroine of PL and Flaubert's Emma Bovary.

Martin Green, *Re-Appraisals* (1963), in an attempted devaluation of James, finds second-rateness and theatricality in PL.

D.W. Jefferson, *Henry James* (1960), perhaps the best of the introductory studies.

Arnold Kettle, *Introduction to the English Novel*, vol. II (1953), argues (surely rightly) that the theme of 'freedom' is central in PL.

Dorothea Krook, *The Ordeal of Consciousness in Henry James* (1962), stresses the religious aspect of James's fiction.

F.R. Leavis, *The Great Tradition* (1948), the most searching of all the critiques of James's work, and especially of PL: a constant stimulus to questions.

F.O. Matthiessen, *Henry James: the Major Phase* (1944), has a valuable chapter on James's revisions of PL for the New York edition.

A.R. Mills, '*The Portrait of a Lady* and Dr. Leavis', *Essays in Criticism*, Oct. 1960, argues that James *meant* to portray Isabel as a romantic egotist.

J.M. Newton is severe on 'Isabel Archer's spiritual disease – and Henry James's', *Cambridge Quarterly*, Winter 1966/7; see also replies by Ian Robinson and Roger Gard in the Summer 1967 number.

W.R. Poirier, *The Comic Sense of Henry James* (1960), is a study of the earlier novels, including PL.

S. Gorley Putt, *Henry James: a Reader's Guide* (1966), informative and balanced.

C.T. Samuels, *The Ambiguity of Henry James* (1971), argues that James in his novels constructed his own ethical system.

William T. Stafford (ed.), *Perspectives on James's Portrait of a Lady* (1967), collects useful articles.

CHAPTER 11   On *The Golden Bowl*

Select Bibliography
On *The Golden Bowl* (henceforth referred to as GB) the following, listed in alphabetical order, are of particular interest:

Allott, Miriam (1953) *'Symbol and image in the later work of Henry James'*, *Essays in Criticism*, July. James meant Adam and Maggie to seem noble, but misjudged their effect on the reader.

Anderson, Quentin (1958) *The American Henry James*. GB seen as based on the 'system' of Henry James's father. Maggie is 'Divine Love', Adam 'Divine Wisdom'.

Barzun, Jacques (1945) 'Henry James, melodramatist' in *The Question of Henry James*, ed. F.W. Dupee. Pro-Maggie. GB shows 'supreme goodness' overcoming 'surreptitious evil'.

Bayley, John (1960) *The Characters of Love*. Contains long and challenging essay on GB. Spiritedly opposes Edith Wharton's view that the characters are 'suspended in a void'.

Berland, Alwyn (1981) *Culture and Conduct in the Novels of Henry James*. GB is a failure: it 'cannot be understood definitively, owing to the absence of the elements necessary for certainty.'

Bradbury, Nicola (1979) *Henry James: The Later Novels*. 'Maggie, at least, we must trust, if we are to follow the novel at all.'

Blackmur, R.P. (1952) 'Introduction' to *The Golden Bowl*. Hagiographical (Maggie-ographical?) about the Ververs: Maggie is 'like Beatrice in the *Divine Comedy*, the Lady of Theology.' She 'suffers the pangs of the highest human love.'

Chatman, Seymour (1972) *The Later Style of Henry James*.

Cox, C.B. (1955) *'The Golden Bowl'*, *Essays in Criticism*, April. Pro-Maggie.

Crews, Frederick C. (1957) *The Tragedy of Manners*. Influential view of GB as Christian allegory.

Dupee, F.W. (1951) *Henry James*. Includes useful summary of GB.

Edgar, Pelham (1927) *Henry James, Man and Author*. Early example of a pro-Charlotte view.

Empson, William (1955) 'Yes and no', *Essays in Criticism*, January. Agrees with the pro-Charlotte reading of Firebaugh (see below), but doubts whether it was intended by James.

Fergusson, Francis (1934) 'The drama in *The Golden Bowl*', *Hound and Horn*, April–June.

Firebaugh, J.J. (1954) 'The Ververs', *Essays in Criticism*, October. Statement of extreme anti-Maggie and anti-Adam view.

Geismar, Maxwell (1964) *Henry James and his Cult*. Vehement indictment of James – and especially of GB. James's art was shaped by his morbid psychological oddities; his world was not a realistic one but the product of his own weird imagination. Well, yes . . .

Girling, H.K. (1973) 'The function of slang in the dramatic poetry of *The Golden Bowl*' in *Henry James's Major Novels*, ed. Lyall H. Powers.

Grover, Philip (1973) *Henry James and the French Novel*. Particularly good on James's debt to Balzac.

Hartsock, Mildred R. (1974) 'Unintentional fallacy critics and *The Golden Bowl*', *Modern Languages Quarterly*, 35.

House, Kay S. (ed.), *Reality and Myth in American Literature*. Helpful in explaining James's idealization of the American businessman.

Hutchinson, Stuart (1982) *Henry James: An American as Modernist*. Pro-Maggie, but emphasizes the complexity of GB.

Jefferson, D.W. (1964) *Henry James and the Modern Reader*. Includes a balanced discussion of GB.

Kimball, J. (1957) 'Henry James's last portrait of a lady: Charlotte Stant in *The Golden Bowl*', *American Literature*, 28 January.

Krook, Dorothea (1962) *The Ordeal of Consciousness in Henry James*. Maggie as scapegoat and redeemer.

Leavis, F.R. (1948) *The Great Tradition*. Pro-Charlotte. His collection *The Common Pursuit* (1952) also contains an essay on James, dealing in part with GB.

Lee, Vernon (Violet Paget) (1923) *The Handling of Words*. Stylistic analysis of late-Jamesian prose. See also the next item.

Lodge, David (1966) *The Language of Fiction*.

Matthiessen, F.O. (1944) *Henry James: The Major Phase*, reprinted with appendix. The 'major phase' consists of *The Ambassadors*, *The Wings of the Dove* and *The Golden Bowl*, but Matthiessen is uneasy about GB and clearly does not care for it. See also his *The James Family* (1948). Includes writings by Henry James Senior and William and Alice James.

Nowell-Smith, Simon (1947) *The Legend of the Master*. Collection of material about James's personal idiosyncrasies, especially in later life.

Nuhn, E. (1942) *The Wind Blew from the East*. Pro-Charlotte: sees Maggie as 'fiendish'.

Owen, Elizabeth (1963) 'The "Given Appearance" of Charlotte Verver', *Essays in Criticism*, October. Anti-Charlotte.

Pearson, Gabriel (1974) 'The novel to end all novels: *The Golden Bowl*' in *The Air of Reality*, ed. John Goode.

Perrin, Edwin N. (1955) '*The Golden Bowl*', *Essays in Criticism*, April. Pro-Maggie.

Putt, Gorley (1966) *The Fiction of Henry James*. Finds many *longueurs* in

GB.

Rose, Alan (1966) 'The spatial form of *The Golden Bowl*', *Modern Fiction Studies*, XII, Spring.

Samuels, C.T. (1971) *The Ambiguity of Henry James.*

Segal, Ora (1969) *The Lucid Reflector: the Observer in Henry James's Fiction.* Defends the Assinghams against Edith Wharton (see below). And cf. the next item.

Sharp, Sister M. Corona (1963) *The Confidante in Henry James.*

Short, R.W. (1946) 'The sentence structure in Henry James', *American Literature*, 18.

Spencer, James L. (1957–8) 'Symbolism in *The Golden Bowl*', *Modern Fiction Studies*, 3, Winter.

Spender, Stephen (1935) *The Destructive Element.* Includes a pioneer 1930s study of James. Shaky on details of GB, but valuable insights.

Stevenson, Elizabeth (1964) *The Crooked Corridor: A Study of Henry James.* Pro-Maggie: 'the good one who pays and expiates, not for the wrong she has done, but for the wrong which has been done to her.'

Tanner, Tony (ed.) (1968) *Henry James: Modern Judgments.*

Watt, Ian (1960) 'The first paragraph of *The Ambassadors*', in *Essays in Criticism*, July. A stylistic study.

Wharton, Edith (1925) *The Writing of Fiction.* Funny about the Assinghams. Her *A Backward Glance* (1934) includes personal recollections of the later James, who called her his 'Angel of Devastation', because, though fascinated by her company and the amusements she devised for him, he needed prolonged recuperation after each encounter with her.

Wright, Walter (1957) 'Maggie Verver: Neither saint nor witch', *Nineteenth-Century Fiction*, 12, June.

Yeazell, Ruth Bernard (1976) *Language and Knowledge in the Late Novels of Henry James.*

CHAPTER 13   E. Nesbit and *The Book of Dragons*

References

E. Nesbit: biographies by Doris Langley Moore, *E. Nesbit: A Biography* (1951) and Julia Briggs, *A Woman of Passion: The Life of E. Nesbit, 1858–1924* (1987).

Other works:

Graham Greene, *A Sort of Life* (1971).

Gore Vidal, *Selected Essays 1952–1972* (1974).

C.N. Manlove, *Modern Fantasy* (1975).

Stephen Prickett, *Victorian Fantasy* (1979).

Humphrey Carpenter, *Secret Gardens* (1985).

CHAPTER 16: The Poetry of C.S. Lewis

Notes
1 My quotations are taken from C.S. Lewis, *Poems*, edited by Walter Hooper (1964).

Index